Telling Tales

Telling Tales

Selected Writing, 1993–2013

Amit Chaudhuri

Union
Books

First published in Great Britain in 2013 by
Union Books
an imprint of Aurum Press Limited
74–77 White Lion Street
London N1 9PF
union-books.co.uk

These essays originally appeared in *Granta*,
the *Guardian*, the *London Review of Books*, the *Dublin Review*, the *Telegraph*,
Index On Censorship, the *Times of India*, and the *Hindustan Times*.

A catalogue record for this book is
available from the British Library.

ISBN 978-1-90-852624-3

1 3 5 7 9 10 8 6 4 2

2013 2015 2017 2016 2014

Printed and bound in Great Britain by
CPI Group (UK) Ltd, Croydon, CR0 4YY

For Arvind Krishna Mehrotra and Karl Miller

Contents

A Note on the Text

Most of the pieces in the first section, 'Telling Tales', come from the column of the same name which I write intermittently for the *Telegraph* in Calcutta. I haven't included every piece I've composed for this column – how I came to write it, and why, are described in an essay in the section called 'In the Back of the Shop'.

The pieces in this section aren't arranged chronologically, except that the first piece is indeed the first thing I wrote for the column – in January 2000 – and the last piece is also, at the time of writing this, my latest addition to it. A few of these were also published elsewhere: 'German Sequence' in the *Dublin Review*, under another title, 'Changing Planes' in the *London Review of Books* blog, and 'La Loge, or "The Theatre Box"' in the *Guardian*. 'Cowboys and Indians' was, in fact, never published in the *Telegraph*, though I've put it in this section; it came out in *Granta*. One of the intentions of putting some of these short pieces together is to hint at the variety of stimuli surrounding me in Calcutta – the invisible milieu of the column – though, oddly, Calcutta is no longer the stimulating place it used to be. The other is to gesture towards a faith that informs my fiction, and, I see with hindsight, these short essays as well: that it is possible to write about anything. The fact that we still don't have a full-blown capitalism in India, shaping and controlling the media, means you can, if you want, get away with writing about anything (even on the editorial page) without almost anyone noticing.

The second section contains, among other things, a tiny selection of disagreements I've had with other writers – usually, writers I read with much pleasure, but whose wrong side I may have found myself on temporarily, or they on mine. Although I'm generally taken to be a friendly sort of person, I find I've had far more of these spats in print than I would have cared to have had. As a result, I've only decided to showcase a couple of disagreements, partly to remind myself that we don't, in India, live in the voluble but dull intellectual consensus that we often seem to, but also because even a wrong-headed argument can help you clarify your thought processes, and your relationship to that putative consensus. 'Partition as Exile' first came out in *Index on Censorship*, and was republished in the *Telegraph*; 'Event, Metaphor, Memory' in the *Telegraph*. 'Planetary Configurations' was published in *The Times* of India.

This section contains some political writing and reportage too: 'Living in the *Mohulla*' appeared in the *Telegraph*, and 'Diary' came out in the *London Review of Books* soon after the Babri Masjid was brought down. 'The Tailor of Gujarat' was published in *Granta*, and 'Hitchens and the Mother' in the *London Review of Books*. 'Our Awful Record' appeared in the *Hindustan Times* in 2012, not long after Salman Rushdie was kept from visiting the Jaipur Literature Festival.

The third section comprises reflections on projects that might well have been abortive ones, but, by some minor miracle or accident, did end up taking shape; and others that seem doomed to remain in perpetual abeyance. 'Interlude', first published in the *Dublin Review*, is about how I ended up being a novelist rather than a poet, as was my original intention. 'Listening', which appeared in the *Guardian*, is about how I ended up becoming a composer in experimental music. 'Writing *Calcutta*', also published in the *Guardian*, is how I ended up writing my first non-fiction book about that city. I repeat the term 'ended up' because none of these ventures was inevitable. 'Art-Delusion' first came out in the Philips de Pury special catalogue, and is about how I have *not* ended up becoming an artist.

The fourth and last section is a small selection of some of the literary journalism and critical writing I have done in the last twenty years. This includes an introduction I wrote for Hesperus Press for a selection of stories by E.M. Forster; an introduction to two novels by Shiva Naipaul, published by Penguin Modern Classics; an introduction to the selected essays of Walter Benjamin, also for Penguin Modern Classics; and a review of a novel by Kazuo Ishiguro, published in the *London Review of Books*. Neither this section nor the rest of the book has the overt critical purpose that the essays in my other collection, *Clearing a Space*, have – to demonstrate the limitations of the term 'postcolonial'; to enquire into how the notion of modernity might open up or realign certain discussions when we reflexively and unthinkingly keep talking about 'Western' and 'Eastern' literatures; to 'clear a space' for writers like myself, who are supposed to be postcolonial writers, but don't bear clear marks of postcoloniality, except our skin colour and our names. The essays in this collection don't have that overt purpose, but they might embody it inadvertently. They're meant to record the mutating conversations and environments in which we have existed in the last two decades, my own physical locations – Calcutta, mainly, and England – and (to fall back on cliché) the locations of the mind. There's a pattern to the record, both in my retrospective rereading of these pieces and in the anticipated habits, enthusiasm and prejudices of the readers they aim to discover.

My thanks to the editors of the various journals I've mentioned, as well as to my editor, Rosalind Porter.

Amit Chaudhuri
Calcutta
21 April 2013

One:
Telling Tales

Invitation to a Voyage

These last days of the century were days of sleeplessness, and of disasters, both real and simulated ones. (The last days: only the other morning I heard a commentator refer to the 'old-fashioned' caps that Australian cricketers wore in the 'last century', and wondered, after a few seconds of blankness, if it was the twentieth century he was speaking of.) One saw the hijacked Indian Airlines flight land, and take off, and land again; the lights winking in its wing and tail reminded me of journeys made in and since childhood. It is an airline that has no mascot (such as Air India's bowing Maharajah); it doesn't even have a compelling logo; and, with other, better airlines now available on the domestic routes, Indian Airlines is like a word in a dead language. Few protagonists more unlikely than it could have emerged, to occupy our attention, at the end of the millennium. A great, heavy miasma of waiting surrounded IC 814. We do not associate Indian Airlines flights with the long haul and insomnia of intercontinental routes; they are anything between half an hour to two and a half hours long, and can be brief as a one-act play or a feature film. Their interiors have less to do with the profound currents than with the banal accessories of human life: cotton wool for earplugs, plastic knives and forks, tea, coffee, peas pulao. What could be a less satisfying and, on the other hand, more apposite emblem for the end of a millennium than a view of the edge of a runway, that little insignificant piece of waste land we never look at before the plane takes off?

There were those who tried hard to give the event an air of simulatedness, and borrowed from the lay vocabulary of theatre in doing so. Apparently one of General Musharraf's earliest remarks was that the hijack was an 'Indian drama'; and former foreign secretaries gathered on chairs in a PTV studio observed, at least towards the beginning, that the whole thing had been 'stage-managed'. Later, obstinately sceptical Indians on Star News accused the Taliban, in their show of compassion, as they filled mineral water bottles with water, of 'putting on an act'.

On another channel, a disaster that truly *was* simulated (though that formulation sounds like an oxymoron) had been unravelling; Star Plus had promised to show its viewers *Titanic*. All week, as the hijacking protracted itself, and as we stared at the frozen images of the Indian Airlines plane on the tarmac, Star Plus flashed clips of the impending disaster involving a vessel more famous than IC 814, which we would all be able to partake of on the night of the 31st. Much planning seemed to have gone into the making of the film; the title itself was the outcome of considerable thought; 'the' of 'the Titanic' had been the first casualty, and thrown overboard, turning the title into an adjective, or a special kind of noun.

Just as the pictures of the hijacked aircraft were repeated again and again, the sinking of the *Titanic* was shown twice on television in the last days of 1999, once on Star Plus and once, a few days earlier, probably on Christmas Day, on a home-grown cable channel. I'd never seen the film before; yet, as I prepared to go out in the evening on Christmas Day, I saw, by accident, while switching channels, the depiction of a more momentous accident, as the ship tilted to one side and water flowed in through the portholes. These were roughly the last twenty minutes of the film. One couldn't help noticing the film had an astonishingly tacky, cut and paste air about it. Its preoccupations seemed not so much the mythic themes of death and love and separation, enacted in the lives of the doomed passengers, and echoed in the story being shown elsewhere daily on Zee and Star News, as the manufactured quality of the ship, and, indeed, the disaster itself: its assemblage from its different parts by set designers and computer technicians, and the way the North Atlantic ocean had been created inside a studio. Everything – the sky, the decks, the water – seemed to belong inside a studio, as in the early days of Hollywood, except that many of the effects would have been achieved on a computer – which, increasingly, has become the studio of the contemporary artist. In Kandahar, the plane refused to take off from the tarmac; here, the ship tilted so it stood upright in the ocean, tall as Sears Tower; people hung from the railings; the hero and the heroine, who'd had the foresight and luck to be on the right side of the sinking ship, lay recumbent on the topmost railings, not far from heaven. In contrast, the swimmers, down below, seemed to be flailing, when seen in close-up, in a large swimming pool. The first-class passengers, on their boats in another part of the swimming pool, stared gravely at the toy ship sinking in the distance. The studio atmosphere of artificiality and enclosedness meant that, even in the presence of the elements, of water and sky, one was reminded of the interior of the hijacked aircraft and a sense of imprisonment; and yet it also gave those scenes from the film the buried feel of the first printed stories we read.

At about six or seven o'clock on New Year's Eve, it was heard that the hostages had been released in exchange for three militants, and that the hijackers were free. I suppose this piece of news must have brought a modicum of relief to the celebrations, and also an element of ambiguity; what, now that such a debatable deal had been struck and executed by some masked men and a nation, had we exactly gained or lost in all those hours on the tarmac? Rupen Katyal was dead; yet there is a strange sanguinity about the popular art of films such as *Titanic*, as we watch the drowning passengers flail about in the shallows, in that we are sure the actors will get up and dry themselves once the shot is over. Tragic art gives us the pleasure of catharsis; real tragedy gives us none; but popular art gives us elements of banal, recyclable material that will never be completely lost to us, but surface repeatedly. As the twentieth century ended, revellers on Park Street saw the *Titanic* go under on a giant Samsung screen, and then witnessed its paradisial and digital resurrection, as the aged actress, supposedly Kate Winslet grown old, dreams of it before she sleeps, or dies. So the year 2000 was born in Calcutta. In the last two years, I have seen the *Titanic* resurface from the depths in the most unexpected places; on the back of state transport buses on Ashutosh Mukherjee Road, where it appears intact and still afloat; and I have heard it was spotted at quite a few Puja *pandals*. Perhaps the stranded IC 814 will also reappear, in spite of the time lag, in the Puja lights in the coming year. It will have become banal and lost the weight of its tragedy; but the lighting artistes during the Pujas are adept at recording, and illuminating, in both senses of the word, the clutter of sensory and informational data that inhabits our psyche and existence, and which our conscious mind cannot always accommodate and often rejects. Will there be anything we know of the bygone century beyond these immense, or trivial, inventions?

Understanding Cats

Cats live in our building. They live in the spaces that have no definition, in the shadowy corners of the garage. Sometimes, deep in the night, you hear them quarrelling; as Durga, in *Pather Panchali*, half asleep when Apu was born, thought she heard a kitten mewling, we can sometimes mistake the sound for a newborn crying inconsolably, and, looking at our sleeping four-year-old, be thankful that the trauma and bewilderment of those months, which seem not so long ago, have passed. By morning, that nocturnal passion is spent; when they are visible in daytime, or you are present, the cats will never give you the benefit of losing their self-possession. Strife and hysteria are their domestic affair; for the public – and you are the public – only an icy stare and an indifferent composedness are appropriate. Cats cultivate privacy and escape the human gaze in a way that celebrities no longer can.

The cat is an enigma. It often inspires distrust and dislike; but, unlike the serpent, occupies no transcendental position in the Judaeo-Christian tradition. It is neither good nor evil; it existed before that historical moment when, in many parts of the world, the human consciousness bifurcated into heaven and hell. Since then, the cat's eluded almost everything, including theology; its home is the folk tale and the proverb. The Bengali saying, 'The cat is the tiger's maternal aunt', suggests that – if the tiger represents Nature, in its energy and splendour – the cat is older than Nature, if related to it. The cat is not quite of Nature, then: so is it then partly construct? But whose construct, and in which language? The great human inventions – gods, demons, angels, devils – have outlived their uses; they have had

7

their day. But the cat continues to puzzle: we still haven't accounted for its appearance and disappearance in our lives.

The cat, on the whole, is seen to be a feminine enthusiasm; and the enthusiasm is one of the reasons why women are slightly unfathomable to men. Passion for cats gives, among other things, women their oddity – not in a comforting, but in a disquieting way. It's this sense of disquiet that moved Arun Kolatkar to write a poem called 'Woman', which begins with the observation: 'a woman may collect cats read thrillers/ Her insomnia may seep through the great walls of history . . .' (The poem's itself a perpetration of feline deception and hide and seek: when it was first anthologised by Dilip Chitre in a collection of Marathi poetry in translation, it was noted it had been translated into English by the poet. The second time it was anthologised, in a selection of Indian verse in English, the editor, Arvind Krishna Mehrotra, pointed out 'the Marathi version has never been committed to paper'.)

In the second stanza, Kolatkar returns to the disturbing obsession: 'a woman may name her cats/ the circulating library/ may lend her new thrillers'. It's women's nebulous private culture that's being speculated upon here, as it is in the disjunctive litany that ends the poem: 'a woman may shave her legs regularly/ a woman may take up landscape painting/ a woman may poison/ twenty three cockroaches . . .' Men play and watch cricket; they drink beer; they preach religion; they kill each other. What do women do? There is fear and curiosity in this question, the ancient uncertainty of being cuckolded; and the cat is part of the woman's dream life, of the perpetual possibility of sexual betrayal, that the man can't quite encompass.

The cat, it has to be said, had slightly different registers in European and Indian modernity. Some time in the nineteenth century, it seems, the cat became, in Europe, a figure for social polish and bourgeois artifice. Since social polish was associated, in England, almost exclusively with the French, the cat became a symbol for Gallic pretentiousness and self-absorption. The cat is not quite of Nature, as we have seen; and, in the nineteenth century, the dichotomy of Nature and Culture was rewritten, in the cat, in terms of Anglo-Saxon directness and roughness, on the one hand, and French polish and obliqueness, on the other, the cat coming to be synonymous with the latter; and becoming involved, then, in its subterranean way, in both a national debate and an aesthetic one.

Thus, Baudelaire, devoted *flâneur* and dandy, the first poet whose inspirations came almost entirely from the artificial world of the city, rather than from the 'natural' universe, dedicates a poem to his muse, the harbinger of artifice: 'A fine strong gentle cat is prowling/ As in his bedroom, in my brain' (Roy Campbell's translation). Many years later, Ted Hughes would revise these lines in his early poem 'The Thought-Fox', replacing the French cat with the English fox, and, in doing so, enter the familiar Nature/artifice debate: '... with a sudden sharp hot stink of fox/ It enters the dark hole of the head'.

With this, the first poem in his first book of poems, Hughes would position himself as a poet of landscape rather than of the city, and inaugurate a visionary career in which he would set the rough, northern, Anglo-Saxon consonant against the soft, cat-like padding of the French and southern English vowel, the 'sudden sharp hot stink' of English against the 'sweet perfume' ('So sweet a perfume seems to swim/ Out of his fur both brown and bright') of France. Hughes's 'Englishness', thus, is an altogether more combative and embattled affair than, for instance, the English identity that the feline Eliot would embrace – Eliot, who began as a Francophile, a French poet, and aimed not for Wordsworth's 'real language of men', but a fastidious diction 'nether pedantic nor vulgar'. There is a cat-like distaste for Anglo-Saxon directness in Eliot; and his homage to artifice would come, even as he was composing the high moral sequence of *Four Quartets*, in a slim book of 'light' verse about cats.

In India, the line dividing Nature from Culture isn't always clear. In contrast to Europe, the cat, in India, is neither entirely a domestic nor a wild animal; there is an intermediary space in our society, occupied by scavengers and parasites, and it's this semi-official, parallel space that the cat inhabits. It's also a space inhabited, in India, by certain paradoxical figures of authority, who are at once appeased for their power and reviled in private: the Brahmin priest, for example, and, increasingly, a certain type of politician. Western modernity is all about doing away with this intermediary parasitic space; its elimination, however, is accompanied by an anxiety about whether the socialisation which comes with modernity is a good or a bad thing, and the cat is often at the centre of this anxiety.

In Indian modernity, this intermediary space has been kept alive, and even given a political function. Those great chroniclers of our emergent democracy, the Kalighat *patuas*, appeared to realise this, and, to commemorate and record the fact, painted full-length portraits of a cat with a stolen tiger prawn in its mouth. It is a deeply political picture: it presages the fact that our democracy would be less about the politics of right and wrong, or of substance, than of survival; that the politician would be partly a parodic figure. Not the official, recognised and educated figureheads and sources of politics, but the surreptitious snatching of the initiative by the parasitic that the cat with the tiger prawn represents – this, the *pat* seems to say, is the form and shape of our democracy. The cat prowls about in the nation's dream consciousness as that elusive, partially shunned, but ever-present initiative to enfranchisement.

Fortune's Favours

This is not an attempt at analysis, but a simple exercise in comparison. The exercise is the result of having had the dubious privilege of watching a particular show on television, *Who Wants to Be a Millionaire?*, in two different countries. The two countries, Britain and India, were once joined to each other by a long and well-known colonial relationship, but that relationship is not the subject of this piece. Of course, the fact that I've lived in both these countries (and, as a consequence, watched two versions of the same show) may have something to do with the fact that such a relationship once existed. My predilection for comparison as a method, however, might have to do with my having been, as an undergraduate, a student of English, and having, almost compulsively, compared texts by Milton to those by Dante, or a poem by Shelley to another one by Shelley, or a story by Kipling to another by Joyce, each comparison intended to illuminate some meaning that the text might convey.

Since my undergraduate days, though, academics, finding themselves in an increasingly global world, have become less interested in comparing one utterance to another than in the relation of one locution to another locution; that is, less interested in comparing Wordsworth's 'I wandered lonely as a cloud . . .' to, say, Shelley's 'Ode to the West Wind' than in comparing the way Wordsworth's poem might be read in Australia to how it is studied in Japan. English literature, after all, has had a way of cropping up in different parts of the world, not all of them with a colonial past. Similarly, *Who Wants to Be a Millionaire?*, like the Wordsworth poem, has relocated itself in country after country, the latest of which, it seems, is India. Its name here, *Kaun Banega Crorepati?*, even manages to preserve the exact number of syllabic stresses – four – that the original name possesses.

About three months ago, eight o'clock in the evening would confront me with Chris Tarrant in a vast, darkened room, wearing a dark suit, asking someone a question that, if answered correctly, would bring them money. Tarrant is no Amitabh Bachchan; Michael Caine might have been Bachchan's equivalent in England, or Harrison Ford in America, but the producers obviously found it difficult, for whatever reason, to think of an ageing actor hosting the show. Tarrant is very much a television man, like our own Shekhar Suman – he belongs to the idiot box, just as orchestras and musicians seemed to us to reside inside the gramophone when we were children.

Who Wants to Be a Millionaire? made him famous; before it, he'd been glimpsed hosting other shows that were always inane and slightly lascivious. His own grin and now-celebrated chuckle (imitated by mimics – or impressionists, as they are artistically called in Britain – like Rory Bremner) also hover, as he asks his question, between the good-natured, the inane and the slightly lascivious. If the contestant happens to be female, he hugs and kisses her, after almost each successful answer, in the manner that has been common for some time to middle-class British social gatherings. He is slightly cheap, although, paradoxically, he is very rich, doles out huge sums of money and wears expensive suits. Unlike some of the influential British popular entertainers of the 1970s and early 1980s, who had Oxbridge educations but used tawdriness, bad taste and anarchy as a means of subversion and provocation, Tarrant's opulent tawdriness is of a benign, even establishment, kind; he looks like an estate agent. Unlike the quiz masters of more conventional quiz shows (say, Magnus Magnusson on *Mastermind*), he presents no illusion of actually *knowing* any of the answers except, perhaps, the simplest ones; he is there to chuckle, to sign the cheque, to complete the deal; he is an agent.

Amitabh Bachchan in *his* dark suit, on the other hand, looks, I discover upon returning to India, like what he might have been had he not been appropriated by popular culture: a distinguished, high-ranking company executive, albeit in the early days of his retirement. He is, after all, a chartered accountant; born into the educated Indian bourgeoisie and into the cradle of 'high' culture, he is the son of a man who is not only one of the Hindi language's most respected poets, but one who, long ago, also acquired a Cambridge doctorate in Yeats's poetry.

In two regards, Bachchan differs from Chris Tarrant and the hosts of *Who Wants to Be a Millionaire?* in other countries; he is the only superannuated 'superstar' from the big screen the show has anywhere; and he (in his career in cinema; in his present incarnation) represents the slightly uneasy compromise 'high' culture makes with 'popular' culture in order to enter the latter's domain. Something fundamental has changed the face beneath the carefully tended but stubbly beard; is it life, or a new pair of dentures? In a country in which every sphere of activity revolves around obsequious pliancies and hierarchies, the contestants look mildly disarmed that Mr Bachchan should be addressing them familiarly rather than commanding them. However, it is notable that, in contrast to the contestants in egalitarian Britain, who call their host 'Chris', as if he were a weekend tennis partner, the Indians don't take Mr Bachchan's name, while the latter teasingly pronounces theirs again and again, like a stereotypical Indian bridegroom dallying with his bride on the wedding night.

What of the contestants? In England, they have a suburban, nervous look about them, and a pleasant and perpetual air of embarrassment probably intended to ward off the evil eye. At least the first five questions are ridiculously simple, even simpler than the ones the Indians are set; they are something of a joke, they make everyone smile, and are meant to ensure that no one leaves empty-handed. There are few questions on mythology; did a character in E.M. Forster observe, regretfully, that the English have no mythologies, only goblins and fairies? On the other hand, the people who've compiled the questions for the Indian programme seem to have gone deep into the more minor chapters of the epics, to come up with divinities as ephemeral as our politicians, possibly presupposing that Muslims, Christians and atheists are unlikely to want to participate in the show.

I have never seen a British contestant go away with nothing; in India, strikingly, I've seen this happen again and again. This seems to defeat the purpose of the show, which is not, really, to test the contestant's knowledge, but to create, briefly, for the space of an hour, the illusion of a happy romance, the romance between man and money, the most one-sided and unrequited infatuation ever experienced by human beings. This show, like a version of pastoral in the capitalist world, is meant to bear the message that the romance is possible, that it can flourish.

That is why Amitabh Bachchan looks so sad when a contestant leaves with nothing; it's as if he's somehow failed. It's not as if the Indian contestants – many of whom are teenagers (not surprising, perhaps, in a country where someone is born every minute) – are stupid, as some have accused them of being; it's just that the early questions are sometimes capricious, forcing them to use two out of three lifelines before five questions have been asked; and because the contestants are reckless. The British are generally prudent; they are content to depart with what they have rather than risk losing 20,000 pounds because a question whose answer they're not certain of offers them the chance of winning another twenty. Even the English proverbs, like 'A bird in the hand etcetera', attest to this venerable tradition of cautiousness. They leave, the cheque warm in their pockets; they retire to their suburban homes.

The Indians think it undignified to do this, just as they do to admitting they don't know the way to a certain street you might have asked directions to; it's not a lack of knowledge that betrays them in the end, but a lack of self-appraisal. Bachchan, agitated, tries to act as nursemaid; he is far more transparent than Tarrant (who can shake his head misleadingly at a correct answer), and usually easy to read. When he says, 'Sure?' and 'Should I lock it?' it means the question has been answered correctly; if the answer is wrong, he sighs deeply, ponders on something, says, 'You still have two lifelines.' The contestant, his or her face bright with certainty, is too impatient to read these signs; he or she is sure of the answer; Indians seem uneducated in the fact that their actions, or words, might have consequences.

Double Trouble

About midway through Henry James's novella, *The Private Life*, the narrator has a strange experience. The story itself seems to be located in familiar Jamesian terrain, and begins by describing the sort of 'international situation' in which characters in many of his tales find themselves. Here, a group of English aristocrats and socialites are gathered, probably at the turn of the nineteenth century or one of the early decades of the twentieth, near a 'great bristling, primeval glacier' in Switzerland, in a 'balconied inn', for what seems like a vacation. Among them is Clarence Vawdrey (Clare Vawdrey to his friends), a famous writer, 'the greatest (in the opinion of many) of our literary glories'. The narrator's description of Vawdrey's dinner-table manner will be read with recognition by those who, among us, have studied famous writers at close quarters: 'I never found him anything but loud and cheerful and copious, and I never heard him utter a paradox or express a shade or play with an idea . . . His opinions were sound and second rate, and of his perceptions it was too mystifying to think. I envied him his magnificent health.'

Midway through the novella, as I said earlier, the story turns from a study of displacement into something like one of those super-natural tales that James was adept at writing, and the narrator has that unsettling experience which suggests to him why one who is a fine writer (in the opinion of many) should be such a dull and garrulous raconteur. After a long evening repast, the narrator, who appears to be unreliable in more senses than one, notices that Vawdrey is occupied with a well-known actress on the terrace; he takes this as an opportunity to go up to Vawdrey's room in order to search for a play that Vawdrey claims he has been writing but, given his incessant socialising, would actually have little time to write. Rummaging among Vawdrey's things in the dimly lit room, the narrator is shocked to discover that the silhouette he thought was a rug draped on a chair is a human figure, and shocked to discover the human figure is Vawdrey. He mumbles something and rushes out. Who, then, was the man downstairs with the well-known actress? The narrator suddenly realises that the answer to this question is also the answer to the problem posed by the discrepancy, in quality, between Vawdrey's writings and his pronouncements; that Vawdrey has a not very intelligent double who performs the public role of the writer, while he sits in private and writes.

James, tactfully, only glosses over, after all, what is common knowledge among the writing fraternity, but is little publicised outside it; that novelists and creative writers often employ doubles to perform their obligations and duties in the public domain. Not only do these doubles shake hands, answer questions and sign copies of books, but are even, while the novelist is engaged in the struggle of creative work, assigned the responsibility of writing reviews, articles and treatises, all the texts that might contain the writer's 'philosophy of life' or his 'point of view'. Thus, a commentator such as Ashis Nandy, to mention only one critic, finds himself frankly bewildered and flummoxed when confronted with the dismaying qualitative gap between H.G. Wells's science fiction, of whose unconventionality and quirkiness he is an admirer, and Wells's 'prim, predictable' pronouncements on science in his more 'serious' non-fiction, such as his *Outline of History*. It's almost as if, Nandy seems to suggest, the considered pronouncements on science had been made by *another man*.

Poor Nandy, in the same essay (which happens to be on Satyajit Ray), proceeds to record other disillusionments; he confesses to having been at a loss (almost as much at a loss as the narrator in James's story must have been) when he realised that another icon, Conan Doyle, creator of the 'dispassionate, rational' Holmes, was, in his spare time, a 'practising spiritualist and theosophist'. Nandy then goes on to speak of the enigma of Rushdie, like Vawdrey 'the greatest (in the opinion of many) of our literary glories'. Nandy is a great admirer of *Midnight's Children*; but, lighting upon Rushdie's more 'formal social and political comments', finds them 'cliché-ridden . . . not even good radical chic', and 'a direct negation of [the] sensitivities' of the novelist he so admires. Is it time, then, to solve this enigma and reveal that there are two men at work here, as James had once hinted at playfully, under the single signifier 'writer', or, in this case, 'Rushdie'? In Rushdie's case, indeed, the life of the double has taken on a tragic resonance. No one has chronicled, least of all Rushdie, what it means to this double to go on shaking hands, to lecture at literary events and be interviewed with the endlessly extending shadow of a fatwa hanging over him; Rushdie tells us little of the double, and the double insists on speaking only about Rushdie. The situation reminds us of how much we see of the writer's double in our everyday life, in the flesh, on television, in newspapers, but of how little we know about the person whom we seem to be acquainted with so intimately; not even his name.

You will ask, How, then, is the writer's double produced? Is he, or she, arrived at by some technological process of which we are not all aware? Or is he too a fiction created by the author in which we've come to believe? A clue might be provided by the texts and works of art that writers themselves have composed, texts that have proliferated, tellingly, with doubles through the centuries, from the *Epic of Gilgamesh*, written on clay tablets in Babylon in the third millennium BC, to *Terminator 2*. The epic tells us of Gilgamesh, created with a perfect body by the gods, a god-like creature who is, however, not entirely invulnerable: 'Two thirds they made him god and one third man.' (In our age, the latter-day superhuman, Arnold Schwarzenegger, is similarly physically perfect, but suffered from a condition called aortic stenosis.) When Gilgamesh becomes too proud, the gods, to subdue him, decide to create his double: a superman called Enkidu. The description, in the epic, of the creation of Enkidu, might provide us with some information as to how doubles come into being: 'So the goddess conceived an image in her mind, and it was of the stuff of Anu of the firmament. She dipped her hands in water and pinched off clay, she let it fall in the wilderness, and noble Enkidu was created' (N.K. Sandars's translation). One might imagine that it was in this way that Dolly the sheep came to find herself upon this extraordinary planet. Like Dolly, 'Enkidu ate grass in the hills with the gazelle and lurked with wild beasts at the water holes.' (I've always thought that, if the *Epic of Gilgamesh* were ever filmed, with its shows of strength and battles of equals, Schwarzenegger must be recruited for the double role.)

Doubles, however, come cheap these days. Although I am not a well-known writer, I too have one, who performs an increasingly alarming number of public functions; unlike me, he is constantly travelling cities and continents. I have spied him in local bookshops once or twice; seen him, from a distance, autograph copies of my book and hesitate, once, before signing, as if he'd momentarily forgotten who, or where, he was; I've then experienced a pang of compassion. The other day he was apparently at a bookshop, meeting people, being photographed and parrying questions; while I was at home, in a gloomy corner, trying to write this article.

Pure Delight

On the 26th of this month, I emerged from a coffee shop on Park Street with a young man whose acquaintance I was making for the first time. We turned right and began to walk towards Middleton Row; and almost immediately came upon a large crowd. It was gathered outside a shop that sold refrigerators, washing machines and television sets. I had temporary amnesia; what were they watching? The cricket series between England and India had still not begun. Then illumination dawned: it was the semi-final between Brazil and Turkey, which I had intended watching myself. The match was on.

The crowd must have been straining to see. Far away, on a shelf, the first half of the match was in progress on what appeared to be a fourteen-inch screen. You saw more of the side of the television set than you did the screen, which faced the wall opposite; the wall was at an angle of ninety degrees to the window. Standing on tiptoe, I barely made out the screen above the heads. To watch the game this way was not unlike following a cricket match from the top of a twenty-storey building. Indians don't mind straining their eyes to look at what they love. The crowd was content; they exchanged bits of information; they clapped and smiled. I knew they had good news. 'What's the score?' I asked. 'Brazil one, Turkey nil,' a man replied. We nodded and moved on.

Before us, there were more crowds. What is Brazil? And in what way did it become a locality in Calcutta? When I see, in television reports, boys from impoverished city neighbourhoods with Brazilian flags painted on their faces, I am astonished by the lovely mockery this makes of national identity; and also by the cheerful one-sidedness of the adoration. Brazil exists in Calcutta, but does not know it.

My companion, who mostly lives in Delhi, was puzzled by the euphoria (although he had been forewarned of it), and rightly so. For it's a puzzling phenomenon, this devotion to a team and, in effect, a country with which one has no cultural or historical ties to speak of, about which the neighbourhood boy with the painted green and yellow colours on his face knows next to nothing; an enthusiasm that, importantly, can result in no direct material benefits to the enthusiasts.

I pointed out certain other oddly Bengali enthusiasms to my companion: Charlie Chaplin, for instance. My companion was intrigued; he didn't know of this. In spite of Raj Kapoor, in spite of the Cherry Blossom commercials, Chaplin does not, in other parts of India, occupy the space he does in the middle-class Bengali imagination. In the country of his birth, Chaplin is scorned for being sentimental and not being funny; it's something of a scandal. I, as a child, was told that Chaplin made you both laugh and cry, a strangely non-utilitarian view to have of a comedian. This particular affection is common to more than one class; portraits of the tramp, melancholy but about to spring to life, can be found on the backs of pulsating state transport buses.

The love for Chaplin is not altogether fathomable. One could attribute it to Chaplin's left-wing sympathies, but that would be too easy; his appeal, for Bengalis, pre-dates the time when Bengal became synonymous with Marxism. Unlike Romain Rolland – another Bengali icon, once refulgent, now on the wane, and largely forgotten in his own country – he had no connection with the likes of Ramakrishna or Tagore; he met Gandhi, but Gandhi is not exactly beloved of Bengalis. No, the love, as in Brazil's case, is slightly unfathomable.

Perhaps, with both Chaplin and the Brazilian team, it has to do with the capacity to move; to move both in the inward, emotional sense, with compassion and wonder, and in the physical one. Rivaldo's amazing goals and passes; Chaplin's astonishing acrobatics, what Satyajit Ray called, in his essay on *The Gold Rush*, a 'precision of action to a degree unknown in the era of sound'. It is Chaplin's physicality that Ray emphasises: 'Chaplin's words have never quite matched the eloquence of his pantomime.' Pure, physical delight, then; it is as if, watching Brazil and Chaplin, an occasionally over-cerebral culture, too reverent of books, degrees, credos, dogmas, awakes to a realm beyond the word.

But is pure, disinterested delight possible? ('Disinterested' is a forgotten adjective made influential by Matthew Arnold; it implies a dispassionate appraisal of a work of art – not, as in the increasingly common, mistaken usage, 'uninterested'.) For more than twenty years now, theories in philosophy and criticism have instructed us that there is no such thing as disinterested admiration; that we admire, or emulate, nothing that does not enhance our own access to power.

It's probably with this in mind that J.M. Coetzee, in an essay called 'What is a Classic?' (a meditation on the question posed by the title, and also on T.S. Eliot's essay of the same name), recalls the first time he heard Bach's music as a teenager. The music is coming from a neighbour's house, and it's like nothing that the young Coetzee has heard before. It is, as it were, his first encounter with a classic; and it changes his life. In retrospect, however, Coetzee gives a less sublime interpretation to the moment. Was he so affected by the music because of Bach's 'greatness', as he once thought; or was he responding to it, subconsciously, as a South African, a colonial, for whom Bach would be an avenue out of the peripheries of the colony?

If we relate this question to the emergence of Bengali modernity, and its engagement with other cultures, we have to admit that we cannot answer it unequivocally. The faculty for wonder and delight seems to have played as important a role in these transactions as the impulse towards power. The composer Salil Chowdhury's love of Mozart, and his audacious borrowing of a phrase from Mozart's Symphony No. 40 for the tune of 'Itna na mujhse tu pyar badha' in a Hindi film, would have gained him the recognition of neither Europe nor his contemporaries, most of whom would not be able to identify the source. It was a creative experiment undertaken almost in secret; just as the love for Chaplin and Brazil is largely an inadvertent secret outside Calcutta. The secret, one-sided transaction, where one party does not know of the existence of the other, goes back in Bengal to the nineteenth century.

The collaboration between Bengali and English culture, so formative in the emergence of Bengali modernity, was, and still is, almost entirely unknown to, and unacknowledged by, the English. No matter; this did not diminish the ardour, or originality, of the experiment; Bengalis were content with an England and Europe of the mind, as they exult in a Brazil of the mind. No doubt the politics of power are involved in these transactions; but so must pure delight, which directs an enthusiasm to be undertaken for its own sake. Even if it is not, I'm moved, watching the men on the pavement outside the shop window, by the illusion that it is.

Laughing Out Loud

What's reading but sensation and physicality? Even the terms we use to describe the way we're affected by words – being 'touched', or 'moved' – is as if reading were not some transcendental mental communion, but an activity of varying degrees of gentleness or violence involving our body, with its limbs and appendages. Housman inserted this perturbed physicality of our response to literature into the mundane domesticity of bourgeois life when he said a good poem was one that, when you heard it read out, would make you inadvertently cut yourself while shaving. It's a vaguely life-threatening image; and it's one that connects me to another train of thought and events.

When compiling an anthology of modern Indian writing, I commissioned a well-known translator to render, for me, two of Rajshekhar Basu's stories into English. Doing the anthology has been a process of discovery and rediscovery; of witnessing the different, often unique, ways in which the heterogeneous realities of India can be written about, the acts, in different languages, of formal daring and of concealment and irony. It also took me back, occasionally, to my childhood, because the name of Parashuram – the Bengali humorist Rajshekhar Basu's pen name – had been made familiar to me by my mother. She couldn't mention his name without a smile on her lips, just as we can't speak of certain relatives without betraying an emotion that's associated with them in particular.

It was while reading, last year in Oxford, two of Parashuram's stories, that I laughed aloud in the silence of an English afternoon – whenever my wife was in my presence, she'd be puzzled by this causeless exhibition of happiness. But each time the laughter came, I was helpless before it. Parashuram was a far greater presence in my mother's childhood than he was in mine; but laughing out loud made me think of how writers and traditions (even if they are, for whatever reason, temporarily forgotten) wait to come back, to live again in our bodies, to tremble and shake with us.

In 1991, two years after my father moved to Calcutta after having worked in Bombay for twenty-seven years, my mother found she was putting on weight. She's been a committed consultant of the weighing scale ever since I can remember; and the slightest plumpness is classified, by her, as 'obesity'. So, concerned but not unduly disturbed, taking the weight gain to be a surplus accrued from starting out, late in life, in another city, a new home, she began to eat less. I was in England at the time.

Eating less didn't help; the family doctor told her she must restrict her meals further, because an increase in weight wasn't advisable at her age. She reconciled herself to more meagre portions, while her stomach grew mysteriously. She began to go for walks downstairs, in the building compound, but they left her fatigued. Her stomach continued to grow; she resolved to cut down her food; the fatigue continued when she was idle. When she went out in the car, her stomach hurt with every bump; staring out of the window of the car, she felt envious of thin people; getting out of the car, she struggled to climb up the three or four steps of the Calcutta Club. She noticed, then, that though her stomach had distended to an enormous size, her arms were still curiously thin. As no one else felt its weight, no one seemed aware of its existence.

In the heat of the summer, she stopped passing urine, and doctors realised her stomach was retaining water. My father and mother then began to go from specialist to specialist, hoping there would be a diagnosis. But there was only bewilderment. A well-known specialist told my father, in private, that it was cancer, and a terminal case. Another doctor suggested the cure needed to be a medical, not a surgical, one, and that some of the water should be removed and sent to a laboratory for a 'culture'. That would provide an answer, he said. Nothing of this sequence of events was relayed to me; but, one morning, she was admitted into the Belle Vue Hospital to have the water taken out. When I heard that she'd been put in hospital from a telephone conversation with Nepal, the cook, I presumed something terrible had happened. Not so; the nightmare was to recede. A test revealed my mother had contracted tuberculosis of the peritoneum.

The first response to the word 'tuberculosis' is fear. Those were the years – the end of the 1980s – that TB, after what seemed like a long moratorium, was returning to the world. It was still a poor person's disease; but since, in Calcutta, the middle class comes into contact with the poor daily, there's no certainty when the disease may infiltrate its lives. My mother's TB was of the non-contagious kind; but she'd most probably got it from Nepal, a recovering alcoholic who was always in and out of employment at our house, and who'd returned from a long stint at home with what sounded like a smoker's cough (he was a chain smoker and a repository of several exemplary habits) but was an infectious tuberculosis of the lungs. So my mother's life and the disreputable cook's came to be linked in this way.

When my mother was a child, no one recovered from tuberculosis; it was for that reason that the cheerless couplet had once been composed: 'Jakkha hole/ Rakkha nahi' – 'There's no hope/ If you have consumption.' That couplet isn't heard any more; in fact, these days, said the doctor, it's better to get tuberculosis than some other disease, because, given the right medication, and provided it isn't a rare strain, it's as curable as toothache.

Both my mother and Nepal were given a thorough and long course of medicine; and my mother, too weak to move about, read in bed as she recuperated. Her reading originated in a past in which death from TB had been common; but now those authors came back to her as seemingly tranquil companions to her recovery. But reading is never tranquil. As she turned the pages of Sharat Chandra Chatterjee, she found reading him painful in more ways than one; she wept as she read him, and, with every sob, her still-tender stomach racked her with pain. 'Don't read Sharat Chandra,' her brother advised her. 'Read something happier, like Bibhuti Bhushan Mukhopadhyaya.' So she began to read *Barjatri* to regain her composure, till episode after episode left her shaking with laughter and in as much pain as before, wondering what she should do next. One wishes, albeit only on certain occasions, that our most beloved writers were duller, or that, while reading, we could dispense with the participation of our bodies.

Picasso in the Capital City

When Picasso didn't come to Calcutta, the city mourned briefly, then recovered. With so much passing it by – in investment and industry – the failure of a major exhibition to arrive should have left no one surprised; and, after all, art and capital are joined to each other inextricably. Yet the insult remained.

One was curious, too, to have known what a Picasso – say, *Portrait of Marie-Thérèse Walter* – would have looked like in Calcutta, with the traffic, the incomplete flyovers and the minibuses at arm's length. It would have added another dimension to the Picasso painting, which, anyway, is usually about the deferral of its meaning. Picasso's guitars, his women, his men with mandolins, break apart and come together again: to view them in Calcutta – the notion so contrary as to, in itself, constitute an aesthetic experience – would have meant to subject them to that breakdown and congealment in yet another way.

It was not to be. Delhi has become our city of exhibitions, of late-night television discussions, state visits, inscrutable policy-making, stentorian speeches, dull, knowing commentaries on those speeches by social scientists, book launches ridden with envy, visiting American and German lecturers who have written books on the history of Indian art, or on Nehru, Black Cat commandos and biannual shoot-outs, endless lunches of *appam* and stew with fresh orange juice at the India International Centre, where more VIPs (that ugly term, India's favourite abbreviation) congregate within spitting distance of each other than they do at parliament. Here are, worryingly, the people in whose hands our country lies. It is a city of inaugurations;

it's only right, then, that Picasso should be inaugurated here, before journeying to Bombay, and not journeying to Calcutta.

The exhibition, naturally, did not have everything. There were none of the 'taciturn and androgynous harlequins', as his friend the poet Apollinaire called them; nothing I noticed from the Blue Period, nor the huge balloon-like women sprinting weightlessly by the seaside. Yet one was still struck by what is most disconcerting in Picasso: his bewildering variety of styles and signatures, from the Cubist representations of stringed instruments, the collages of the same, the black and white etchings of the Minotaur series, the distorted, garishly coloured faces of his women friends, the early imitations of Cézanne, the sculptures. He is not so much a Renaissance man, a master of competing genres, as an incorrigible dabbler in different modes of painting, from Surrealism to the Cubism he inherited from Cézanne; he is a sort of Auden of art.

What reminds one of Auden as one wanders through the exhibition is the evidence of indefatigability, the need to be *seen* to be always at work. Both Auden and Picasso are the great peddlers and vendors of their respective art forms, Auden bringing to his clientele an array of wares – the short lyric, the long discursive poem, the love poem, the political poem, the ballad, 'light verse', reworkings of Shakespeare and of Christian mythologies; in their restlessness and promiscuity, both painter and poet embarrass those of us who believe in the focused but circumscribed dignity of the artist's vocation. Unlike Cézanne, for instance, who removed himself from the public eye and worked in controlled bursts of activity, revising and revising a single painting, Picasso, like Auden, not only reinvented himself constantly, but reinvented himself in public; his revisions, and departures, *are* his paintings.

It is always difficult to view a classic; it doesn't explode in your face; you have to work your way towards it. If you ignore its prickliness, you will, depending on your temperament, or your mood at the moment, give it a curt glance, or a few moments' devoted obeisance, then move on. You're hindered, further, by an absolute lack of familiarity with the original, and over-familiarity with its reproductions; its several incarnations in histories of art, encyclopedias and posters. Like the 'Ode to a Nightingale', you've already memorised it in childhood and can no longer know it afresh.

The work of art loses its aura in the age of mechanical reproduction, said Walter Benjamin once; this is almost true, but not quite. Instead, the aura gets transferred to the bric-a-brac, generated by the artist, which we have inadvertently hoarded; the Picasso postcards and prints that have become besmirched and hallowed with time, and with the phases in our lives made up of forgotten social interchanges, sexual quickenings and disappointments: for it was at that moment that we discovered Picasso. To confront the original after this is to almost come face to face with a Platonic idea, something removed from the world of the flesh.

My first disappointment with the original of a masterpiece came when I was eleven years old. I was in the Louvre in Paris; the *Mona Lisa* was not far away from me and my parents. I had seen her picture in school; perplexed, I had discussed with my friends the reason for this being the most famous painting in the world. Only one of them could enlighten me. 'From whichever direction or spot you look at it,' he said, 'it seems to be looking at you.' This seemed to be true. I put other portraits, even photographs, to this test, and it seemed to be equally true of them; still, I decided it was more true of the *Mona Lisa*. Nevertheless, by the time I was in the Louvre, I was ready to be left unmoved by the masterpieces of Western civilisation. The *Mona Lisa* was being mobbed, and was impossible to approach. When we finally did reach her, my disillusionment was complete. I said to my mother in my Cathedral School intonation (the line was once repeated to me often, both for its earnest comedy and its no nonsense tone), 'Ma, what's so great about it?'

A degree of scepticism about Picasso survives even today; I saw it in the faces of the passers-by in the exhibition. It poses itself as an unspoken but pressing question: 'Am I being had – is this really a painting?' The question has not lost its force with familiarity or the passage of time; it is as if Picasso were less a painter than an illusionist, his business less art than sleight of hand. But the misgiving it voices is a perfectly valid, and respectable, constituent of our response to Picasso. For illusionism, or legitimate trickery, is an integral part of modern Western art, if we discount works of realists like the American Edward Hopper. It is there in the Impressionists; it made their early critics snarl that the human figures on their canvases were 'tongues or smudges'. It is there in Dalí, who turns Mae West's lips into a sofa; in Magritte, in one of whose paintings a window looking out on a landscape doubles as a canvas and easel.

Nowhere in Picasso's work is his illusionism, his instinct for trickery, put to better use than in his sculpture: into the bicycle seat turned into an antelope's head, or the magnificently pregnant she-goat made from scrap iron and a wicker basket (both were displayed in the exhibition). Looking at the series of photographs of Picasso in the first gallery, I was reminded – perhaps by the neatly combed hair and the predominance of the black suit – that his world was not so distant from the world of the professional performer or magician. The black and white photographs also took me back to the early black and white French films, and, in particular, to the figure of Michel Simon in Jean Vigo's wonderful film, first released in 1936 after his death, L'Atalante.

This is a film, Truffaut said, whose feet smell; it captures something of the dilettanteish bohemian life of magic tricks and carnal desire from which Picasso's art sprang, and which he discovered, in Montmartre in Paris, in 1900. In it, a newlywed couple decide to spend their honeymoon upon a barge (called L'Atalante) going down the river, in the company of kittens and an old layabout played by Michel Simon. Simon, one day, takes the bride to his room below the deck, and shows her his cabinet of curiosities. Here is a Picasso-like assortment: 'rattles, tinkling musical boxes, a sawfish bone, hats from places faraway . . . a fan, photographs, an elephant tusk,' to quote from Marina Warner's little book on the film. Suspended in a bottle full of liquid is a severed hand.

Terrified and charmed, Juliette, our heroine, looks on as the old man displays to her the tattoos on his body. On his stomach is a face, its lips drawn around Simon's navel. When Simon inserts a cigarette into his navel and moves his stomach muscles, the cigarette seems to move in the mouth of the painted face. This tomfoolery, this frivolous inventiveness and amateur magic, this refusal to let a square inch of the universe go to waste in the production of a work of art, is pure Picasso; and Juliette's shock of physical delight at that moment is not too far from our own response to the Spaniard's achievement.

Kalighat Revisited

Early last week, Dr Jyotindra Jain, Director of the Crafts Museum at Delhi, gave a quite enthralling lecture at the art gallery in Oxford Bookshop. The subject was Kalighat painting, supplemented and illustrated by slides of pictures in Dr Jain's book on the same subject.

The aim of the lecture was to show us how the paintings of the Kalighat *patuas* were embedded, artistically and psychologically, in the popular culture and history of the time; how the profane and the contemporary elements of urban existence – an existence whose provenance lay in colonial contact and capitalism – entered the space of paintings whose function would otherwise have been the straightforward retelling of mythological narratives about Hindu gods and goddesses. The paintings, then, reflect, embody and opportunely exploit the birth of the urban modernity in nineteenth-century Calcutta with which its own birth is concordant.

Dr Jain tells us, for instance, how gossip and scandal, as a sort of 'low' form of history, are incorporated as subject matter by the *patuas*. There are hilarious scenes from babu life which depict the babu as an ineffectual male dominated, and even physically abused, by his wife or mistress. (Surprisingly, these representations of the babu as a neutered male are not too far from the British colonialist stereotype of the effeminate *bhadralok*.)

The series of paintings about the seduction of Elokeshi, wife of Nabin, an employee at a printing press, by the head priest at Tarakeshwar, a bearded, ardent, pot-bellied specimen of unreconstructed nineteenth-century manhood, is not unrelated to this subject;

the series culminates with pictures of Elokeshi's subsequent murder by her jealous husband, and, finally, of the trial of Nabin and the head priest. This incursion of scandal and gossip – the kind of thing that would belong to the more prurient among our tabloids and magazines – is not, after all, unknown to the stylised and remote universe of the imagination. Dante's *Inferno* provides an early and illustrious example of such an incursion; being part an epic account of hell and part a dubious tabloid populated with the feuds and jealousies of the time.

But the Kalighat painting refers not only to contemporary events and figures, but to other forms of art that were at the time in the ascendant – like proscenium theatre, for example – and it's in the uncovering of these references that the heart of Dr Jain's argument lies. The Elokeshi affair was, indeed, the subject of twenty or so plays at the time, and the Kalighat paintings on this subject (and, as we see, on other ones) also comprise, then, a homage to contemporary theatre. Certain scenes are borrowed straight from the stage; and it's interesting that a figure in a certain painting, bent low before the feet of another figure, asking for forgiveness, should, instead of directing her attention to the feet, be giving us the benefit of a frontal view of her face, as if she were appraising her audience.

Dr Jain cites other examples of the interface between the paintings and theatre, too numerous to list here; the most notable among these is the pleated curtains of proscenium theatre which form the border of many of the Kalighat paintings, as if the scene depicted in them were a scene from a play. Dr Jain points out with some relish how even the saris that some of the female figures wear are made to resemble theatre curtains. In yet another gesture towards theatre, the faces of well-known actresses on the stage were used, not infrequently, by the *patuas* for the women in their paintings.

Proscenium theatre and babu society aren't the only urban discourses that the paintings refer to. The *patuas* didn't hesitate to borrow images and motifs from the urban ephemera of the time – labels, postcards and photographs. Many of the painters, Dr Jain also claims, were potters and artisans, or collaborated with potters; the shading of the Kalighat paintings, he argues, is less an acknowledgement of the chiaroscuro of Western painting than it is intended to suggest the rounded surfaces of the clay figures that the *patuas* were also, otherwise, engaged in producing, or painting.

Finally, the paintings are often implicitly located in the bazaars of Kalighat where the *patuas* sat. Dr Jain showed us a painting of Shiva and Parvati taking Ganesh out on a family outing, looking rather like a lower-middle-class family in Marxist Bengal, a listless Shiva carrying the small, elephant-headed child in his arms, using the damru as a rattle to placate his son. The disorienting cosmopolitan world of colonial Calcutta, too, is everywhere in these paintings; in one of them, the god Kartik wears the Westernised buckled shoes that were then in fashion.

Listening to Dr Jain's lecture, I felt with renewed force something I've felt before: that the inheritors of the Kalighat *patuas* are the craftsmen and artisans who transform the Durga Puja from a harvest festival into a creative exploration, and occasionally an outrageous comment, on urban reality. As the scandals of Calcutta, the embarrassments of middle-class life, and a vivacious degree of cosmopolitanism marked the world of Kalighat painting, our contemporary scandals and public events – the death of Princess Diana in an automobile accident; Satyajit Ray receiving the Oscar; the so-called 'plague' in India in the mid-1990s; a scene from *Kaun Banega Crorepati?* or *Titanic* – form the subject matter of the men from Chandannagar who do the lighting for the Pujas. These are our *patuas*, though their medium is at once brighter and more evanescent than the Kalighat *pat* ever was; like the *pats*, these lights are part social comment and part parody. Again, as in Kalighat, the proximity of the sacred seems to actuate, rather than impede, these artists' (for they are artists) embracing of the profane elements of contemporary urban culture.

Moreover, does not the *pandal* itself echo, subliminally, the proscenium? We enter it – seeking *darshan* – as if entering an auditorium; and Parvati, her family, and the *asura* appear before us like actors upon a stage gathered at curtain call. And just as the figures in Kalighat paintings (often inspired, Dr Jain reminds us, by clay figures) are inscribed into urban reality, women made to resemble actresses, Shiva made to look like an itinerant family man in a bazaar, so with the Puja images; over the years, one would have confronted, not infrequently, a Durga whose face was uncannily like Hema Malini's, or an *asura* that seemed to be the twin of the taxi driver who took you home yesterday. After the Kargil conflict, some of the *asuras* came to resemble Nawaz Sharif closely, in a typical Kalighat-type metamorphosis of the sacred into the political.

Finally, the chaos and hurly-burly of the Pujas recreate, almost unwittingly, the ambulant bazaar atmosphere of Kalighat. In his essay 'On Some Motifs in Baudelaire', Walter Benjamin notes how the 'amorphous crowd of passers-by, the people in the street', is imprinted on Baudelaire's creativity as a 'hidden figure', and how it is also a significant constituent of nineteenth-century modernity in capitalist Europe. 'The crowd – no subject was more entitled,' says Benjamin, 'to the attention of nineteenth-century writers. It was getting ready to take shape as a public in broad strata who had acquired facility in reading. It became a customer; it wished to find itself portrayed in the contemporary novel, as the patrons did in the paintings of the Middle Ages.' Among the people in this 'amorphous crowd' is, Benjamin points out, the *flâneur*, a typical figure in the urban landscape, the loiterer – often a gentleman of leisure or citified dandy – who plunges into the crowd for no particular reason, except to window-shop, observe and survey the various ephemeral items of urban paraphernalia displayed on pavements and in windows.

If the crowd is the 'hidden figure' imprinted upon Baudelaire's creativity, it is the 'hidden figure' in the Kalighat paintings as well; and it is through these paintings we realise that, as in Paris, the crowd is an all-important element in the construction of modernity in nineteenth-century Calcutta. The crowd, in modern, bourgeois India, often operates in families; and the picture of Parvati, Shiva and Ganesha out on a stroll portrays the sort of family that would loiter in, and pass through, the long stretch of Kalighat with its bazaar, part devotee, part aimless, urban spectators. Kartik, too, is represented as a nouveau riche, leisured dandy, with his buckled shoes and Prince Albert-style haircut. The crowd is customer; like Benjamin's novel readers in nineteenth-century France, who wanted to read about their own fictionalised incarnations, and like the erstwhile courtly European patrons who would have their likenesses painted by professionals, the customers in the bazaar crowds of nineteenth-century Calcutta too must have demanded to see themselves in the *pat*; to see the divine family become as themselves, secularised, itinerant and slightly louche.

The chaos of the Pujas, too, agglomerates us, even at the beginning of the twenty-first century, into crowds and *flâneurs*, forcing us to abandon our immobile, traffic-stalled cars and take to the streets, contained and disciplined only by bamboo barricades; it turns entire areas of present-day Calcutta into something like the bazaars of nineteenth-century Kalighat. This is almost a conscious homage to what the modern metropolis used to be like; for most postmodern cities in the developed world are inimical to the sort of exploration on foot that was once a fundamental part of urban life, and have become suburban enclaves connected to each other by motorways. There are exceptions – for instance, New York, Berlin, London; the death of Princess Diana witnessed, again, a mapping of London by crowds, on foot, as the hearse made its way out of London.

During the Pujas, the crowd is both loiterer and customer; as it moves towards the *pandal*, it pauses at stalls selling fast food, soft drinks, balloons. The crowd wishes to pay obeisance to the deity, but it also wishes to consume its own image and its concerns – the films it is familiar with; the reports in the newspapers it reads – in what it sees around it. Thus the Durgas who still look like Hema Malini (or some appropriately contemporary equivalent), the *asura* who resembles Nawaz Sharif, the stories in lights about Princess Diana and Satyajit Ray. And we relive the illusion, as the crowds in the bazaar did, of inhabiting an extraordinary city.

Motherland – As She is Written

I have before me an under-publicised book of poems which I bought recently from a local bookshop. It is called *Motherland*, and first appeared in 1998 from Dey's Publishing; I picked it up from a fairly munificent poetry shelf for its slightly tawdry cover, and because the author's name was Mamata Banerjee. 'Who is this other Mamata Banerjee?' I asked myself; and found, on the dust jacket, a photograph of the Trinamul Congress leader, her head resting upon the open palm of her hand in frowning, Rodin-like cogitation. That hand, which we've grown accustomed to seeing constricted into a fist punching the air, or waving at crowds in rallies, has here become an indispensable accessory of a writerly pose.

I have seen no reviews of this book in Calcutta or elsewhere, and (unless I've missed them) have to wonder why; did literary editors concur that it would be impossible for anyone to say anything worthwhile about it in a 600- or 700-word review? Certainly, the book presents us with a dimension to Ms Banerjee that at least I wasn't aware of before – and its publication poses, again, a few familiar questions.

'*Motherland,*' says the author in her short foreword, 'is a collection of poems written by me at different times, arising out of different sorts of emotions. I am afraid, the collection may not find readers' attention as far as the quality of verses is concerned, but I may expect appreciation for their simplicity and emotional content.' The first half of the second sentence strikes an unMamata-Banerjeeish note of hesitancy, amplified by that redundant comma after 'afraid'; yet her bluntness about her limitations as a practitioner is the kind of 'straight talk' that has endeared her to some people in the past.

The second half is uttered by the Mamata we've come to know, the politician who will make, intermittently, righteous demands for our approbation, and likes to think even her failures are made memorable by her courage and sincerity: 'I may expect appreciation.'

We – all of us who are the offspring of the marriage between Western history and our own – are deeply uncomfortable about politicians, or people in power, writing poetry, or, indeed, dabbling in any of the arts. The discomfiture originates in the Romantic idea of poetry, an idea we've thoroughly internalised, and whose residue still informs our responses; Shelley's poets were 'unacknowledged legislators of the world', and, ever since that pronouncement was made, it has become difficult for people in the English-speaking world to reconcile themselves to an acknowledged legislator – like Ms Banerjee – being a poet. The non-English-speaking world is impeded by no such embarrassment; the playwright Vaclav Havel has been president of the Czech Republic; Mario Vargas Llosa has run for president in Peru. The pre-Romantic, Renaissance universe of England is, of course, full of figures, like Milton and Donne, who were, at one time or another in their lives, politically active or influential office bearers besides being poets.

In Mughal and medieval India, there was no apparent contradiction in great kings, like Bahadur Shah Zafar or Wajid Ali Shah, being great poets, even if they *were* accused, by the British, of being poor administrators. The incredulity and contempt with which the British regarded Wajid Ali Shah, not least for his habit of composing verse, are a study in the nineteenth-century English disquiet about Art, as an emotional, feminised mode at odds with the vigorous enterprise of Empire. Whatever the flaws of Ray's *Shatranj Ke Khiladi*, it does convey, rather well, the unease of a hyper-male British officer when confronted with the androgyny of a king who dances, sings and recites poetry.

Like other successful women politicians – it isn't difficult to recall Mrs Gandhi or Mrs Thatcher being referred to both wistfully and maliciously as 'the only man in the party' or 'in the cabinet' – Ms Banerjee is an androgynous figure, her maleness and aggression an indispensable part of her political persona. But readers who expect to find in this book a softer, more feminine side to Ms Banerjee, a side concealed from her political life, will be frequently disappointed. The titles of many of the poems – 'Motherland', 'The new generation', 'Hindu Muslims', 'Casteism', 'Arrogance of power', 'Hunger', 'Determination', 'Achievements', 'Cowardice', 'Politics', 'Corruption' – declare, unequivocally, that Ms Banerjee might have agreed with Wilfred Owen when he said, 'Above all I am not concerned with Poetry.' For Owen, the 'pity of War' was both his subject and his medium, and poetry an incidental offshoot; for Ms Banerjee, the subject that overpowers mere poetry is not so much political engagement as that amorphous area covered by the heading, 'the burning issues of the day'.

Like some poets greater than she (for instance, Lawrence), she is often undone by the conflict between the demands of prosody and the compulsion to rhyme. The first two lines of the title poem, with which the book begins, clearly bear the mark of the pressure exerted by this conflict: 'India is our Motherland/ Friendship with other countries is our stand.' She redeems herself somewhat in the subsequent couplet, where the unpromising rhyme 'mother' and 'fathers' is used more interestingly than I can remember it being used recently: 'Everybody loves their Motherland as they love their mother/ But selfish people have some selfish fathers.' In the next line, 'happiness' is mauled as much by the typesetter as it is by these 'selfish people': 'They cannot tolerate the happiners [sic] of others.' While the sentiment expressed in the penultimate couplet is indisputable, and explains her frequent, self-contradictory, populist outbursts, 'We must love people of the neglected sector/ For they are the main pillars and the main factor', the conclusion might either be a general reflection or a veiled remonstrance to the Chief Minister, Jyoti Basu, who is so thoroughly dismissive of her: 'We should have respect for each other/ Because everybody is our brother and sister.'

There's something for everyone. 'Hindu Muslims' takes on the official, secular line of the party she abandoned (or which, she'd perhaps have it, abandoned her), and begins with an optimistic tautology:

'Severance cannot divide Hindu-Muslims.' That hyphen is striking, as if the two communities were Siamese twins conjoined at birth, unable to pursue their independent and respective lives. But the next poem, 'Future', which gropes its way through a *Four Quartets*-like beginning – 'Future thinks about future/ Present thinks about the present/ Past always kept aside' – ends with what is dangerously close to a ringing BJP credo, 'Let us think of unity, speak about unity/ And fight out the Evils who want disunity', where such 'Evils' are not infrequently synonymous with aberrations from the (Hindu) mainstream.

There are one or two touching things here, like the poem 'Torn Paper and Soiled Paper', about the boy going from house to house, collecting rubbish on the day of the Bengali New Year. 'Whilst I sat my glance on the newspaper/ Suddenly I heard/ Didi, may I take the torn papers, the soiled papers?' Ignoring the awkwardness of phrasing for a moment, and the hovering figure of the boy, one realises that this is how Ms Banerjee sees herself, dreams of herself – 'Didi', 'older sister' – and one can't grudge dreams their poignancy, however removed they may be from reality.

The author tells us she's published in Bengali in the past, but suggests this is her first foray into the English language; her graceful admission – 'yet I would like to present my English renderings with much humality [*sic*]' – is, again, made ridiculous by the typesetter, leading one to speculate as to whether he's a CPI(M) worker. She calls the poems, one notes, 'renderings', raising the question as to whether they are translations, or versions loosely based on poems written originally in Bengali, or, indeed, whether these poems came into existence in English, as they well might have. Yet why English? It's the great post-colonial question that is never answered satisfactorily. To say that Ms Banerjee turned to this language only to widen her audience and constituency is to discount the deep and puzzling urge that Indians feel to express themselves in English, and the way they often indulge in it, like a terrible vice. Ms Banerjee might have been advised to exercise greater self-control; but she's never been known to set much store by those who are circumspect in their actions.

Thieves, Gangsters, Poets

My friend and his wife went to see *Takshak* the other day. The word was apparently chosen by the director, Govind Nihalani, not so much because of its meaning but its sound. The film represents Nihalani's excursion from middle-of-the-road realist cinema into the territory of popular film. It's interesting that Nihalani should herald this crossing over into the realm of popular art with sound taking precedence over sense; decades ago, Shobhaa De, then Kilachand, sanctified lowbrow film journalism, in the hypnotic argot of her column 'Neeta's Natter', with the feline syllable: 'Meeeow'. Assonances and sounds multiply everywhere in popular culture; even the early dicta describing it are themselves alliterative, assonantal and self-repeating – 'The medium is the message'; 'Celebrities are people who are famous for being famous'.

Takshak, my friend told me, was enjoyable, as long as you accepted it was a copy of the Mafia and gangster films of Hollywood. 'Copying' and theft have, indeed, an honourable lineage in Hindi cinema. Zeenat Aman, strumming the guitar and singing the words *'Chura liya hai tumne jo dil'* ('You've stolen my heart'), may not have been aware that it wasn't only her heart that had been stolen, but the tune as well, from 'If it's Tuesday, it must be Belgium'; if Eliot once declared, 'Mature poets steal; immature poets imitate', or words to that effect, R.D. Burman's *'Chura liya'* was no less a manifesto and a proclamation.

The idea of plagiarism is probably not as fundamental to our culture as it has been in the post-Romantic West; one might imagine the number of lawsuits that might have proliferated among the bhakti poets and Kalighat *patuas*, for instance, if it had been so. In his *Collected Essays*, A.K. Ramanujan meditates on the fact that a number of stock lines, phrases, images and sentiments are transferred from poem to poem, like a kind of currency, a form of free trade, in classical Tamil poetry, without, in their poets' eyes, compromising the individuality of each poem; here, the original and the borrowed are not in opposition to each other.

The Hindi gangster films – what little I have seen of them on television; *Satya*, excerpts from *Arjun*, others I don't know the names of – are a form of translation. One set of codes – in this case, to do with the underworld of Chicago or New York – is transferred on to another – the representation of the Mumbai underworld. We have heard of the term 'pale imitation'; yet perhaps 'pale original' would be more in order here. For Hollywood has become increasingly inward-looking, its films arrested by their formulae; increasingly, they ignore material reality and are distinguished only by their preoccupation with special effects and 'aliens'. Even relatively successful gangster films like *The Untouchables*, which is really a period piece, a *noir* film dressed up by Merchant–Ivory, pursue, with a few exceptions, the old 'feel-good' Hollywood verities of heroes and villains. Those very formulae, transplanted on to recent Hindi cinema, have served as a kind of release, an opening up of these films to contemporary India. Translation, here, is a way of looking at a changed, hybrid reality. These new films about psychotics or underworld dons let in the contemporary, ambiguous, banal, globalised world – of, for instance, cellphones and one-day cricket matches – into their composition in a way that neither films like *The Silence of the Lambs* nor more respectable genres such as the novel do.

But another group of practitioners in the arts, besides the film-makers of Bombay, has studied America closely, and borrowed from its language and forms for its own purposes. I am thinking of the Indian poets who wrote in English in the 1960s, 1970s and 1980s. Two of the most notable among them, Arvind Krishna Mehrotra and A.K. Ramanujan, have used a diction that bears the self-evident impress of American poetry: Ramanujan, in his unsettlingly quirky line endings and his misleadingly chatty, confiding tone, takes something from Marianne Moore, and Mehrotra has himself pointed out the importance of Gregory Corso, Ferlinghetti, Ginsberg and Hart Crane to his work. There is only one poet, though, who, like the Mumbai film-makers, seemed to have realised the potential that the language of the Hollywood gangster films has, and probably used it creatively some time before they did; I am thinking of Arun Kolatkar. Thus, while Kolatkar has a predecessor in William Carlos Williams, he also has a possible ally in Martin Scorsese. More than once, Kolatkar has used the slang spoken in the streets of New York and Chicago to map the psychological terrain of 1970s Mumbai. Surely the most striking example of the language and structure of the Hollywood Mafia film transplanted on to an Indian work of art is not some Bollywood film but the poem 'Ajamil and the Tigers', which occurs in Kolatkar's great sequence of poems *Jejuri* (1976). This narrates the arrival of a middle-class, ironic but observant loiterer at an inconsequential pilgrimage town, Jejuri, in Maharashtra. Though the place abounds in myths, it has no important shrines or monuments; the priests and guides themselves don't seem to know the stories they tell too well; yet the narrator, who is not obviously religious, occasionally traverses the distance between irony and wonder. 'Ajamil and the Tigers' is a retelling of a mystical tale that the narrator may possibly have heard in Jejuri. It is about a pure-hearted shepherd, Ajamil, whose sheep are always threatened by the marauding tigers in the area; the tigers have no success in purloining the sheep mainly because of Ajamil's fearless sheepdog, who vanquishes them again and again. The tale is narrated in the idiom of the Hollywood gangster movie. Ajamil and his sheepdog play the unassailable policeman and his deputy; the leader of the tigers a kind of Mafia don who, at one point, promises, 'I'm gonna teach that sheepdog a lesson he'll never forget.' 'Nice dog you got there,' the 'tiger king' tells Ajamil at last, after a battle, 'spitting out a tooth'. And he complains to Ajamil that his tigers are starving to death, thanks to the intrepid sheepdog. In its mixture of mysticism and machismo, the poem looks forward to the globalised, Hindu-revivalist Mumbai of the 1990s, where religion and terror went hand in hand. But a benign humour prevails in Kolatkar's poem. The solution Ajamil proposes to the tiger king is both ecologically sound and a parodic inversion of the culture of Mafia protectionism; he gifts the tigers a few of his sheep in return for the rest being left in peace. For, as the narrator points out, 'Like all good shepherds he knew/ that even tigers have got to eat some time.' This conclusion, both reminiscent and parodic of Blake, who spoke of the tiger in proximity to the lamb, is also a subtle comment on the act of creation as translation, from which the poem itself springs; instructing us, as it does, that it's impossible for something to originate without it being involved in a transaction with other points of view, other selves, other languages.

Family Secrets

Families have their secrets and treasures. Some of the secrets might be a source of shame, and might even be known to only one or two of the family members; the treasures can be a cause for continuing pride, and also pulse with disappointments, as reputations dwindle and promise remains unfulfilled. The family, then, becomes a site that struggles, through its folklore and memories, against the amnesia of history.

Marriage is an exchange of these treasures and secrets. The principal treasure in my wife's family is the painter, Sudhir Khastgir (1907–74). Some time before we were married, my wife told me that her grandfather, Satish Ranjan Khastgir, the distinguished physicist, had a younger brother, a painter whose work she liked very much. I hadn't heard the name before, but when I repeated it to my parents, they spoke of him admiringly, although they said they hadn't seen his paintings in a long time. In a couple of generations, the reputation had faded; the family's treasure had become one of its secrets.

The first time I saw a Sudhir Khastgir painting was in 1991, when my wife took me to Shantiniketan a few months before our wedding. She wanted me to see her grandfather's house in Purba palli, with its courtyard of jhau trees, and amloki, custard-apple and other trees in the orchard at the back. It was a house she used to dream about even then. We went there in the summer; it was end of term in Oxford, where we had met about eight months ago. She showed me the faint Bengali lettering by the gate, which spelt 'Subhoshree', the name her grandfather had given her, before her grandmother gave her the name I had first known her by, Rosinka.

One looks upon one's wife's family with a mixture of curiosity, tenderness, and a certain lack of indulgence. I remember being disappointed by this house, the house my wife still visited in her dreams. It was in decay, and soon to be sold. Shantiniketan itself was dead, a place with a history but no present, to which retired people moved and where the rich built winter retreats, but otherwise without life or purpose; and we had the summer to contend with by day, and the lack of electricity by night. The bathroom was in disrepair, and I bathed in cold water collected in a pail, the first time I did so in almost two decades. Some of my wife's grandmother's things were still here (she had lived here after her husband died, and once fractured her femur), among them a wide bedpan made for people with osteopathic problems.

When my mother was a girl, she might have come to Shantiniketan, and learnt singing; she might have met Tagore. (She has one of the most perfect singing voices I have heard, and is a respected artiste in her own right.) But that was not to be; her father died when she was a child, and the family fell into straitened circumstances, and lacked the means to send her anywhere outside the Sylhet and Shillong in which she grew up. Who knows; if she had come to Shantiniketan and entered its magic circle her pitch-perfect voice might be heard more widely today. But Shantiniketan, which gave Bengal some singers, remained out of reach for some others, like my mother. Now, on this visit, I saw how Shantiniketan had become a small town of no particular distinction; how it was struggling for visibility, as my mother had when she was a young woman; history had come full circle.

We ate with my wife's aunt, Shyamoli Khastgir, the artist's daughter, in her house in Purba palli, not far from where we were. She had been married to Lee Tan, architect and son of the man who was once head of China Bhavan, from whom she was now separated; she herself was an environmental activist, and was convinced technology was taking the world towards its own destruction. Around us, scattered on the floor or leaning against walls, were the works of the painter to whom I felt, uncomfortably, I was about to be related by an imminent marriage.

My immediate impression of his work was that it was different from anything I'd seen before, and that it diverged strikingly from much of the painting of the Bengal school. For one thing, the medium was oil; and the work had little of the nostalgic meditativeness of the Bengal school painting. A large painting of the Buddha confronted me; yet it had not been executed in the expected (given the subject) delicate Far Eastern or Japanese style which the illustrious Bengali masters frequently dabbled in, but boldly, in oil; this Buddha looked like a hero, or a great actor. It began to rain around us, the lights were switched on, and when I looked at the face, it seemed as if it were illuminated by stage lights.

That night, we slept without electricity behind a mosquito net; my wife's aunt slept in the next room, our custodian, the door between us open. In the morning, my wife showed me the accessories of her grandparents' lives, the table where her grandfather worked, the old grandfather clock, none of which she would actually see again in that setting; and nor would I.

Among the things she showed me was a painting in a rudimentary frame that had been gathering dust, of two branches of palash flowers, by her grand-uncle, a painting she told me she had always loved. This was gifted to her later by her father after the house was sold, and now hangs, in a new frame, on a wall in our flat. Again, it is a startling picture, the brush strokes rapid and unhesitant and almost reminiscent of Van Gogh; yet the flower depicted in it is the untranslatable, Tagorean palash, redolent of Bolpur and Bengal. But the painting has none of that stillness or lyrical inwardness that the landscape studies of the Bengal school often have; like the portrait of the Buddha, it is a theatrical work, and the branch of palash is a protagonist, rather than a detail alluded to or briefly touched upon.

Over the years, I have absorbed, and come to have a high regard for, the individuality and power of this painter's genius. One misses him in exhibitions; he was a great and unremarked absence in the *Art of Bengal* exhibition at the CIMA gallery; I find him, instead, in people's homes, and three or four of his paintings hang on the walls of my parents-in-law's flat in Mandeville Gardens. One of them is a picture of a waterfall by a gulmohur tree; all the other pictures have magnificently drawn dancing figures in them.

Among them is a painting of a couple, a frontal view of a man and a woman, dancing, their arms outstretched, their hands poised in a mudra, the urgent brush strokes making them shimmer as they move sideways. The background is dark; but there is a light in the painting which feels not so much like moonlight as the lighting on a stage, especially since the faces of the figures are made bright, seemingly, by a source of light before them. When my mother-in-law saw this painting after her marriage, she apparently said to the painter, 'You must have been thinking of the lines, *"Premero jowaare bhashabe dohare"* when you painted this', quoting from a song from Tagore's dance-drama, *'Shyama'*; and the painter was sufficiently pleased by the identification to give her the painting. The lines are not easy to translate: 'You will set these two adrift/ Upon the high tide of love.' The lines, with their invocation of 'high tide' and of 'casting adrift', are as much about the onward motion and stream of actions that are the substance of theatre as they are about love.

The anecdote suggests to me what I have come to feel about Sudhir Khastgir's imagination: that it was suffused with the world of theatre, the Tagore dance-drama, and music; that is, the world of performance. Even his landscapes, in the vigorous movement which is their true subject, seem to allude to the flux and hurry of the stage. This interest was confirmed to me when I was told by his family that he was a singer, and that he also directed some of Tagore's dance-dramas when he was an art teacher in Dehradun. In situating his art in the metaphor of performance, he seems almost unique among Indian painters of his time. He is, in effect, an artist who has rebelled against his art; for the impulse of the painting is to record a scene and preserve it for eternity, while the impulse of performance is to race to its conclusion, so that it may begin, on another occasion, again. Art is timeless, still, and eternal; performance is transient, mobile and recurrent. To discover how these two opposing impulses converge in the genius of one artist, we must view Sudhir Khastgir's singular paintings again.

The Lion's Roar

Once a week, the lion roared. He was hungry. By prior consensus, the creatures of the forest met and voted for who, among them, would be the lion's dinner. This saved them a lot of unnecessary introspection, and gave life in the forest a semblance of orderliness. The decision to arrive at this arrangement with the lion had been made by a council many years ago, no one remembered exactly when. If the lion were kept happy, there would be peace in the forest.

Naturally, there was, as a result, peace in the forest; the creatures gambolled, pranced, grazed, reproduced, and were free to do whatever they pleased; only, once a week, when the lion roared, one of them was required to present himself before him at mealtime. Despite the occasional tears and protests this offering of oneself involved, it had become a routine soothing in its predictability, and preferable to greater, and less premeditated, calamities. Risk, chance, the unknown, chaos, were the main enemies of the forest, it was concluded, and not the lion; the lion was much loved for having banished risk from its life, and wielding his appetite as a judicious form of governance.

One day, it fell on a monkey to satisfy the lion's hunger. He spent all night devising ways of getting out of this situation, because he had no intention of being the lion's repast. The next day, he arrived late at his doorstep. The lion, tossing his mane angrily, said, 'What on earth do you mean by keeping me waiting? Have you any idea of how hungry I am? Besides,' he said contemptuously, looking him up and down, 'you're a morsel. I could eat another five of you.'

The monkey trembled and confessed, 'I set out quite early, sire. But I was met by another lion on the way. He was going to eat me immediately, but, after entreaties and prayers on my part, has allowed me to come to you with his message before I go back to him.'

'*Another* lion?' said the lion.

'Very nasty and mean,' said the monkey nervously.

'Nastier and meaner than *I* am!' exclaimed the lion, getting angrier all the time. 'And what did he have to say?'

'That, henceforth,' stammered the monkey, 'you will have to take permission from him for all your dinners and lunches.'

The lion leapt up as if someone had pulled his tail. 'Where is he? Take me to the impostor!'

The monkey led the way for a while through the forest. He stopped at a well. 'Sire, he lives down there,' he whispered. The lion stood up eagerly on its hind legs and peered down, and caught a glimpse of a face that was large and threatening. He roared at it; the creature below bellowed back. Enraged, the lion leapt into the dark, and was drowned. Nothing more was heard of him. The monkey informed a few others of what had happened, and news spread to different parts of the forest; celebrations began to take place.

We are all familiar with some version of this story. Its magic lies, for us, precisely in its story-like quality, its unrealisability; if something like it were to happen in what we call 'real life', that event itself would become story-like, enchanted, fabular. Well, something like it did happen this week, in the Eden Gardens stadium. The lion – the antipodean beast, the Australian team; Steve Waugh – arrived in India in February, having lunched on fifteen Test matches and several teams; and, digesting them all thoroughly, was still agile and playful as a cub, and ready for its next dinner.

Having said that, let me admit that there is no lion I admire more than Steve Waugh, his apparent slowness disguising his alarming feline spring when he darts equally to his left or right to take catches, and then settles into repose again; his eyes, when batting, seeming to diminish with drowsiness, but actually narrowed in focus and appraisal. He is a creature who seems to inhabit the animal world between physical rest and mental calculation, and is never not sizing up a prey; yet he is far more intelligent than the lion in the story I have retold above, and is admired, at least in this city, by both its underclass and its bourgeoisie as perhaps no other player, not even Tendulkar, is.

The lion had an unsurprising and easy dinner at Bombay; the creatures of the forest – rabbits; monkeys; pigeons; deer – offered themselves, as they've long been accustomed to, to his insouciant jaws, with the appropriate dressing or sauce; the jaws masticated, then became still. By the time the lion had come to Calcutta, he was ready to eat again. He roared; the forest creatures assembled; but the spectators had begun to tire of this story; one saw them leaving Eden Gardens in droves at the end of the second day, an even sadder sight than what was happening on the field.

But, in the gap of the night that followed, someone like the monkey in the story had decided he didn't want to be dinner; a relatively junior Hyderabadi batsman, the impeccably mannered and deeply intelligent V.V.S. Laxman, once protégé of the now-disgraced Azharuddin. He kept the lion waiting; then escorted him to the well, where he heard his own loud roar and attacked himself, and was drowned. Laxman's primary cunning, even more than his single-minded achievement, was to arrange for the lion to become his own, insurmountable opponent.

Unlike in the story, of course, this lion will roar again, and the forest creatures will wish to queue up before it, nostalgic for the symmetry and logic of a narrative they've grown used to. The little monkey will not always survive. Epics and fables are not real life; but, as the second Test in Calcutta reminds us (as Yeats once did: 'Those masterful images . . ./ Grew in pure mind, but out of what began?/ A mound of refuse or the sweepings of a street'), they owe at least something of their insubstantial stardust to the toil and sweat and uncertainty of our actual existence.

In the Back of the Shop

Not long after I returned to Calcutta, and to India, in 1999, the *Telegraph* asked me to write for its pages. This was my brief: to write twice a month, on Sundays, but to depart from this regime when it was necessary; and to write, more or less, whatever I wished to write about. The brief was temptingly put; but most alluring was the idea of writing for a Calcutta newspaper and an immediate readership.

'Immediate' in the sense that a newspaper readership is immediate, but also perhaps in the sense that writer and presumed reader would belong to the same physical and cultural vicinity. I was reminded of the feeling of metropolitan completeness that newspapers once conjured up, and which T.S. Eliot captured in the lines, 'The readers of the *Boston Evening Transcript*/ Sway in the wind like a field of ripe corn.' The image is too bucolic for Calcutta; but Eliot is writing these lines at one remove, as a cosmopolitan American in London, about to remake himself as an Englishman, reminiscing about his origins. No wonder that the poem ends with an exaggerated sense of distance and exile: 'I mount the steps and ring the bell, turning/ Wearily, as one would turn to nod good-bye to La Rochefoucauld,/ If the street were time and he at the end of the street,/ And I say, "Cousin Harriet, here is the *Boston Evening Transcript*."'

Returning to Calcutta, I had brought with me that sense of distance. I had written for British newspapers, and still wrote essays and articles principally for the *London Review of Books* and the *Times Literary Supplement*; but writing for the *Telegraph* would be different. I was not sure how. Different contexts bring into being different possibilities. It was with that sense of possibility that I said 'Yes' to the editors, keeping in mind that between the *London Review of Books* and the *Telegraph* lay something like La Rochefoucauld's puzzlingly endless avenue.

I have been writing this column for almost two and a half years. This anniversary issue gives me an opportunity to consider what, at different moments, I envisaged the column to be, to re-experience that minor pulse of excitement. From the beginning, I knew it was a 'column' I wanted to write; that is, not only produce individual pieces and articles, but situate them, even if they were noticeably unlike each other, in a continuum in which they would be related to each other – and this continuum would be that imaginary space called the 'column'.

A column is not only a space on a page that is filled with words; it is something that exists in time (that is, on the day of its publication) and outside it. Having identified that it was a column I wanted to write, I now searched for a name for it; for a column, like a character in a story, is incomplete without one. I don't know when human beings began to name themselves; but one presumes it was around the same time that stories came into existence. Which came first, names or stories, is difficult to tell; it is like the chicken and egg joke; certainly, human beings, from the very beginning, have named themselves after the legendary and mythical beings they have created.

What did I want to write about? The answer to that question might, I thought, suggest the name I required. It quickly became clear that my subject matter should comprise things that did not fit anywhere else: in a novel, in a poem, or a story, or even a critical essay. They would not be 'true' subjects, in a sense; they would have existed greyly, neither significant nor insignificant, and would have had the potential of becoming subjects suddenly conferred on them by the imminent existence of the column.

It was not their significance I wished to mine, but their continual persistence in my life; like someone who is at peace, having buried a corpse in his backyard, but finds it has an ability to sprout vegetation.

Every writer's life – perhaps everybody's life – has a sort of mental junkyard, full of things not entirely discarded; as the years pass, the junkyard grows. Many things inhabit my junkyard, including certain lines from Eliot, a poet, unsurprisingly for the time I grew up in, I loved as a teenager; they come to me unprompted, for instance, when I am exercising and my muscles are fatigued, or when I am in a traffic jam: 'Till human voices wake us, and we drown' or 'I grow old . . . I grow old . . .' They come without meaning, the way we mutter expletives or prayers. Was it possible to write of such inexplicable sensations, of thoughts that were really not thoughts, in a column?

When I mentioned to a literary friend at the *Telegraph* the notion of the junkyard, he took me back to the figure of Montaigne, the inventor of the essay as we know it. 'You could call it "The Back of the Shop",' he said. Montaigne lived in the sixteenth century; but one could call him a very early Romantic. A lawyer and scholar, he would retire frequently to a tower near Bordeaux to compose his essays, which grew out of stray quotations he had put together, adding commentaries that finally subsumed the quotations and became the essays. (As a method of composition, it still largely holds good today.)

The 'back of the shop' the friend referred to was, in Montaigne's words, the *'arrière boutique'*; an early Romantic delineation of the artistic private space defined against the bonds of society and family. In the following quotation, from Montaigne's 'Of Solitude', it is translated as 'storehouse': 'A man that is able may have wives, children, goods, and chiefly health, but not so tie himself unto them that his felicity depend on them. We should reserve a storehouse for ourselves, what need soever chance, altogether ours and wholly free, wherein we may hoard up and establish true liberty and principal retreat and solitariness . . . there to discourse, to meditate and laugh, as without wife, without children and goods, without train or servants . . . We have a mind moving and turning in itself; it may keep itself company . . .'

We tend to associate such extreme demands and moods with poets. The *'arrière boutique'* – the 'back of the shop' or 'storehouse' in the passage – might be Montaigne's tower near Bordeaux (and – who knows – it could be where the term 'ivory tower' originates); but it is also, as John Hollander and Frank Kermode point out in their introduction to the Oxford anthology *The Literature of Renaissance England*, what became 'for humanist meditative writers more than merely a locale, a room, a place, but rather a whole region of the mind . . .' It is a gendered space, of course, and one that would be annexed, a few centuries later, by Virginia Woolf in the feminist cause.

By the time I returned from England, I was what is called a 'full-time writer'; I needed to retreat from neither home nor work, and I had no tower to retire to. Home was where I worked; and even this essay has been written with my child, now almost four years old, in earshot, and in proximity of my wife and parents (the European man, even in the sixteenth century, did not, after all, live with his parents). The 'back of the shop' is no longer a physical locale; it has truly become, even in Calcutta, a 'region of the mind'. But it was not really that romantic space I desired when I thought of the column; it was a junkyard in which the flotsam and jetsam of both the public and private worlds might congregate.

I have not always adhered to that conception. My first column appeared at a time both auspicious and apocalyptic: at the end of the old millennium and the beginning of the new one. Two of the final images of the twentieth century, flight IC 814 on a runway in Kandahar, and the *Titanic*, sinking in an artificial ocean, became the subject of my first piece. After some thought, I named the column 'Telling Tales'.

Two pieces I wanted to write at the outset, one on twins (based on Ketaki Sheth's mysterious pictures of twins in the Patel community in England), the other on the shortage of small change in India, remained unwritten; as did a spoof column which I wanted an alter ego to author when I was on 'holiday' (for I was anyway always travelling outside Calcutta), berating me for my lack of engagement with 'real' issues. These aborted attempts are, for me, part of my column's dream life. One thing I learned in the process of writing these pieces was to let myself start with an image or thought without completely knowing where I was going; so that the piece would not be a report of what I already knew, but the record of a discovery made in the span of its writing. This essay, too, has been written with the same principle in mind.

Localities

'I can give you some material for your column,' my mother said to me recently. I nodded; people are always suggesting to me what to write. I'm not talking about the people who review my books; I mean ordinary people. Ordinary people give me their manuscripts – their novels or stories – and want me to tell them how to write better, or that they write well, or in what way they might get published and become famous, or at least read by others. But some – relatives; strangers – might ask me to fictionalise their life stories, or someone else's. They seem to sense, rightly, that the burden, and the material, of the writer is anonymity; not only his own, but others'.

My mother's offer came to me from a sense of affront and outrage. She has a greater faith in the efficacy of newsprint than I do. She has an unarticulated belief that newsprint is an instrument of social and political change; and whenever she encounters something appalling or unjust in this city, she turns to me and says, *'Tui likhbi na?'* This time it was no injustice, but her driver's room that had moved her – she perhaps saw it as a form of injustice.

'You must go and see it,' she said. 'It's not far away.' The previous day she and my father had been to Ravinder's room. Ravinder (I have changed his name), the tall, rather gangly driver of the Maruti Esteem, has been working for them for about eight years now. He was there, in the front, behind the steering wheel, when we brought our newborn daughter home from the Belle Vue nursing home.

But from time to time he disappears, always leaving my parents at a loss, searching for a replacement. Something at home beckons: his wife; his two children; a relative's illness; a problem with *'sampatti'*.

Off he goes to a village near Giridih, and comes back thinner and darker, expecting re-employment. He is always taken back after the first admonitory noises. The last time he returned, he resolved to put an end to this back and forth movement, which was being caused by his father's inability to get on with his wife. 'Khali jhaada kore,' he said: 'jhaada' (to shake) is his way of pronouncing 'jhagda' (quarrel); it captures the violence of these domestic differences. So he decided to move to a room that would accommodate his family.

Once, when he was absent, we looked him up in a room on Broad Street which he was sharing with six other people; later, he shifted to a room near the Ruby Hospital, the area in which the driver of my car, a young Bihari boy, now lives. In other words, Ravinder, during his employment, has never lived very far from where we do; he's always been a walk or a short drive away. It has to do with the extraordinariness of this city, where neighbouring localities can be so different from one another, economically and socially, and the way the inhabitants of one locality, or even a corner of a locality, become familiar with another neighbourhood and yet remain in a sense strangers to it; this is true, for instance, of both Ravinder and myself, and will continue to be true for us in the 'foreseeable future', as they say.

Giridih or its environs is where, as I've said, Ravinder comes from. A good-looking young man who stands outside the Emami shopping centre on Lord Sinha Road, wearing spotless white kurta and pyjamas and a Gandhi cap, and who assiduously tries to sell me flattened chana garam in a packet, tells me he comes from Sitamarhi in Bihar, which is, he informs me, 'Janaki's birthplace'. Two older men, dressed identically, stand with him outside the mall in the evenings. The young man expounded a theory to me once: that most Biharis in this city come from Sitamarhi and— but I can't remember what the other place is. So I went looking for him, but was disappointed to hear he'd gone home to a relative's wedding. 'Not his own?' I asked. 'Oh no, he's married with children.' Later, I took a solitary walk in my own 'district', passing the Birla temple into Queen's Park. This lane still has the quietude of affluence; as I was walking back, I saw a man pulling a rickshaw. Why was he here? Would he have plied the Japanese Consul General, or Mr Khaitan, or Mr Todi home? I asked him; he told me he'd delivered a fan – a *'pankha'* – from Ballygunge Phaadi. He'd been pulling a rickshaw for 'ten-twelve years' now, and he came from Giridih. 'From Giridih? Or near there?' 'Oh, near – just like here and Park Circus,' he smiled, 'or like here and Gariahat.'

In my head, thus, proximities, distances, localities have been confused of late: I run into Giridih in Ballygunge; and a driver's room in the middle of the national elections. 'My room is near *"chaar nambar bridge"*,' said Ravinder, 'not at all far from here.' A few evenings ago he took me there: as you descend the *'chaar nambar bridge'*, you go a little way into the bypass and turn left into a lane. The lane winds past the high walls of granite and pharmaceutical factories till it comes to an open field with water on one side; and beyond the water is the bypass again, on which cars dart swiftly towards the ITC Sonar Bangla or Lake Town or the airport, or, on the other side, back to the south.

Ravinder parked the car here; it is very quiet in the field. It struck me I'd often glanced idly in this direction, across the water, while being driven down the bypass. To stand here, looking back, was like irrevocably entering a mirror. Ravinder took me back down the lane and we reached, in less than a minute, a gate on the left that displayed a poster asking for votes for Mohammed Salim. Then a short, narrow alley, with a series of rooms on one side. I think Ravinder's was the third room on the right; a room three-quarters the size of my bedroom, with a large double bed that had no mattress, lit by a tube light, and a fan – transplanted from the 'servant's quarter' in our flat to this ceiling – whirling overhead. A two-year-old girl was tottering on the bed, surrounded by the puffed rice she had evidently scattered. And here was the diminutive wife, shy, standing on one side, with whom Ravinder's father found it so difficult to come to an agreement. A pillow was offered to me to sit on: I recognised the pillow cover. Just as we were about to leave – for Ravinder's working day was not over – his seven-year-old son wandered in.

'Do you know,' said my mother, her memory of the room still

fresh, 'they have a tiny shared toilet at the back of the alley. But they have no closed space to bathe in. Which is all right for Ravinder. But the wife has to bathe in the room itself. There's a drain in the corner through which the water flows out into the alley.' She sighed, and added with a faintly bewildered smile: 'They're so *boka*, you know, they're very happy. They think they've found a wonderful room to live in . . .'

Articles of Faith

Earlier this year, I was rereading, for a purpose I won't elaborate here, Gayatri Chakraborty Spivak's preface to the book she famously translated into English, Jacques Derrida's *De la grammatologie*; or, in her translation, *Of Grammatology*. This commentary on Derrida, and the German philosophers who precede him and with whom he finds himself in a kind of Oedipal conflict, is one of Spivak's more lucid and sustained pieces of writing. It was composed in the relatively early days of post-structuralism, and before her own discourse both inaugurated and embedded itself in the extravagant entanglements and syntactically tortuous articulations of post-colonial theory.

Is it odd that I should be thinking of her, and about that preface to *Of Grammatology*, now, in the returning din and activities of the Pujas? Certainly it is odd; unexpected, too, is Spivak's own interest, as a 'non-believer', in the Mother Goddess, via the songs of Ramprasad, which she has lately translated. Not long ago, I saw her on a Calcutta television channel, with her short, sheared hair, in a cotton sari, singing, half-abstractedly, at the behest of the interviewer, a Shyama sangeet in a voice unpractised but not unpleasant, looking a little like a Bengali widow in Kashi; there was not a hint of jet lag in her eyes.

There is a brief meditation, at the beginning of the 'Translator's Preface' she wrote about three decades ago, on the convention of the preface itself. Indeed, the first, flamboyant sentence points the reader in this direction: 'If you have been reading Derrida, you will know that a plausible gesture would be to begin with a consideration of "the question of the preface".' Spivak then provides an outline of the trajectory of Derrida's career for those who are unfamiliar with his work (as most of the Anglo-Saxon academy would have been at the time) before returning once more to 'the question of the preface'. It is this section that has a peculiar resonance for me now, during the Pujas.

What Spivak draws her readers' attention to, quoting from Hegel and Derrida, is pertinent enough: she dwells on the small deceit that is perpetrated when a text that is composed some time after the principal text, or book, is named a 'preface'. The positioning of the preface at the beginning of the text, too, creates the illusion that it, as an utterance, came *before* the text, not after it. 'It is clear,' says Spivak, 'that, as it is commonly understood, the preface harbours a lie. "Prae fatio" is "a saying before hand" (Oxford English Dictionary – OED).' And yet, she says, 'it is accepted and natural' at the same time that the 'preface' is a retrospective exercise, an afterthought expressed with the benefit of hindsight.

The 'question of the preface', then, gives the text, or book, a kind of doubleness. The text is related to its preface, according to Derrida, as a father is to his son, because it is in the text, and its content, that the preface originates; the text, in effect, produces the preface, as father does son. But the preface, in positioning itself at the beginning of the text, and pretending to be anterior to it, questions the father's originary power; instead, it pretends, itself, to be the originary point from which the text proceeds or emanates; and thereby, in Derrida's ostentatious imagery, it commits an act of parricide, overturning and slaying the father. Derrida's and Spivak's meditation on the 'question of the preface', then, becomes a meditation on the myth of origins, and also an overturning of that myth, in which the point of origin shifts from text to preface, and back to text again.

The five days in which the Pujas are celebrated, too, are a meditation on doubleness, the doubleness that characterises the narratives of the Pujas and our own relationship, either as devotees or secular bystanders, to those narratives; they are both an affirmation and an overturning of a myth of origins. If, in Derrida's metaphor, the relation of the preface to the text is analogous to that between father and son, in which preface and text, alternatingly, vie to play the role of the father, in the Pujas, it is the roles of son and mother, and parent and daughter, that are inscribed simultaneously into the mythic narrative, and exemplify the strange relation man has to his gods, as both their creator and their progeny.

Did Durga exist before us, as a preface from which the text of our lives seems to emanate, or was she written and inserted later as an afterthought, as the preface cunningly is? We cannot know: that is the necessary, ambiguous fiction. We do not know, in our Pujas, if we originate in the gods we worship, or if they originate in our worship of, and need for, them; both human being and deity change places constantly as preface and text, originator and creation, in the continuum, the fabric, we call the Pujas. The mythology of the Pujas dramatises this doubleness thus: on the one hand, the deity is the mother, come to the world to rid it of evil and vanquish the *asura*, and to save us, her mortal progeny. On the other hand, she is Uma, visiting earth, her father's home, from Kailash; as she is immersed at the end of the Pujas, the worshipper finds himself thinking of her not as mother, but daughter, with that odd ache that fathers, or parents, experience on the eve of their married daughter's departure; the devotee becomes as the father, the originator, bidding his daughter farewell; the deity becomes his progeny, his creation.

The locus of the originary, in the course of the Pujas, moves, then, back and forth from deity to mortal – text and preface, parent and offspring, creator and creation, exchange roles and incarnations. In ordinary domestic parlance in Bengal, fathers sometimes, tenderly, call their daughters 'ma'; here, again, they unwittingly subvert the authority of the originator, and the linear flow of time, and transform from father into child, from creator into progeny. Time, in this formulation, is, like the Pujas, and like Durga immersed in the water, ever returning, as it is in Wordsworth's curious assertion about 'the Child' being 'father of the Man'. Was it Hopkins who confessed in his diaries that, try as he might, he could not understand that statement?

Sir Geoffrey's Lives

Where is Geoffrey Boycott these days? Any prolonged spell of absence on the Yorkshireman's part induces an odd kind of hunger – a hunger for Boycott, for that stream of admonishments emanating from the side of the mouth. Never has a Yorkshire accent sounded better – especially in its ability to metamorphose a limited English vocabulary into a credo. Is there a likeness, you wonder, of Boycott at Madame Tussaud's, commemorating the blue eyes and the angle of the mouth? Those who had been missing him for too long might, if they were passing through London, stop to hover around his replica in Baker Street. But they may not find it there; Boycott, after all, is an Indian invention.

While the public, in this country, has bestowed a knighthood upon Boycott – it is not unusual to hear him referred to as 'Sir Geoffrey' in India – in England he is, at the very least, unpopular, and at best a figure of fun. For Rory Bremner, the impressionist, both Geoffrey Boycott talking about cricket and Prince Charles conversing with his plants are soft targets. Doing Charles, he conjures up a faraway loquaciousness befitting an heir apparent who will seemingly never ascend the throne; doing Boycott, he invokes a scowl of earnest disdain.

We know why Charles has few friends; but why does Boycott not have more? There are reasons. For one thing, Boycott's dogged and meticulous way of hoarding runs never endeared him to his contemporaries. There is the rumour, too, that Boycott's best friend was his mother; in the eyes of the English, a cardinal sin. Then there is the conjecture, untrue but plausible, that he used to sleep with his bat.

Indeed, there was an uncomfortable air of homoerotic concealment about him that did not quite fit in with the vigorously heterosexual and matey ethos of the team sport he was a participant in. Whatever doubts one might have had about his sexuality were dispelled, in a regrettably unambiguous way, with his girlfriend taking him to court for assaulting her. In response to his evident misogyny (in spite of his not very convincing protestations of innocence), the British press turned upon him with headlines that sounded like tautologies: 'Ban Boycott'.

But bad behaviour has never been allowed to come between the British public and its heroes; if that were so, Botham, guilty of adultery and other deadly sins, would not be Britain's most popular sporting icon. Both 'high' art (for example, *Paradise Lost*) and the popular imagination are, in the Anglo-Saxon tradition, at least agreed on this: the glamour of badness and the dullness of virtue. No, Boycott's deadly sin, which makes him such a gauche figure in British society, is his lack of irony, his fundamental seriousness.

Everyone else, though they may be from divergent social back-grounds – as are Botham and Gower – is playing the game, whether on the field or off it. In contrast, Boycott, as a commentator, is as unflinching in his pursuit of 'truth' as he once was in amassing runs, as if he had some special access to it that others did not; this makes him an irritant and a source of discomfort to his colleagues. Tom Paulin, the Irish poet and critic, a maverick who now teaches, slightly uneasily, at Oxford, told me not long ago that the way British committees deal with crises and unpleasant problems is 'containment': evade and smooth over the issue if you can, rather than confront it. Boycott, unlike his colleagues on the commentary team, is a bad committee member; his impulse is to confront an issue and hammer at it, rather than come to some implicit agreement over it, as the others do. To them, he is, one senses, an embarrassment.

Left to Britain, and to the Anglo-Saxon cricketing world, Boycott would have continued to be an embarrassment, a minor figure of ridicule in the annals of the game. Thank God for the Indian subcontinent, for it has allowed us to discover the marvellous tonic and breath of fresh air that Boycott really is. Indian cricket, and the commentary that has become an all-important part of it, would be a moribund affair were it not for Boycott. Cricket in India, like every other walk of life here, revolves around egos, factions and politics; it is a sphere where, too familiarly, achievement is outdone by desire, perceptiveness by self-delusion. If one were to expect that the commentary team would be a disinterested observer of the scene, one would be mistaken; it brings to the scene the half-truths, evasions and factional loyalties that are already endemic to it.

The non-Indian commentators – for instance, Tony Greig, Ian Chappell, Barry Richards – are no better, and are probably worse, quick to sniff out the local rivalries and play up to them, as the colonials once did, and, with the air of foreigners plunging into a necessary and ancient ritual, join enthusiastically in the monotonous and sycophantic chorus of praise for Sachin Tendulkar. At the same time, they can be unashamedly partisan, though the white man has another name for partisanship, 'objectivity'; Botham, especially, exemplifies again and again that the English are wonderful sports in victory, and ungenerous in defeat.

Gone are the days when commentaries were merely descriptive; these days, they are prescriptive – the most boring thing about them is not the way the commentators, mostly former captains, reel out statistics, but how they, both Indian and non-Indian, sit in judgement of the players, tell them how to sit, run and eat, and continually give both them and, really, us, the spectators or viewers, the benefit of their ideas on moral and physical self-improvement. In this regard, Ian Chappell has always a homily to offer, the homily of a hardened, unappeasable committee man speaking in polite but unforgiving committee language. The Indian commentators, like Ravi Shastri, utter slightly vacuous platitudes, while offering solemn obeisance to Tendulkar – an obeisance that, like all forms of obeisance, has a violent undertone to it, suggesting implicitly that anyone who disagrees must face the consequences. Indeed, the whole tone of these discussions has the air of an eschatological meeting between established clerics.

In the midst of all this, the awkward, loud-voiced Yorkshireman, Boycott, is the one redeeming figure. He has little time for the English team; he is not shy of criticising Tendulkar. While the others damn with faint praise, he either damns or praises. In his excessive championing of the Prince of Calcutta, he has been an embarrassment to his colleagues. It isn't, thus, as if he doesn't have advice or praise to give; but that he seems to give it to all the wrong people. But, for his independent-mindedness and his instinctive dislike of bullshit ('Roobish,' as he musically puts it), the Indian public has turned to him with love and gratitude; neglected and parodied in his own country, in India he has become a post-colonial hero. Without Boycott, Indian cricket would be intolerable; without India, Boycott would not be the contemporary classic he is. It is as if two singular and slightly disreputable entities had met, and succeeded in augmenting each other's mythologies.

Doing Busyness

The principal mode of our epoch isn't business, but busyness. It's to realise with a start in the middle of the day that we don't have enough time on our hands. This has little do with apprehensions of mortality; those apprehensions and their ancient, poetic intimations have never before seemed so containable and, in the end, literary. Our anxieties have to do with our management of the day, the increasingly compressed portions of which it's constituted.

To not be busy is, in a sense, to be superfluous. Which is why it's so difficult to encounter people who aren't constrained for time, or to come upon an actual day in which you're entirely 'free'. What makes us – not keeps us, but makes us – busy? In the answer to this question lies, you suspect, the key to its obverse, the near-unnegotiable query: why are we superfluous? As to what *keeps* us busy, the answer is simple, if long: jobs, business lunches, post-lunch coffees, checking email, filling cheques, investments, telephone conversations, loans, planned and unplanned expenditure, the pursuit, for some, of extramarital enthusiasms, the pursuit, for others, of a client, the purchase of a new car, a visit to the cinema, selling a property, a trip to the hospital, the education of our children and the welfare of older relatives.

In what way, though, is time at a greater premium now than it was a hundred years ago, when it was not unusual for people to die at the age of thirty or forty? To review the projects that Derozio and Kaliprasanna Singha had taken up and completed in different periods in our own nineteenth century, before their death at the age of twenty-two and thirty respectively, is chastening. To look back at what Henry James – inadvertently bequeathed, unlike many of his characters, a long life – wrote only in the last three decades of that century is to confront bewildering effort and profusion. As it is to think of D.H. Lawrence's dense and restive bibliography, a list of poems, stories, novels, essays and travelogues (not to mention letters) he undertook and completed before he turned forty-five, dying when he was about a year younger than I am now. Interesting, also, to (closer to today) remind ourselves of what Naipaul had written by the time he was thirty. Were these people busy? There is hardly a mention of the word. Even in letters and diaries (and it's in our conversations with friends and acquaintances, and while thinking aloud, that we use the term: 'I'm sorry, I've been very busy'; 'She must be busy now'), where there is mention of frustration and exhaustion, there's almost no consciousness, or invocation, of busyness. The word occurs, almost always with a pedagogical mock solemnity, in Renaissance poetry, but very rarely in the personal record of modernity. Many of the great works of the last two centuries, and of some of the writers I've mentioned, seem to carry within and around them a deceptive afflatus, an air of expansiveness and redundancy, of special opportunities for receptivity to the world. But, given their itineraries and output, where did these writers find time for anything other than work? Their oeuvres, their biographies, their health, are marked by continual, even frightful, toil. Are toil and labour, then, distinct from 'busyness'? In what way?

And what, for that matter, are the signs of busyness? Often, they are brief messages. 'Will call later'; or, characteristically, 'In a meeting will call later'. What is a 'meeting'? It's one of the mysteries of the contemporary lifestyle; something that others do and define, something we interrupt or understand incompletely. Once, meetings had a ponderousness and weight; like journeys and appointments, they were planned and prepared for. Today, they are multifarious, and, in a simultaneously interconnected world, a form of deferral, a way of indicating a hierarchy of conversations. Until even the late 1990s, the main thing that kept people waiting was bureaucracy; in the first decade of the new millennium, it's probably safe to say that bureaucracy has been replaced by the condition of being busy. Not Kafka's door-keeper, but the unanswered email, the text message, hold us up, keep us outside. In the context of busyness, advertisement and information, two cardinal features of modernity and, then, globalisation, are near irrelevant, just as the bureaucratic injunction and the governmental edict are near obsolete; the language it works through is the mirage of interpersonal contact, and the contentless but disarmingly direct message: 'In a meeting will call later'. In Kafka's parable of bureaucracy, *The Trial*, K. realises belatedly, and with a precipitous intuition of doom, that the door-keeper who he thought was appointed to keep everyone out had really been appointed 'for him alone'; in our epoch of busyness, this is parodied utterly: the personal message is not meant only for us; it's for everyone. 'In a meeting . . .' is a default text, sent out by pressing a button.

Time shrinks with busyness, but so do objects. Our telephones turn into mobiles, our mobiles into BlackBerrys, our CD players into Walkmans, our Walkmans into iPods and who knows what spidery, weightless appurtenance. And, while certain technologies become obsolete, so, of course, do some pastimes. For instance, it's almost inconceivable to think now of sitting in front of a music system, listening, as we used to do when we were children; the archaic ritual of the family gathered round the hi-fi. In the West, but, more and more, here too, music – like business, like communicating with friends and clients – is what we do in cars, on buses and trains, in aeroplanes. Busy, we have to squeeze a great deal, music included, into the spaces that exist between locations; and a time may come when we are not only always busy, but when (and this is increasingly foreseeable) the distinction between the workplace and the site of recreation no longer holds – none of this happening in an extraordinary transformation, as in a science-fiction film, but in the humdrum, inalienable form in which most changes take place. With busyness, certain kinds of magic must cease to exist; for example, can children listening to music on the iPod believe in the necessity of tiny performers, as we once did? For the simulation of a concert to occur, with a miniature, make-believe but compellingly credible orchestra intact, we must recreate some of the ceremonies of performance: of identifying a time when we're doing nothing, of deferring to the source of music, of giving it, for a while, our attention. Is it possible to attend a concert when one is moving?

Money Matters

O ne of the things that's long intrigued me about this country is its curious, grudging relationship to money – by which I mean not markets, capital, financial gain or material success, but, specifically, the individual banknote and small change. I was reminded of this when, a few days ago, taking out a new 500-rupee note to pay a bill at a nursing home, I was made to notice the razor-thin tear in the crisp paper, and given it back. 'I just got this from an ATM,' I said, shaking my head; the receptionist, noticing my look of exasperation, and mistaking it for pique at the cash machine, commiserated by sharing his own experiences with me: 'These days even banks aren't reliable. They . . .' and continued with words I couldn't hear properly.

I gave him a comparably crisp note, a flawless one this time; and suppressed the urgent question I often feel like asking and sometimes have: Why will a note with blemishes not do? People's responses are varied: some grin, as if, like a child, I've gone straight to the heart of the matter without any understanding of what it is that makes our lives what they are: complex and sometimes opaque. Others, with downcast eyes, pretend not to hear; they are helpless – silent adherents to a law that only a fool or a saint or a foreigner would have no inkling of.

What was the next sensible step, though? Would I have to go to a bank, in the near-forty-degree Celsius brunt of the morning, and return this note for another one? Instead, I had a cappuccino at one of those coffee shop chains, where the note changed hands without comment or scrutiny or judgement. Maybe the thin, placatory young man (little more than a teenager) hadn't seen the tear, which was almost invisible unless you shook the note. Or maybe he'd noticed it, but both he and the chain he worked for and for that matter the coffee he served represented a new order, to which the physical state of the banknote had suddenly become irrelevant. This development had occurred belatedly, unevenly, but it's possible to hazard a guess and say it has occurred, at least in some enclaves of the rapidly changing metropolis we now inhabit. The only other party in this city that will accept a damaged looking note occupies an axis opposite to the one the coffee chain represents: I mean the much-resented parking attendant. This ghost of the licence raj, darkened and attenuated by exposure to the elements, but impelled by a sudden breathless energy that can make him cover half the length of a street in seconds, knows the money he collects from the car isn't seen as a legitimate fee at all, but as gratuitous commission. Though he's seldom tested – because the imprimatur of the state clings to him like a faint film – he's aware he has little authority. He will accept any kind of note at all, new or aged or tattered. He represents the rarely but oddly accommodating nature of the old order; of how it's based on a mixture of complicity, mistrust and mutual understanding – a DNA of cooperation that's changing, but hasn't gone away.

The realisation that the physical condition of a banknote is unimportant came to me in my years in England – not in a flash of light, but over time, semi-conscious, semi-attentive, as ragged five- or ten-pound notes, a few even rescued by a simple and firm band of Sellotape, changed hands without a word. At some point, nations made the transition from coins – which, in their weight, their detailed, minted appearance, the longevity for which they'd been designed, seemed to contain the value they represented – to notes, which no one could confuse for having any value at all. There lay the paradox of money as we've understood it – why the world abounds in it, and why so little of it's available. To ascribe value to a piece of paper is, of course, to be part of a contract, as well as to be involved in a willing suspension of disbelief. The sheer literal worthlessness of the frayed note makes its symbolic value transcendental and near indestructible.

In India, though, this isn't the case. The symbolic worth of the note is almost overwhelmed by its physical, worldly incarnation, and by the loose but inescapable aesthetic guidelines that inform our scrutiny. As the torn, perishable note threatens to fall apart, so does the value it represents; in this, it almost becomes indistinguishable from the commodities in the market it was assigned to purchase. Only yesterday, I heard my mother, taking out a fatigued-looking twenty-rupee note from her purse, complain, 'Where does he get them from?', referring to the driver of her car. She was speaking of the note as it were a vegetable or a fruit the driver had brought back home; it had begun to wither; it lacked freshness.

This leads me to the other mystery in our daily lives related to the monetary: the curiously perennial shortage of change. Give a 500-rupee note to a shopkeeper (it used to be a 100-rupee one) and he will close ranks, his expression giving away nothing and everything. Then there's the inscrutable, sly, adamant refusal to part with coins, leading to the swift, across the counter, yogic calculations peculiar to Indians; for instance, if, on being presented with a bill for sixty-two rupees, you were to give the shopkeeper 100 rupees, he will say, 'Do you have two rupees?' This is the default query; if you don't have two rupees, it results in a mixture of accusatory silence and introspection. And who can forget those pregnant moments in taxis our lives expand to make room for, when the driver, having been handed a large note, first rummages tiredly in one pocket, then another, then takes out a carefully folded wad and looks at it in the half-light? Then the coins appear in one palm; money is broken into smaller and smaller units because you had no change; almost a minute passes in the heat, and nothing happens. This is when you might wonder where all the change goes; what causes this constant paucity; why we all hoard coins and notes of smaller denominations, and lie about not possessing change even when we have it in our wallets; that the paucity doesn't even necessarily have anything to do with the general or literal or metaphorical lack of wealth in circulation.

The poet C.P. Surendran once gave me an insight, in Delhi, into why the situation as we know it exists. We'd arrived in Khan Market late in the morning; we had to pay the fare; not a single auto driver, though, among the line of autos parked in the front, could give us change for 100 rupees. My old puzzlement came back: 'How can not one of them have the money?' C.P. said, 'These people don't bring the last day's earnings when they return to work. They begin each day afresh.' And this was the first time someone had said something illuminating to me on the subject, and opened my eyes to the most common sort of employee around us: the daily wage earner. This person goes back home at night, possibly having spent part of his money on beedis, gutka or drink, possibly giving some of it to the family, or part to an employer to whom he owes a species of mortgage. The next day he's back, like a migrant, to whom the business of livelihood is old and inevitable, but to whom money is always new. He could be anywhere. Having money doesn't mean owning it; it means to relentlessly make or break the makeshift rules of exchange. Change isn't hoarded for the purposes of saving or spending, but because it constantly needs to be earned. Others, in the salaried middle classes, or in trade or business, have to deal with this person in their own manner: by outwitting or outwaiting him, or – what's more common – by mimicking him.

Who's Afraid of Jane Austen?

So Mira Nair is filming *Vanity Fair* next. This engagement with nineteenth-century Englishness is not as startling as it at first appears. It was implicit in her last film, the flawed but captivating *Monsoon Wedding*. For *Monsoon Wedding* is an Austenesque film; its existence would be near impossible without the space Jane Austen opened up with her novels in the nineteenth century. That space was large with fictional possibility, but Austen never failed to emphasise its actual smallness; when Nair expressed surprise at the success of her film, because it was, after all, a 'small film', she was speaking in terms that echoed Austen's quiet pride in her 'little bit of ivory, two inches square'. '3 or 4 Families in a Country Village is the very thing to work on,' Austen wrote in a letter once; and, in the course of her film, Nair reveals how the atmosphere and hidden delights and suffocations of a country town pertain to her characters even though, or precisely because, they belong to the Indian diaspora.

The mid-1990s saw an Austen revival, culminating in the great commercial success of another film, *Sense and Sensibility*, based on the first novel that Austen had, with a mixture of modesty and adroit reserve, published anonymously. Why was Emma Thompson's film, actually based on an Austen novel, and laboriously devoted to recreating the physical details of the time, less Austenesque in temperament than *Monsoon Wedding*? W.H. Auden summarises Austen's achievement rather well in 'Letter to Lord Byron'. Like many poets, and 'poetic' novelists, including Nabokov, Auden is slightly afraid of Austen's decorum and sanity. Nevertheless, in a stanza in which he registers his admiration for this 'English spinster of the middle class', he arrives at a pretty fair description of what she's doing: Austen, he says, reveals 'so frankly and with such sobriety / The economic basis of society'.

Austen's fascination with marriage, and the circumstances that lead to it, is related to her analysis of the 'economic basis of society'; but this isn't something that interests Emma Thompson. She is more interested in the 'love story', in the forces that separate the couples and bring them together. The 'economic basis of society' plays a part in the film, certainly, but in the way that the horses and corsets do, as a piece of verisimilitude. In order to further her intention – to narrate a gentle romance in the style of the old Hollywood musicals, transplanted on to a landscape of English country houses – Thompson takes liberties with the text: not, in itself, taboo to a film-maker. In essence, though, she uses the text and banishes Austen – not through the changes wrought upon the story, but through her lack of interest in, and comprehension of, what's characteristically Austenesque.

Although *Monsoon Wedding* wasn't written by Austen, it could, or should, have been written by her. In spite of the charming (a little too charming) subplot about the relationship between the servant girl and the man contracted to erect the wedding podium, in spite of the highly charged emotions of the main story, to do with incest and betrayal, Nair shares with Austen a basic disregard for both excessive charm and excessive emotion, and seems to have Austen's conviction that, by studying in a dewdrop the reflections of a few families of a newly mercantilised class, she will discover a universe.

Austen's social knowingness ('Beside her Joyce is as innocent as grass': Auden again) was partly a reaction against Romanticism. There is a similar reaction, I think, in *Monsoon Wedding*, which constitutes a turn – comparable to Austen's location of Englishness in bourgeois interrelationship rather than Romantic vision – towards 'Punjabiness' as a synecdoche for postmodern Indian identity. There's a wonderful snatch of dialogue in the film, spoken as a couple of guests arrive at the wedding. One of them says, 'You Punjabis are so ostentatious!'; to which someone replies, 'You Bengalis are so pretentious!'

This smart exchange hints at the critical thrust of Nair's 'small' film; at its timeliness. What is Bengaliness? I think it was, and still is, almost exclusively a metaphor for Indian modernity; as much so in the domain of culture as the 'Nehruvian' is in the domain of politics. Its temperament is liberal humanistic; its predilections 'high' cultural. It abhors bad taste and the lowbrow; socially, it abhors commerce and trade. It inhabits seemingly uninhabitable contradictions, in the way that classical modernity does everywhere; that is, its provenance is deeply cosmopolitan, but its raison d'être is an authenticity of experience – it despises fakeness. Its relationship to the self is ambivalent; to the world, romantic. It is, while being deeply embedded in bourgeois society, oddly ill at ease in the world; it partly desires, echoing Tagore, to be 'not here, but elsewhere'.

And what is Punjabiness? It is, in its most popular construction, all that modernity, and Bengaliness, once officially rejected. It is at home in the present; it is at ease with ostentation and what was once called 'bad taste'; it has little time for nostalgia; it is driven by the energy of popular rather than 'high' culture; it optimistically believes in upward mobility; it embraces, with a peculiar joie de vivre, the material benefits of the world. Bengaliness, and classical modernity, looked down upon Punjabiness; but, with postmodernity, and with India entering the age of global capital, the latter's time has come. Postmodernity rehabilitates the popular and the materialistic; and Punjabiness, in Mira Nair's film, becomes an integer of Indian postmodernity and its recent power.

By celebrating Punjabiness, by taking a dig at Bengaliness, Nair is making a break with the past. In order to discover her métier, she is decisively leaving behind the high cultural, modernist, Bengali impetus of Indian art-house cinema, embodied by the early films of Satyajit Ray, whose influence is palpable in *Salaam Bombay*. In identifying Punjabiness with the postmodern Indian *Zeitgeist*, she is taking a risk, is going against the romantic modernism that must have formed her sensibility as it did that of other film-makers of her generation. And we realise that Austen, whose realism we now think of as classical and timeless, must have been making a similarly radical break in rejecting Romanticism and arriving at her sane and worldly discourse.

Why was Auden afraid of Austen, and of the sort of novelist she represented? In 'Letter to Lord Byron', he remarks, tongue in cheek, 'I don't know whether/ You will agree, but novel writing is/ A higher art than poetry altogether/ In my opinion, and success implies/ Both finer character and faculties.' And the 'average poet by comparison/ Is unobservant, immature, and lazy/ . . . I Iis sense of other people's very hazy . . .' I think it's safe to say that it's a quality of 'grown-upness', of citizenly responsibility that's reflected not only in the subject but in the craft of the nineteenth-century realist novelist, that intimidates Auden. I once had a conversation with the Irish poet Paul Muldoon, during which I told him that I'd started out by writing poetry, then turned to prose. Muldoon, nine years older than me, said ruefully, 'You grew up. I never grew up.'

To fully enjoy Austen and a certain kind of novel, one must be 'grown up', a participant in a society and even a nation-state: one must abjure the solitary, daydreaming, irresponsible child's vision of the world. But there is a kind of novelist who, like Muldoon's poet, never fully grew up, who engages with the social but compulsively transforms it into a private dreamscape, who is uncomfortable with Austenesque 'maturity'. Nabokov was one of these – and he resisted reading Austen until Edmund Wilson exhorted him to do so, and never had anything but a grudging admiration for her; rather like an idler's insincere respect for a pillar of society. Proust, whose subject matter – bourgeois society – was ostensibly similar to Austen's, was another who converted the social into regressive private fantasy; into – in other words – poetry.

Frank O'Connor, the great Irish critic and short-story writer, once made a distinction between the novel and the short story: the former emerges, he said, from an entrenched mainstream culture, the latter from societies in which an underground subculture still exists. But I don't think O'Connor is speaking so much of two genres here, as of two kinds of sensibility; one, addressing society and even allegorising it, the other transforming it, almost like a child, within the circumference of its self-consciousness. Have underground subcultures ceased to exist in our globalised community? While one thinks of the answer to that question, one can be grateful for Nair's apotheosis of our new-found maturity and adulthood.

In Ordinary Circumstances

A few years ago, my wife and I had gone to see *Split Wide Open*. We'd bought expensive tickets; but the man who'd sold them to us had, inexplicably, given us seats in the second to last row, while the first two rows in the dress circle were largely empty. After the intermission, we decided to move up. We appropriated two seats in the second row; we were alone, except for a middle-aged couple before us. It was too dark to catch their faces; before us hovered the figure of Rahul Bose. I sensed the man was displeased he was no longer alone with his lady friend on his island. While I'd been groping my way towards my seat in the dark, I had caught the man sniffing the woman's hair; sensing my presence (unexpected and unwanted after the intermission), he stiffly raised his head and returned, outwardly at least, to the film. This over-emphatic revision of posture, rather than the hair-sniffing, had, for me, all the incongruous awkwardness of youth and adventure; it determined, for me, that these two people were not married.

I whispered to my wife, 'I think we're disturbing this couple.' She peered hard at them, and said, 'You know, I know the man – he's a friend of a friend. He *is* married, but not to this woman, I think.' Later, after the film, we emerged into daylight and blinked; leaving behind the film's precipitous fantasy, and also the cinema hall's artificial middle-class nocturnal dark, with its buried, inappropriate desires. The middle-aged couple, descending before us, casually disappeared. 'What is that man doing?' my wife laughed. 'He's not separated from his wife.' Daylight excited us with these questions.

Calcutta: moving here has instructed me that the Bengali middle-class family is a stranger entity than I had thought. It is capable, every now and again, of becoming its own parodic, or alter, self. In the West, the oppositions and dichotomies are fairly clear, or at least clearer than they are here. There is the 'happy family', which largely exists now in the manifestos of conservative political parties. Then there is the dysfunctional family; and, finally, the break-up of the dysfunctional family into its individual components. In marriage, there are fidelity and unfaithfulness; there is the (increasingly rare) happy and fulfilled marriage on the one hand, with its long-drawn-out contentment, and, on the other, the 'affair', with its brief impetuosity and intensity.

In many middle-class families in this city, I find these oppositions don't hold; nor does the dichotomy implicit in Tolstoy's great opening sentence: 'All happy families are the same, but each unhappy family is unhappy after its own fashion.' Marriage itself (unlike the marriages in *Anna Karenina*, in which happy and unhappy families are apportioned to parallel narratives) is the site of the sort of contradictions that should enervate and annul it: affection, indifference, individualism, empathy, dependence, deception, routine. For some people in this city, conjugal happiness seems not to be a legitimate or even a realistic or useful aspiration. Marriage has its uses: oddly, as a context, and platform, for the search for individual happiness, and the fulfilment of individual desire. The 'affair' itself is a euphemism for something more complicated, which I still can't pretend to understand: 'affairs' aren't always affairs in the Western sense, because they are sometimes not consummated.

It is a half-adult, half-childish world we are speaking of, then; but, since we have only one life, it is the only life that some people will, or do, have. People subscribe to their own definition of loyalty; I know those who have been in a series of exhausting emotional entanglements, but can't and won't abandon their spouse because of some deep sense of compassion and commitment: what, in ordinary circumstances, would be called 'love'. Although adultery isn't sanctioned by society, it appears to be occasionally sanctioned by the spouse – who will neither acknowledge it, nor deny it, nor confront it. Can we say that this is one of the many definitions of a happy marriage? Jibanananda Das asked this question in his comfortless, strangely beautiful prose writings. In his fiction (unpublished in his lifetime), Das is not so much a chronicler of the conventional marital breakdown, as an anatomiser of marriage becoming its alter self. On the evidence of his prose, it would appear that the *bhadralok* marriage, as a site of alterity, of otherness, is not exactly a recent phenomenon.

The other site of alterity is sanity itself. I remember looking, once, at family photographs of a friend of my father-in-law's. This friend is now dead, and I always saw him alone, as if he were a bachelor. 'This is Ajitesh uncle's wife,' I was told, as I held a colour photograph in my hand (Ajitesh, of course, is not his real name). 'This is his son. This one is his daughter.' There was something slightly strange about these people, as if they were in the middle of a birthday party, or taking part in amateur theatricals. 'They're not all there,' said my wife. 'The wife and the son are a bit mad.' But they lived at home, I was told; not in a home.

Madness is ascribed to people too easily in our culture; or not acknowledged at all. It is both the abnegation and the assumption of a role. Like adultery, it doesn't seem to exist at all in *bhadralok* society, except as fiction or in private conversation; and sometimes it seems to exist everywhere – and even that all-permeating existence has a disquieting fictionality about it.

At one point, after moving to Calcutta, it seemed all the stories I heard from friends and acquaintances were either to do with marital unfaithfulness or personality disorders; either their own or others'. The bourgeois family in Calcutta appeared to me a doorway through which the 'normal' and 'abnormal' had free and constant passage. Ajitesh uncle's life, with hindsight, is no less remarkable than that of his family members; the way he'd go out in the evenings for a drink with his friends, discuss politics, reminisce about America, offer an opinion or two on music; his penchant for wearing striking kurtas. Was this entirely normal? Just as he'd allowed 'madness' to reside at home, his family too seems to have acquiesced to his own aberrant behaviour.

Rangakarmi's latest play, *Khunje Naao*, taps into the stream of alterity that runs through bourgeois Bengali life. I saw it about two weeks ago – it is a harrowing play; harrowing, not because of its difficult subject – a few years in the life of a gifted but psychologically disturbed girl, played marvellously by Sohini Haldar, and her family – but because, like Das's fiction, it maps the way – one possible way – in which the Bengali family slips into its alter incarnation. It is not as if this is *not* a happy family; it's not as if this is *not* a happy child: the play is held together by the logic and glue of Diwali parties, swimming competitions, classroom lessons, restaurant outings (with a particularly terrific and disastrous scene of soup eating). All this is punctuated by visits to hospitals, doctors, asylums, and epiphanic instants of disorder and violence: the same sparse props metamorphose, guided by Swatilekha Sengupta's superb and self-effacing directorial instinct, from social and festive spaces into pathological ones.

The play is a translation; but the very act of translation can lend cultural specificity to a work. The pain and power of Sohini Haldar's performance doesn't only have to do with the tragedy of madness; it has to do with the paradox of the Bengali *bhadralok* family being a space for what it can't wholly and unconditionally love, nor wholly disown. The Bengali family, as yet, has found no other, or easier, definition.

German Sequence

1. A Walk Around Schoeneberg

Once, in 1973, a Switzerland-bound train I was in with my parents stopped for a few minutes at Bonn. A soldier came into our compartment and sat opposite us, and got off at the next stop: it seemed fantastic, but it was true. For many years, this was my only claim to having been in Germany.

It's now more than a month ago that I entered Berlin for the first time. We flew into the Tegel airport; oddly, for a capital city, there is no pre-eminent international airport in Berlin. This is in keeping with its history; its once-lapsed status, its division into two cities, its rehabilitation after reunification. Even its lack of a single international airport seems to be located in its inward, traumatic complexity; its shyness of landmarks and its proliferation of them; its dubious but continuing fascination with its emblems of the past; its being situated in this constant narrative of relocation – mental, ideological, physical, geographic. So, there is the 'old' city centre and the 'new' city centre, the 'old' town hall and the 'new' town hall; but these inscriptions of 'old' and 'new' are themselves fairly recent, and don't pre-date reunification. The expected movements of history have been compressed unnaturally; it's a little like being in Calcutta during the Pujas, but on a long-term basis, so that one might almost hope to become inured (who knows?) to this intertwining of the fantastic and the factual, this encounter with the banal, the historic, the allegorical, the domestic, and the proximity between them.

It was a brilliant summer. It took me by surprise: this natural affluence of daylight in the midst of such palpable material affluence was difficult to digest. I thought, blinking in the sun, of, at once, those pre-war summers when Stephen Spender and company descended on Berlin, to sunbathe with god-like blond boys, and also of the vanishing, in an instant, of sensual innocence, political blindness, devastating pain, into the vacancy of this present-day, new-millennial happiness. Bathed in light, I was there with Spender, in the 1930s, as I could never have been if I had lived then, and I was here, in post-unification, post-Schroeder, post-Iraq Berlin.

We stayed in a lovely flat in Schoeneberg ('beautiful hill', apparently, though there was no hill in sight) with large windows and wooden floors, and that most unEnglish of promontories, a balcony; the flat spacious enough for a dog, let alone humans, to be content in. There was no dog; but my new friend's 'children' – a blond sixteen-year-old boy and a dark-haired nineteen-year-old girl – kept coming in, going out. My friend and his wife no longer lived with each other; they spoke to each other on the phone and shared the children; they had become blood relations. His name was Reinhold ('Call me Reini'), and he taught English at the University of Magdeburg in the former East Germany, where, in four days, I was to read my stories.

I went out and stood on the balcony and surveyed the buildings opposite. I looked greedily; more reticent but no less compelling than cathedrals and temples, they wouldn't give up their secrets in a glance. Schoeneberg, Reini said, had been a mixture of economic classes and religions before the war; people of varying income groups had lived here, and not a small number of Jews. (I discovered later that the area used to be called the 'Jewish Switzerland', and had a sizeable upper-middle-class Jewish population at the turn of the century.) 'Tagore might have come here,' he beamed. Why? 'Einstein lived here. If they met in Berlin, it might have been here!'

The houses I saw from the balcony, like the building I was in, had been erected in the 1920s; they had miraculously survived the bombing. Thus, some of the residential areas of Berlin, which escaped both the bombs and the social levelling of East Berlin, have an extraordinarily ambiguous 'inner weather'. There are certain cities where the houses in which people live and whose residential districts are even more revelatory to the outsider than their monuments and landmarks. Calcutta, I'd say, is one, for a walk in Mandeville Gardens or a drive through Bhowanipore or Alipore is much more instructive and charged with excitement for the visitor than a pilgrimage to the Victoria Memorial. Berlin, I think, is another.

Next morning (again, glorious), Reini said he'd take us – me, my wife, our daughter – for a walk around Schoeneberg. On a plaque at the bottom of the façade of a nearby block of flats, partly hidden by the undergrowth, was the message that Einstein had resided here. We crossed the main road, further rows of buildings, and a bridge. We came to the 'old' town hall and the 'old' city centre. Before the wall fell, the Schoeneberg town hall had been the town hall of West Berlin. Happy, indeed secure, to be at the centre of an American colony, it displayed lapidary words from John F. Kennedy addressed to West Germans. At midday, the stentorian chimes of the 'freedom bell' rang out, as it had for fifty years, once a signal to benighted East Berliners that liberty and democracy would one day be theirs. Unlike the Iraqis, the West Germans, till recently, were happy with their liberators (and had chosen to forget their Russian ones); liberated not only from Nazism, but the dreariness of socialism and enforced equality.

On our way back our companion pointed out signs that hung from posts on the pavement, black German words on a white background. I recognised only 'Juden' as common to them all. These signs were meant to remind you of the exact day when, say, Jews became barred from taking PhDs. Another proclaimed the date when they were deemed ineligible to become professional classical musicians. Another recorded the day when Jews were denied access to well-known areas of recreation. The dates ranged from the late 1920s to the late 1930s: no one (and I mean here, really, the German liberals of the time) could claim that they didn't know what was coming.

Thinking of those signs, I'm reminded of Walter Benjamin and his essay 'Theses on the Philosophy of History' for two related reasons. The first is obvious; Benjamin's own history, his destiny and aborted career, are inextricable from the history the signs narrate. Unable to become a professor because of his religion, driven to suicide by fear after the fall of Paris in 1940, it is only after walking around Schoeneberg that I understand something of the panic that fuelled his eloquence: 'The tradition of the oppressed teaches us that the "state of emergency" in which we live is not an exception but the rule'; and 'The current amazement that the things we are experiencing [that is, fascism] are "still" possible in the twentieth century is not philosophical'.

Part of Benjamin's critique of what he calls the 'empty, homogeneous time' of Western history – of the idea that Western history, with its narrative of rationality and progress, stands as a universal paradigm of history itself – surely involves his violently endangered Jewish identity. It was the inability of German liberals and opponents of fascism to imagine outside that paradigm, to imagine in what way fascism might be happening beyond and outside it, that helps bring fascism, in Benjamin's eyes, into existence. The same might be said of many secular individuals and political parties in India – the problem is not just the calculated connivance with fascism, but the inability to imagine it is really present, to acknowledge that it is not an element in our 'empty, homogeneous' secular history with which we can quarrel on our own terms.

The other thing that struck me gradually, as I looked at these signs – astonishing, estranging and puzzling – is the profound, as yet unfathomed importance of the Holocaust to European identity and self-consciousness. This is something I hadn't quite grasped till I travelled to Berlin. Obscene though it might be to say so, it seems that the obsessive righteousness, memorialisation and remorse surrounding the Holocaust – in Berlin, in Germany, but also everywhere in Europe – suggest that it, too, has become an all-important component of that 'empty, homogeneous time' without which history would be unimaginable (although it is imaginable without many other traumas in the twentieth century) – a development that Benjamin, naturally, didn't live to see; nor can we know whether, as a once-divided Zionist, he would have wanted to. The Holocaust cannot be replicated or repeated; it has been universalised, almost aestheticised, with the authority only Europe has, or has had, to universalise and aestheticise. Both Jew and European non-Jew are hurt and outraged if any equivalence is made, say, between what is happening in Israel and Palestine and what happened in Europe. The ' "state of emergency" in which we live is not the exception but the rule', but, ironically, this statement is doomed to be proven true only in retrospect.

2. The Shadow Line

In the afternoon, we slept. We were heavy with jet lag. When we woke, we found Reini was waiting for us. We set out in his car from Schoeneberg at about half past four; summer days in Europe are interminable. As the afternoon expanded, it seemed we'd woken up at an untimely hour in the latter half of the day not only to a new time zone, but to the extension of possibility.

Reini drove us to Nollendorfstrasse, where, in a rented room, Isherwood met and became familiar with some of the characters in *Goodbye to Berlin*, and with the 'deep, solemn, massive street' itself. His pressing reason for being in Berlin – his search for working-class boys – is, of course, mentioned in neither of the Berlin novels. Is it this story of unspoken desire, this unsaid, that gives the language of these novels, especially *Goodbye to Berlin*, its character, its deceptive transparency, its constant, low-key melody; for what's literary style but a negotiation between the sayable and the unsayable? The unsayable, in the 1930s, was not just a word, or a phrase, but a way of life.

The next day, I'd return here with my wife and daughter, walk down Nollendorfplatz, with its shops and restaurants, eat there, and walk back to Nollendorfstrasse. Not far from Isherwood's abode, a man was arranging things for a jumble sale. Mainly furniture and household objects, which had an exquisiteness that, my wife observed, only European objects once had. We asked him how much a small white porcelain swan, its neck and head bent over the edge of a table as if it were about to drink, would cost us. Its delicacy – the pleated wings, the pale yellow of the beak, its whiteness, which, if it were an illustration in a book, would have made it merge into the page – made it look like something from the 1920s. It would need to be placed always at the edge of something, like a basin in a bathroom, because its head and neck were stooped at such an angle that they must necessarily inhabit empty space. We waited for a vast figure. Four euros, came the reply. We decided to buy it. It was wrapped in a polythene bag for travel.

That brief encounter with bric-a-brac dislocated me. Recounting the experience of walking in the Parisian arcades, Walter Benjamin had said, famously, that some time in the late nineteenth century Paris had become a great interior; the introduction of gas-lit lamps had, in a sense, removed the sky over the city, turning it into a ceiling; to stroll as *flâneur* or dandy through the arcades was in a way to roam about in your own room; interior and exterior were confused with one another. In Nollendorfstrasse, buying the swan, hovering over the furniture, I felt something of that confusion, and felt, too, that my being there was charged with significance. It was as if I were in someone's house, but the house had been made invisible – by history. On Nollendorfstrasse itself, buildings had been razed in the bombing, then swiftly replaced in post-war reconstruction by what Reini pointed out as prefabricated houses. These were juxtaposed to the buildings that had survived, with their balconies, their drawing rooms with chandeliers.

The swan might have belonged to one of those houses. In my mind, the history of the bombing had set it free. Certainly, the bombing must have once added to the *flâneur's* experience of urban rambling, with its interchangeability of inside and outside, a dimension Benjamin couldn't have imagined. This ambiguous extra dimension informs this sentence, about London after the war, from Muriel Spark's *The Girls of Slender Means*: 'Some bomb ripped buildings looked like the ruins of ancient castles until, at a closer view, the wallpapers of various quite normal rooms would be visible, room above room, exposed, as on a stage, with one wall missing; sometimes a lavatory chain would dangle over nothing from a fourth- or fifth-floor ceiling; most of all the staircases survived, like a new art form, leading up and up to an unspecified destination . . .' This self-aware aestheticisation, with its comedy of absences and its juxtapositions of castles and wallpaper, takes me back to Benjamin's view of bourgeois Paris. The meandering sentence might not know it, but it is a child of that vision.

That sentence, which I'd read several years ago, prepared me for the Kaiser Wilhelm Memorial Church in the Kurfurstendamm. The latter is a long avenue of shops, cafés and restaurants, Berlin's Champs-Elysées, albeit on a smaller scale; the church, built at the end of the nineteenth century in memory of Wilhelm II, was bombed in the war. The main structure has been largely left as it was; 'left as it was' is perhaps a better way of describing it than calling it a 'ruin', with its suggestion of slow, timeless attrition; here, although it looks very like a ruin, the sudden impact of devastation, the bruises wrought by a single moment, are permanently on display. It has been added to later, and its interior is open to tourists; before it, like a futuristic offspring, is a new bell tower, modernist in conception, a tall hexagon. The contiguity between the two buildings is astonishing and provocative. The old church, perhaps affectionately, is called the 'rotten tooth'; it looked to me uncannily like Brueghel's picture of the Tower of Babel, with its burst centre, except that it, unlike the Tower, overwhelmingly represents silence.

From here, Reini drove us to the Reichstag, which, during the era of the two Berlins, had been disowned by both sides, partly because it stood on the border that separated them; it was now revived as a conference centre and a tourist attraction. We stared at it and walked across the now-impalpable dividing line; there was no wall here; it was at this point that the border most approximated the phrase with which Isherwood so movingly evoked it in his account of a post-war visit: the 'shadow line'.

I have never encountered the past as I did when I was in Berlin.

It was not only I who saw the ghost; my wife did too. 'It's amazing,' she said. If only one of us had seen it, we could say that the person in question had imagined it; but *both* of us couldn't have had the same dream. Every city gives you a past which is, of course, a construct: London, Paris, Delhi. But, here, the construct is curious. You are meant to confront the past everywhere; but are kept from what is surely the universal human instinct towards it – to mourn it; to commemorate it. Instead, you are dislocated by it in a series of encounters.

We crossed the 'shadow line' in Reini's blue car as the sun began to go down; he took us into the former East Berlin and showed us rows of prefabricated houses, and old official buildings the government still didn't know what to do with; like some East Bengali refugees, they are still awaiting rehabilitation in some apocryphal narrative of migration. 'Don't quote me,' said Reini, 'but some of the profit-making companies of the East were bought over and discontinued by companies from the West to weed out competition.' From there to Checkpoint Charlie, the wall inscribed with artists' graffiti, the avenue of resplendent and still-threatening 'Stalinist' architecture, the Muscovite buildings looking like a great army without a general.

Can one see a city in a day? Can one absorb it? Certainly, in great modernist texts – *Ulysses, Mrs Dalloway, Under the Volcano* – a day is all that is given; and, in that day, a break is made in Benjamin's 'empty, homogeneous time of history'. Benjamin conceived of that break as a 'now': *'Jetztzeit'*; a revolutionary, but also a mystical, moment in the present. The following is from his eighteenth thesis on the 'philosophy of history': ' "In relation to the history of organic life on earth," writes a modern biologist, "the paltry fifty millennia of *Homo sapiens* constitute something like two seconds at the close of a twenty-four-hour day. On this scale, the history of civilised mankind would fill one fifth of the last second of the last hour." The present, which . . . comprises the entire history of mankind in an enormous abridgement, coincides exactly with the stature which the history of mankind has in the universe.' This is a bit like the Hindu notion of human history as a blink in the eye of a yuga; it is also a fair definition of the day in a modernist classic. A day is at once infinitesimal and endless.

3. Portrait of Reini

Magdeburg is in what was called vaguely, until fourteen years ago, 'East Germany'. It is well known for being an important pre-war industrial town; for being thoroughly bombed during the war; for a very old cathedral; and for Otto von Guericke, after whom the university is named. This man was a scientist who is renowned for an experiment: he joined two empty hemispheres together and filled them with a vacuum. Then, in an odd tug of war, he had teams of horses try to pull them apart. They failed.

As we stepped out of the railway station into the strong light of six o'clock in the evening, Reini made us turn around and look at the building. It was the most magnificent structure in the area, something that might have been erected at the end of the nineteenth century; one could imagine it as a great terminus for horse-drawn carriages. From it to our hotel was a mere two minutes' walk. The hotel resembled an American motel, and was just the place for the conference visitor: well-equipped, efficient, unlovely and turn of the century (the twentieth, not the nineteenth). We washed our faces and combed our hair in a brightly lit bathroom before emerging for our walk with Reini.

Our walks give me the illusion of knowing Reini better than I do. His beard, his granny glasses, his long hair, coming down to well below his collar, suggest – and I confirmed this from a black and white picture in his kitchen – that, although he's probably modulated his politics, he's largely left the incarnation he found himself in during the student radicalism of the late 1960s, when he was at Berlin's Free University, untouched.

Naturally, he's put on weight. No sign of his residual left-wing propensities is to be found in his beautiful Berlin flat. Only, in the course of conversation, a professed enthusiasm for Stuart Hall and

Raymond Williams betrays not so much an allegiance to a programme as a private romanticism. He has travelled; he lived for years in China; he has been to India; among the pictures in his kitchen is a postcard that shows a place I believed I'd seen before – was it Rome? Only after repeated glances at the brown-stone buildings, the lovely urban arc of traffic around an ancient European statue, did I recognise the Flora Fountain in Bombay I'd pass every day on my way to school.

In the black and white photo, Reini is smoking a cigarette. I think he's given up this habit. Like radicalism, cigarette smoking made an exit from bourgeois European society in the 1980s. The new religion is life; not just the pursuit of happiness, but of health. In this regard, Reini's unfashionable paunch – I could see, from old photographs, that he'd had it for a while – proclaims, more than any political opinion, his anomalousness. I don't know what his relationship to the contemporary world is, but I suspect it isn't an entirely normal one; I suspect that, in spite of his joviality, his apparent satisfaction with his routine of work and leisure, he is secretly bemused by the fallout of the Cold War.

I think that he belonged to a particular subgroup in that generation of Europeans that was defined by the Cold War in profound and contradictory ways; that, while he'd never have given up the pleasures and freedoms of capitalist society, or doubted the veracity of democracy, or doubted the futility of the division of Europe into East or West, or the bane of the Iron Curtain, the flame of some pure, Marxist nostalgia would have been fed, without his being even fully conscious of it, by the existence of the Soviet Union that otherwise, in the daylight of reason, so appalled him. The fall of the wall and the collapse of the Soviet Union must have left him off kilter; ever so slightly, in comparison to his counterpart in the East, but off kilter nevertheless.

That's why, maybe, he likes taking visitors for these walks; why he's such a good guide. I wouldn't mind him as a companion in purgatory. I asked him if he ever found it a nuisance showing people around. He said no, he enjoyed seeing familiar things through others' eyes. I think the walks, punctuated by jokes and gestures of the hand, are a sort of circling round history, a pattern of confirmation and distancing. Because they are an improvised, rather than an actual, form of mapping, they must accrue, rather than lose, significance with repetition.

The walk that sunlit evening too traced a sort of circle. We started from the hotel, went past the station, turned right at Pizza Hut – a signpost of post-Cold War Magdeburg – passed a group of academics who'd come here for the conference on post-colonial literatures, walked down an immense road with tramlines in the middle, then right, into a long featureless avenue that led us to the cathedral – dark, huge, one of Europe's oldest. From there we turned back, past another old and peculiar building, the General Post Office, and, finally, made our way through a path that, by some sleight of hand, returned us to our postmodern hotel.

By our second evening, our last, my wife and I had become well acquainted with this arc. Nowadays, I find it takes me only a day or two to form an emotional link with a place I'm passing through. It's as if I've entered yet another suburb of an indefinite but persistent metropolis I'll never escape. This suburb is different from the one I was last in, but not wholly strange. I begin to find my way in it; at first, like a blind man; then, with a mixture of circumspection and trepidation, like someone who's never strayed from the route to a particular destination over many years, but who has never found that route boring. All this happens in approximately a day. When I was a child, I recall, I went to Athens, but never felt like seeing the Parthenon. Now, I find that a city such as Magdeburg compels me to discover it.

My reading, on the second day, was at 7 p.m.; we had the rest of the day to ourselves. We visited a pharmacy; chanced upon an open market in a town square; photographed the statue of a man on horseback; and ran, astonishingly, into an Indian selling knick-knacks. He told me he'd been a taxi driver in Punjab; he had married a German tourist and come here eleven years ago. They were now divorced; he'd stayed on. My discovery of this man, my compatriot, was, to me, incredible; for I'd begun to imagine I was the only Indian man in Magdeburg. These days, no one stares at you in the West; eye contact is a potential precursor to assault; when it occurs, it's nearly always domesticated by a nod and a smile. In Magdeburg, though, my family and I were stared at intently. During that stare, I became aware not only of my own extraordinariness, but of the extraordinariness of history. These feelings were complicated by a conversation I had had five minutes prior to meeting the Indian vendor.

We were resting, then, on a bench before a fountain; a tramp with a can of lager in one hand sat on the neighbouring bench. '*Indien?*' he said suddenly. Disarmed, I nodded. He then asked me a series of questions in German. 'No Deutsch, no Deutsch,' I replied. He embarked upon a hoarse, rapid monologue. Finally, he raised his arm in the old Nazi salute. What had this man done and thought, I wondered, during those forty odd years of communism?

Reini tells me that most East Germans, in a fit of collective amnesia, forgot the legacy of socialism overnight. Although an Indian friend says that she found an older generation in Dresden still insisting on speaking Russian as a second language, the second language in question now is not Russian, but English; and, as the Head of the English Department shrugged and sighed, 'These Easterners know no English.'

It seems a knowledge of English, or the lack of it, has become a metaphor, in certain circles in Germany, for a figurative barrier, a silence that keeps, like Isherwood's 'shadow line', one side from the other. Most of the teachers at Magdeburg's English department are, indeed, 'Westerners', and, thus, commuters. Just as Reini's life was an intersection in my journey, my journey must have been an intersection in the constant travelling of which his life is composed, the weekly toing and froing on the autobahn between West Berlin and what he once laughingly called, in a moment of levity, 'darkest Europe'.

Changing Planes

Three judges (including myself) – gathered together in May this year at a posh Edwardian hotel on Bloomsbury Street, London, to argue over a book prize – would emerge at different times to stroll about the area. All of us had glanced at our neighbour, the Socialist Bookshop, but Jane Smiley, the tallest (in every sense) among us, had noticed an air of quiet celebration in its window displays. The effects of the crash were still reverberating in the Western world (though India had recovered more quickly than expected); and a new complex of emotions seemed to have surfaced in the bourgeois of almost every political persuasion – a mix of panic; rage; a strange, sweet *Schadenfreude*; a nostalgia for erstwhile simplicity; a sudden premonition of the inevitable.

In Calcutta, I knew, however, socialism had never gone away. Hemmed in on every side by an onward-marching, post-liberalisation capitalism, compromised by its own exhaustion and self-doubt, the Communist Party of India (Marxist) was, nevertheless, still presiding over the state of West Bengal after more than thirty years – none of my fellow judges had any idea of this singular trajectory. It had, in fact, been trying madly to attract investment. And the bludgeoning way it went about doing this – snatching land from the peasantry it had once 'redistributed' it to, giving it to Tata for his 'small car' factory – has at long last alienated its unusually long-suffering, tolerant electorate. Just when people in the West have begun to luxuriantly fiddle with the notion of bringing back some form of socialism to their economies and lives (see the latest issue of the journal *n+1*), the people of West Bengal seem finally to have made their mind up (on the evidence of several by-elections in the past few months) that they've had enough of socialism.

This is not the only way in which Bengal, and Calcutta, have made it a point to be out of tune with the rest of the world. While the big cities in India have been increasingly inlaid with the textures of globalisation, Calcutta resists, even while being transformed by them inescapably. New shopping malls appear near the wetlands every few months; but, while Bombay and Delhi have several flights to London every day, Calcutta has – since about eight months now – not one direct flight out to Heathrow. And that's why, of late, I have been passing through Dubai.

In Nehruvian India, with its envious foreign-exchange regulations, its life of parsimony and high thinking, Dubai was famous for its airport and duty-free shopping. J.G. Ballard, reflecting on Heathrow, said that surely cities in the future would be suburbs of airports, rather than airports inhabit the suburbs of cities. Dubai, at least from the aerial vantage point of a cabin window, appears to have been planned on this principle well before Ballard arrived at his formulation. Among Western travellers, there is a noticeable intake of breath, an air of arrested wonder, as the plane descends into the city and then the airport itself. (Compare this with the view, as the plane hovers over Calcutta, of the shattered bucolic carpet of Bengal, with its green and golden patchwork, until the colourless, frayed fabric of the city becomes increasingly visible.)

Two months ago, before the so-called (and oft-denied) crash in Dubai's economy, I saw, rushing to catch a connecting flight, Western tourists gaping at, even photographing, the immense granite walls in the airport, with perfectly measured sheets of water cascading down them. I was reminded briefly of the Bengali proverb clearly descended from colonial modernity: 'Bangal ke high court dekhano' – 'To show a Bangal the High Court'. 'Bangal', in Bengali (as we know), means, strictly speaking, 'East Bengali'. But we also know that regions within nations have country-specific, often prejudicial, connotations; a northern Briton is a more edgy and impoverished national variant than the refined, well-to-do, possibly sly product of the south; while in the US, the Southerner, like the *'Bangal'*, denotes a yokel, or the opposite of a sophisticate. Bengal's East, for historical reasons, was seen as agrarian, feudal and less developed in ideas and institutions, notwithstanding the fact that, ironically, a great deal of Bengali 'high' modernism was the work of East Bengali migrants. (London's eastern boroughs are, in a slightly different but contiguous way, supposed to be, historically, poor, primordial and lively, and possess today, as it happens – an unforeseen modulation on that history – a substantial population of *Bangals*.)

To take a *'Bangal'* to see the High Court, then, presumably, was to confront the uncomprehending oaf with modernity and power. While watching Western tourists at Dubai airport, I reflected on how many Europeans remain *'Bangals'* at heart. Development generates its own simple but profound enchantment. I recalled my first visit to Toronto, when my wife and I were driven by a Canadian friend whom I knew from Oxford (a graduate in law) to admire an unremarkable-looking building, the Sears Tower, then the 'highest free-standing structure in the world'. Here, invoked momentarily (and innocently) by my friend John, was the *Bangal* component of wonder in the beating heart of European modernity: an important – and occasionally intimidating – constituent. I say 'intimidating' because that's what it can be, as we might remember still from the US–Iraq war, when the rhetoric of 'shock and awe' was rehearsed constantly by the American generals, by Rumsfeld and that great *Bangal* Bush, as if war were essentially a display of technology (which is probably what it is) rather than the consequence of conflict or ideology. It may have been in recognition of this that Gandhi decided to perform a subversive riff on playing the *Bangal*, to cultivate a different form of philistinism, when, in his autobiography, he admitted to being unmoved by the Eiffel Tower: 'So long as we are children we are attracted by toys.'

As for myself (and this too may be an oafish anomaly, as I am of *Bangal* extraction; but it may also contain a residue of the *Bangal's* long involvement with the shape of modernism), I go looking for old buildings and doors when I find myself in new cities. In Fribourg in Switzerland, I found versions of the speckled mosaic floors we have in middle-class apartments in India; in the Palais de Beaux-Arts (or 'Bozar') in Brussels there were red stone floors identical to those in my uncle's (now destroyed) house in south Calcutta; and, almost everywhere in Europe, there are balconies. Again, in Europe, apartment buildings do not necessarily have the negative and minatory implications they do in Britain, but can, as in India, be a place where a genteel and yet observable (through those balconies and windows) existence unfolds. However, in Cheltenham, noticing balconies, I couldn't decide whether some memory of light among retired colonials had led to these (for England) unique additions, or whether the balconies themselves produced a special effect of light in Cheltenham. In turn, I'm surprised that more Western people who visit India – or Dubai, for that matter – don't chance upon buildings, cornices and windows that stir some buried, unlooked-for correspondence that tells them more about themselves and their histories than their guidebooks (which are about famous monuments) can. The South African novelist Dan Jacobson once told me that this was a habit of looking that migrants have: as we stopped to stare at an astonishing old bench on Hampstead Heath, he observed resignedly, 'The locals don't see this.' A few days ago, on my way back to India, my flight via Dubai was cancelled and rerouted because of a technical glitch. I can't think – with that 'crash' having happened before I would have changed planes again – that it will be any different from how I now imagine it.

A Sense of Elsewhere

It was 1979 when I first visited New York. The city was in decline; the decline took the form of a shabby grandeur. Walking between those gigantic buildings with my parents, I felt not as if I was in the new world, but as if I were trespassing on the remnants of a civilisation; the buildings on the avenues on the Lower East Side had a Jurassic air. That the inhabitants of Mohenjodaro were short was deduced by measuring the doorways of the ruins; what did these buildings tell us about those who lived here?

To the immigrant approaching it by ferry, the skyline must have looked eerie. Apparently Fritz Lang had a vision of what the frightening but astonishing futuristic city in his film *Metropolis* would look like when he saw Manhattan for the first time from a ship. But I was glad to arrive in New York in 1979; Californian prettiness had been killing me in the first part of my journey. New York reminded me of Calcutta, a city to which, then, I still didn't belong; and I remember the discovery of this perception pleased me almost as much as the discovery of the city.

It wasn't just the decay, casually exhibited, the distracted streams of passers-by, the anarchy at traffic lights; it was the way both cities bore the marks of being born of, and mutilated by, modernity. The allure and aesthetic of the ugly: the modern mind's recuperation, in both Europe and India, of Hinduism's odd dialectic with the ugly and the terrifying, in which these are attributes of divinity rather than of the satanic – the period of this recuperation is roughly coincidental with the rise of the industrial metropolis in both the old world and its colonies, and in the new. The paradoxical and transcendental beauty of the ravaged city in Eliot's *The Waste Land*, the equally puzzling and riveting hymn of praise by Hart Crane to the enormously ugly Brooklyn Bridge, in which it becomes 'harp and altar' and 'a myth to God', Allen Ginsberg's delirious, ecstatic apostrophes to the terrors of Manhattan (Ginsberg, the amateur dabbler in tantra and Kali worship) – you feel these poets' relationship to the modern city has been prepared, and shaped, by their readings of Hindu texts not long ago brought into currency, and the latter's renewing dialectic with the ugly.

The New York I revisited in 2000, very briefly, had moved on from the city of Ginsberg and Crane; it was in the midst of a long economic boom. It had a new mayor in Rudy Giuliani, who was intent, zealously, on cleaning up the city. Giuliani was opposed to ugliness; interestingly, he was also opposed to ugliness in art. Long before 11 September, he became internationally known for his rage against a painting exhibited in the Brooklyn Art Gallery. The painter was a British artist, Chris Ofili; the subject of his painting was the Madonna, but the Madonna was black, and painted in oils and elephant dung – a sort of Kali/Madonna figure. Giuliani, as part of his larger plan to clean up New York, wanted this painting withdrawn, as it probably was; he also blocked a subsidy to the art gallery. Giuliani is a different sort of New Yorker from Crane and Ginsberg; he represents the city's desire to move away from its past, from its spiritually ambivalent relationship with ugliness.

Under Giuliani's tutelage, New York has become a safer and marginally calmer place. Many of its areas have been 'gentrified'. This is a word I had, for some reason, never encountered until I travelled to New York in August 2002 on a longer visit. Yet it is used almost compulsively by educated white New Yorkers in their conversation, with a strange mixture of ruefulness, censure and approbation. Brooklyn has become gentrified, I was told; the West Village and the once-seedy, bohemian neighbourhoods around New York University were now gentrified; even Harlem, with its black ghetto, would be gentrified soon.

What exactly is 'gentrification'? Certainly, it has to do with the acquisition of wealth, with the enhancement of property prices. But it is more than these things; it is a style of living and an attitude to history. Cities, when they revive after a long slump, find ways of rewriting, and even denying, history; it is almost an inevitable process.

Earlier that year in Hong Kong, I found the roads had colonial names, but there was not a single colonial building in sight; we might have been in Toronto. The colonial building had been replaced by concrete and glass extremities; colonial history had been erased, not by ideology, but by capitalist resurgence. No one belonged to Hong Kong, I was told; people came here to make money; the population was largely migrant – not just European or American, but largely migrant Chinese. A fellow Indian writer and I, gawping at the buildings, reflected that Hong Kong and Calcutta had been more or less on a par in the early decades of the last century. And yet I wouldn't like Calcutta to become Hong Kong; to revive itself by decimating its past, to transform itself so strikingly and unforgivingly.

Gentrification in New York is not a decimation of history, but a repackaging of it. The gentrified neighbourhoods have gone neither the way of the classic American suburb, with its functional residential featurelessness, nor of Hong Kong, with its crusading destruction of history. Instead, they cultivate a mood of old-fashioned European haut-bourgeois gentility, a history and gentility that have ceased to exist except in this repackaged incarnation. It is fictional, and has a fairy-tale glow, and I think well-to-do New Yorkers feel slightly ashamed of 'gentrification' because they recognise its fictionality, and also because they feel comfortable in it.

The criss-cross grid of avenues and intersecting streets that makes up much of Manhattan means that gentrification and inner-city dereliction are both far away and never too far away from each other; from locality to locality, there is a persistent sense of elsewhere. Madison Avenue, opulent and celebrated around 55th Street, is, on 118th Street, another city, of boarded-up shops, empty diners and ruminating African-Americans. This is still Madison Avenue.

The street I lived on, 108th, on the Upper West Side, led on one side to Amsterdam Avenue and to Broadway on the other. These were two distinct worlds. Broadway was a model for gentrification; expensive restaurants, terrific bookshops, second-hand copies of Lorca and Pessoa being sold on the pavement, and an absence of the large American chain stores. The newsagents here sell not only the *New Yorker*, but the *Hudson Review*.

If you went down Amsterdam Avenue from 108th, you would meet non-gentrified New York; this is where the Hispanics live, confabulate, and ply their business. The avenue at this point proliferates with barbershops, 99 cents discount stores and Chinese fast-food outlets. Non-gentrification is denoted here by an absence of English; by the predominance of Spanish and occasional Mandarin. But I mainly experienced the difference as music; 'Candela' by the Buena Vista Social Club, a song of joy and yearning from the Cuba that America had long tried to humble, which, on Saturday evenings, was played endlessly and kept me up till dawn.

The Decline of Bengali Food

Two recent encounters with the food at Oh! Calcutta led me to return to Orwell's famous essay 'The Decline of English Cooking'. Except there was no such essay. The piece I'd confused it with is a brief, lovely thing called 'The Decline of the English Murder' – in which Orwell reviews the passing of a certain form of domestic homicide in England (involving adultery or jealousy, undertaken in stealth by respectable members of society) in favour of a new species of gratuitous violence. No, the essay I was looking for is called 'In Defence of English Cooking' – for how could the reputation of that entity (cuisine is too posh a word for it) possibly have 'declined' any further? In 1945, when Orwell wrote this piece, that reputation had already reached its lowest nadir; as he points out: 'It is commonly said, even by the English themselves, that English cooking is the worst in the world.' Orwell then launches into his 'defence', describing a lineage of Keatsian plenty – by 'Keatsian', I mean a plenty which, even at its best, is tinged with lack: as it would have been in the England of rationing in 1945. And yet the array he invokes is, for that very reason, delightful – as is the groundbreaking impropriety of the essay itself, because English cooking doesn't seem like a fit subject for any kind of writing: literary, journalistic, or culinary. So it's with pleasure we attend to 'kippers, Yorkshire pudding, Devonshire cream, muffins and crumpets . . . treacle tart and apple dumplings . . . innumerable kinds of biscuit . . . new potatoes [cooked] in the English way – that is, boiled with mint . . . not to mention redcurrant jelly . . . [t]hen there are the English cheeses.'

I thought of this essay when I realised that almost the only restaurant that served anything like consistently good Bengali food – Oh! Calcutta – had lapsed into mediocrity. (May I digress here and remark on the Bengali tendency to take labels pertaining to their city out of context, and to reuse them guilelessly, without a trace of irony. *Oh! Calcutta*, as we know, is the name of a semi-pornographic West End production from the early 1970s. Thankfully, the term 'city of joy', from the ghastly book and film of that name, seems to have gone out of circulation; and, for some reason, it hasn't occurred to anyone to name a bar City of the Dreadful Night. But this is a puzzling tendency that deserves a separate essay.)

I suppose I should start by saying that Bengali cuisine is a great cuisine, although it's a great unknown. I mean, besides the one restaurant I've cited, there are no retail chains or outlets on a national scale to promote Bengali food; only, in various cities, private delivery services set up by someone's aunt. In this, it's like two other distinguished Indian cuisines that, in spite of their delectable quality, have never been properly marketed – the Goan and the Parsi. Goan food at least bustles in its own region; but Parsi food, belonging to a community of historical exiles, is only available at a few cultish restaurants in Bombay, and at ceremonies and weddings no one but Parsis and their close friends have access to. Bengali food, though, outdoes both these cuisines in terms of range and variety, especially in the amazingly intricate and fragrant gradations of its vegetarian fare. But, until not very long ago, Bengal didn't even have a proper Bengali restaurant. The real custodians of Bengali food are not famous chefs (though the extinction of a strain of Oriya cooks who made the terrific food at Bengali weddings has been a real tragedy), but families – possibly, today, relatively few families. But there was always a great divide between the families that produced and consumed good Bengali food, and the great majority that dutifully and daily cooked food to be eaten unmindfully, and forgotten quickly. And even the dogged attempts of the majority are now replaced by the food rustled up by the part-time cook, who arrives in the morning, creates some daily variation of the cuisine and leaves after two hours, possibly for another house.

Often, Bengali home-cooking, which is still the incarnation in which this food is mainly found, is watery and insipid: very different, in this regard, from the spiced-up cooking of the rest of India, and more congruent, oddly, with the reputation English food had before it became chicken tikka masala. There may be many reasons for this. The influence of Bengali puritanism shouldn't be underestimated. Given its zealous agenda, from the nineteenth century onwards, to do with self-denial, austerity, suggestiveness and the implicit in life, literature and taste (in every sense of that word), I'm surprised that more scholarly energy hasn't been expended on the genealogy of this entirely modern moral domain of Bengali life. It must to a great extent be responsible for the colourless gravies in which fish swim unappetisingly in many of our homes. Secondly, there's the imputation that food from West Bengal is sweetish and bland; from the East, robust, spicy and full of flavour. This is probably a reminder that the West, being the cultural centre of Bengal for some two hundred years, embraced that reformist puritanism more completely than the East, which occupied the margins, remained eccentric and feudal, its cuisine benefiting from the Muslim influence that the West had more thoroughly supplanted. But even the provocative sauces of the East must have sprung from a mysterious syncreticism, because, if you go to Bangladesh today, you find little evidence of the old and superlative technology of East Bengali food.

There's a third reason for the aura of austerity around Bengali cuisine, and it's fairly well known; paradoxically, it's what engendered plenty. I mean the cruel dietary regime imposed on Hindu widows, forbidding them not only meat and fish, but various things including the putatively aphrodisiac onion and garlic. These bizarre strictures (now, surely, less adhered to) have led to a vegetarian repertoire unparalleled, I think, in its subtlety, with a range of condiments, ingredients and approaches peculiar to the region: *chhana*, inaccurately and persistently translated as 'cottage cheese', and mashed in a way that makes it distinct from *paneer*; *paanch phoron*, the fragrant mix of aniseed, cumin, fenugreek and the untranslatable *radhuni* and *kalonji*; the use of unground elements of *garam masala* without the frontal assault of onions and garlic. Unrelated to the widows is the ubiquitous use of mustard: mustard oil, which you have to be careful to heat to boiling unless you want an incongruous undertaste to the meal; ground mustard, which you must grind not only with energy but with a pinch of salt if it's not to taste bitter. Raw mustard oil, of course, with either *mudi* or boiled rice has provided a wasabi-like kick to generations of every class, from the destitute to the leisured. This is not to forget the other recurrent ingredient: the addictive, infinitesimal poppy seed or *posto*. Bengali food, in its deceptive way, is all about aroma and reticence. No doubt it was the aroma that caught the English writer Geoff Dyer unawares when he was in Calcutta earlier this year. 'It looked like green gunk,' he said in surprise of the vegetables he'd had at Oh! Calcutta, 'but tasted really good.' The food can seem unpromising, then, massed and overdone (the Bengali word for this is the expressive *'ghaynt'*), but the array of preparations, defined mainly by strange, serio-comic, two-syllabled words (*labda, chaanchda, shukto, ghanto, dalna, chhakka*, the exception being the evocative *rasha*), is a delicate combination of the vernacular and the sublime.

I wish to distinguish, quickly, between the decline I'm suggesting here and the well-worn tale of decline that is now Bengal's. Unlike Bengali literature, cinema, music, and even science, Bengali food is a well-guarded secret. As a result, it isn't actually seen to be in decline, and regularly receives endorsements from celebrity visitors who are searching hard, in Calcutta, for nice things to say: 'I love *mishti doi*'; 'I just love the fish here.' Leave aside the devastation of *hilsa* fish (how prescient Buddhadeva Basu's poem, where he described their 'gleaming corpses', now seems!), we know Bengal's *pabda* and *tangda* are not what they once were. The venue for the best Bengali food – the wedding – is now a nightmare. There's the hybrid catered food, of course, whose advent began twenty-five years ago with chilli fish fry; but, even when Bengali food is served, it's often served cold. The sensory outrage of cold food and gravy is something that Bengalis, with their 'good boy' exam-oriented values, seem wholly indifferent to. Then, occasionally, there's the spectacle of food being improvised not far from the toilet. If it's a buffet, you're confronted, finally, with a basin full of other people's plates into which you must lower your own. The Bengali is now blind to this kind of ugliness. He has only, as Satyajit Ray once said to the Indian film-maker, to open his eyes.

A Country Ramble

A t Hay-on-Wye to play at the Brecon Jazz Festival, I found myself
at the Rhydspence, where my wife and I had stayed on one
of our visits to Hay – probably fifteen years ago. The Rhydspence
dates back to the fourteenth century, with characteristically uneven
white and black walls; and Brecon's only about twenty miles away.
I'd arrived a day early; the Jazz Festival would begin the following
day. The inn was, for the moment – except for proprietor and staff –
empty; and the day, wet to begin with, had turned into one of those
afternoons that give much pleasure downtown, but which, in semi-
rural Britain (I was now in Wales), emphasise a hinterland of quiet, a
watchful stillness.

Summertime, stretching the day from June to September with
an unfulfillable leisureliness, brings back, without the melancholy of
the original observation, Wordsworth's memorable phrase: 'earth's
diurnal course'. So, when I decided to go out for a walk at half past
six, to confront the stillness, it was unnaturally bright. It was about
thirty hours since I'd been in Calcutta; both nothing and a great deal
seemed to have happened in the meanwhile; I felt no fatigue. I called
my wife on my mobile; given that large swathes of the beautiful
landscape around Hay offer no signal, I knew it would probably be
our last conversation for now. It was close to her bedtime; she was
watching television, about to fall asleep. I went up a narrow road that
rose up a hill almost bang opposite the Rhydspence; at some point, the
five small gradations of the signal disappeared consecutively, and the
mobile became a dead weight in my palm. But I'd already said 'Good
night' before silence and the day reasserted themselves around me.

The silence actually had a low undertone. On my right and left, I'd passed two or three pert, nostalgically cocooned houses on the hillside, with a view, for the occupants on the right, of the hills, horizon and panoramic fields. But the relationship between inner and outer worlds kept changing on that narrow road, so that at one point I was passing through a mournful avenue of trees, with light a photographic glare in the distance; and then I was out where there was a field on the left, and, on my right, no view, but dark undergrowth falling below, fenced in with frail wires, hinting, through the sound of a constant laundry-like drainage, at the movement of water.

The walk was making me feel despondent; it was starting to gather the lugubrious symbolism that country excursions have for me in England (and now, it seemed, in Wales). As usual, I felt shut out, and guided by an invisible but firm hand. Did it have to do with what Naipaul once called, in *The Enigma of Arrival*, his meditation on the Wiltshire countryside, the 'colonial's raw nerves'? That, if I remembered correctly, was a consequence of the glances of people on buses, on streets; but here, it was the landscape – not because of its wildness; there are few wild places left in Britain outside the inner city – with its reprimanding gaze. The strong guiding hand that had designed this – not God's – was evident; it made me adhere to my path. Walter Benjamin said that getting lost in a city one knew was a skill – but, here, the countryside seemed not so much inhospitable to the wayfarer as to the idea of accidentally losing one's way.

I paused next to the open plot of tilled land on my left, undulating upward into the sky; I climbed towards its edge, where the hay had been twisted and rolled into a great confection, and from where expanses of green, carpet-brushed, rose up the incline. A few cows, like idols, stood in the distance; I checked the signal strength on my mobile. Nothing. It was now that I sensed a presence in the silence around me, something I was on the border of beholding, the sweating, buzzing stillness of summer like a declaration, and the heavy vacancy of the sky. Again – because everything was so composed – it's not a making contact with the 'natural' I'm speaking of; it was like entering an old mansion, and becoming aware of a ghostly interloper in the drawing room – an intuition that makes you forget, momentarily, that it's *you* who are the interloper. The intruder or guest will not go away, although they've outlived their meaning and original function; they're now simply waiting, again, to be discovered. The light on the field was unlike the light in India, where you hardly notice it; it was like a silvery pall on the earth.

This was not a moment I could have experienced in company; because my default mode, in the English countryside, is philistinism. In company in the midst of the English rural, you feel like a spectator in an art gallery, always being called upon to attend, by middle-class convention, to accredited wonders. For me, though, nature is not perfection, but disorder and the unexpected – and to find the natural in Britain in that sense one must go to the downtown areas of Newcastle and Edinburgh, and, in London, to districts like Camden Town, Angel, Hackney and Southall. There, the 'natural' flourishes uncontainably, inextricable from the manufactured. Nature itself, in Britain, is too orderly; it is, often, manufactured.

That manufactured quality is both echoed and captured by Thomas Gainsborough; his landscapes, even when he's recording a disappearing rural England, have an artful composure. In this, he's different from his successor John Constable, whom we unfailingly invoke when confronting an actual English landscape. And yet, beyond the pastel-like similarities of reality and representation, there's a slight mismatch between our experience of the landscape and our memory of Constable. He's a connoisseur of the accidental detail, of the act of noticing itself; his paintings, spacious though they are, are all about secrecy – the eye providing the vantage point is itself, you feel, hidden. Working in the heart of the imperialist age, Constable's response to the world – and to imperialism – is almost a forerunner of modernism; it involves a new sort of regionalism, which, in the midst of colonialism's epic journeys, makes the familiar foreign, and the local appear undiscovered and distant. This view of the regional is crucial to modernism's way of assigning meaning; it informs the works of writers and artists in the American South, in Ireland, in Bengal; it suffuses Eudora Welty, Joyce and Jibanananda Das. Constable, strikingly, is exploring that particular regional sensibility early on, through nature and, extraordinarily, through England – the impulse is very different, say, in George Eliot or the late Turner or even Wordsworth.

But the walk in Brecon didn't reveal Constable's world to me. Instead, it's taken me again to Gainsborough, who was working from roughly the middle to the second half of the eighteenth century. And, in both his well-known capacities – as landscape painter and a painter of portraits – his response to the gathering energies of imperialism is surely palpable. His landscapes, even when they show obscure villages, have a premeditated calm; it's as if England were already becoming iconic. But it's his great portrait *Mr and Mrs Andrews* which must count as a prescient study of colonial power. The couple pose beneath a tree, flanked by their dog, Mr Andrews, his eyes unappeasable, with his hunting rifle. To the right are obedient bales of hay, behind, sunlight, clouds, and the gorgeous landscape that comprises the Andrews's property. Gainsborough, here, has brought his refulgent gifts as a landscape painter to the bounded, mastered nature of the 'open'. Long before the project of colonialism, the enclosure laws, from the thirteenth century onwards, became instrumental in segregating 'landscape' into private property in England and Wales, becoming punitive around and after the time of this painting. Enclosure shapes what we know of nature in Britain today – what Tom Paulin calls 'that artificially "natural" world of thick hedges and rectangles which our ordinary experience tells us has been there, eternally'.

That Gainsborough's exploration of landscape's relationship to its human owners has a colonial bearing is brought to light in a later painting, Johan Zoffany's *Warren Hastings and His Second Wife*. Zoffany, a contemporary of Gainsborough's, was German, but spent decades in England as a portrait painter; and then found a market in India. *Warren Hastings and His Second Wife* (in possession of the Victoria Memorial) is a portrait of the couple under a tree, in their Belvedere estate, days before Mrs Hastings's departure, the spaces of Alipore in the background. It's an undeniable reworking of the Gainsborough; a continuity is established between England's enclosed landscape and the domain of India; only the dog (I know this sounds crass) is replaced by an Indian maid. I don't necessarily believe, following Edward Said, in, say, uncovering concealed West Indian plantations in the fiction of Jane Austen. But that there is a historical anteriority to what Paulin calls 'the glumness and suffocation' we feel in much of the English countryside, there's no doubt. India, however, with its vague aleatoriness, its deceptive light, was, as the colonial watercolourists discovered, always going to be hard to enclose.

La Loge, or 'The Theatre Box'

Pierre Auguste Renoir was never my favourite Impressionist. I studied him in a cursory way as a teenager for the same reason I studied the Post-Impressionists and late Turner: for the release they constituted from the glossy, over-ripe representational quality of Renaissance art. The teenage soul in Bombay (without quite knowing it was doing so) rejoiced at no longer having to gaze at nudes that purportedly looked like real, flawless nude women, at Venuses and Davids that closely resembled, right down to the tendon, the real Venus and David, at dead pheasants that glowed like actual dead pheasants in a gentleman's kitchen. 'Humankind cannot bear very much reality,' said T.S. Eliot; and he might well have been speaking of a certain revulsion against the Renaissance. Part of my antipathy must have come from what I saw as my cultural inheritance. Whatever was 'Indian' in me couldn't recognise the pheasants and reclining nudes. This didn't prevent me from participating, intimately, in Van Gogh's fields and cafés and studios, in Cézanne's hillsides, in the elements that combined to produce Turner's mysterious steam engine. Like the cities of the world from the end of the nineteenth century onwards – London, Paris, Berlin, Calcutta, Cairo – the new painting was a place of frenetic cultural intermingling which we could all, in various identities and guises, inhabit.

With Renoir, Europe still seemed very distant. An Indian contemporary of Monet's or Alfred Sisley's might have encountered, in Bengal, some of the very things they did: a semi-industrial sunset, where context and disintegration are at once concealed and implied; an elusive vantage point glimpsed at the end of a canal in the middle of a city. Sisley's and Monet's pictures contain a new awareness of the momentary and mysterious in the midst of the everyday that's also in evidence, a couple of decades later, in Tagore's songs and in the works of the poets and artists who follow him. But that Indian would have probably seen the sort of people gathered at the Moulin de la Galette in Renoir's famous picture of a café only within a colonial setting. The crowd in the café and on the square almost provoke, unfairly, the question you might legitimately ask yourself when you watch the film *Notting Hill*: 'Where are the immigrants?' You don't ask this of the Sisley painting because the intercultural contact that's characteristic of modernity's abandon – bringing together styles from the Parisian street, Bali, Japan, Africa and India – has already begun to animate its technique. You turn to Renoir's café – especially because it's a café scene – expecting that abandon and play. But you are disappointed. The painting has none of the provisionality, the air of estrangement and migrancy of, for instance, Van Gogh's cafés and rooms. Instead, it's a painstaking, penetrating study of a frozen society, demarcated and fixed by class, a bourgeoisie that, even while drinking and dancing outdoors, is unaware of anything but itself, and apparently unconscious of the conflicted world of imperial France it thrives in.

'All great civilisations have been based on loitering,' said Renoir's son Jean, the filmmaker, in relation, as it happens, to his first experience of India. But it could also be a statement about Paris, and a certain response to Paris, of which Impressionism, Post-Impressionism, the writings of Walter Benjamin and some of Renoir's own films are cardinal examples. But it would be wrong to look in Pierre-Auguste's paintings for the *flânerie* and the casual sense of discovery you find in his son's work, or in the works of his own contemporaries, or in Frenchmen of a later generation, like Jacques Tati. This came home to me when I saw, for the first time, the original of *La Loge* at the Courtauld – with the painting described above, *Bal au Moulin de la Galette*, Renoir's most powerful meditation on the French bourgeoisie. Unlike Sisley, Monet, Cézanne or Gauguin, Renoir isn't concerned with the outdoors, or the street, or the aura of migrancy and unfamiliarity that is inherent in everyday locations in the modern world: he's fascinated by interiority – not the interiority of individuals, but of a class. It's a class intent upon studying, admiring, and spying upon itself from various angles, and, in doing so, in keeping at bay or denying the momentous change that surrounds, defines and will superannuate it. The theatre box is a sort of fragile social cocoon; the shared glance, even if it has a private, erotic charge, confirms the artificially inviolate and self-regarding nature of this world. No 'elsewhere' penetrates it; the man has trained his binoculars on others in the audience, while the woman tentatively acknowledges a stranger who's already part of the microcosm. When you view the original, you notice the light in the box, which makes Renoir's picture comparable to, say, a contemporary photograph of a couple watching television: it's an artificial glow in which a class shelters itself. Benjamin, referring to the rise of the novel, said that, by the nineteenth century, the public no longer wanted mythic or sacred subjects; it wanted to read about itself. The same could be said of theatre at the time *La Loge* was painted (1874), with Ibsen's gradual pre-eminence. But the figures, as has been pointed out before, are not looking at the stage. They – as the painter knows – constitute the pulse and tissue of theatre itself. In this way, Renoir inaugurates a line taken up by his son – not in the short films full of idiosyncrasy and wonder – but in *La Règle du Jeu*, the incisive dissection of the French bourgeoisie's relentless fashioning, and preservation, of its own universe.

Madmen, Lovers, Artists

It's now more than a month since I was drenched, like others, in the deluge of *Chokher Bali*. I apologise for putting my response on record somewhat belatedly; but I've been waiting for the tide to recede. My concern is not so much with the film's fidelity to the book (Tagore himself was one of the first to suggest that cinema, to come into its own, must become independent of the literary) but with its own language.

The venue at which I saw the film is the Priya Cinema, that old haven for south Calcutta outings. The morality of community is, you feel in the darkness of the hall, a thin veneer; and it was as absorbing to observe the old women and daughters-in-law in the audience as it was to watch the ones in the film. The audience here is seldom absolutely silent; and, for a while, I kept confusing the sounds in the audience with the background noise on the soundtrack. At one point, I thought the 'madman' from Nandan cinema (I use scare quotes because he is probably sane), the one who wanders like a dervish singing Rabindrasangeet – at one point I thought he was in the auditorium. Then I realised that the loud singing, heard in snatches behind the conversation, was, like many other noises, coming from the film; it was part of the perpetual 'elsewhere' that surrounded the characters.

The constant presence of background noise in *Chokher Bali* is, I think, one of its many instances of homage to Satyajit Ray; and, like the other instances, its purpose seems partly parodic. These acts of homage, for example, are very different from Ray's own homage to Jean Renoir. Ray lovingly translated the party games played by the

French haute bourgeoisie in a country manor in *La Règle du Jeu* into the antics of a group of Calcutta Bengalis in a forest officer's bungalow in *Aranyer Din Ratri*; or, more directly, reworked the astonishing scene with a woman on a swing in *Une Partie de Campagne* into the one in *Charulata*. Ghosh's quotations of Ray – Binodini on a swing, or staring through binoculars; the long verandas of Mahendra's house – are not homage, really. They are more like a domestication, a taming, of some of Ray's most liberating moments in the extravagant and slightly wild palace of *Chokher Bali*; here, in this palace, these moments, like cockatoos or imported eunuchs, are neither at home and nor do they have anywhere else to go to; they sit around with an air of foreignness and ostentatiousness that they never possessed in their original habitat.

One is never, in India, completely alone. Even as I write this, I can hear hammering, birdcall and, further away, traffic. I first became aware of the auditory dimension of our lives on visits home from England; perhaps it takes an outsider to hear that perennial punctuation of sound. The first filmmaker to capture that mysterious, irreducible noise was a Frenchman, Renoir, in the lovely, underrated *The River*. It's there that the auditory possibilities of elsewhere – the cry of a bird, the whistle of a steamboat are captured in a living archive for the first time. It's from this film, I believe, that Renoir's Bengali acolyte (Ray attended its filming in Bengal) inherited his ear for the semi-audible sound in the next street, or beyond the river or the railway tracks.

Ghosh's soundtrack at first seems in Ray's lineage; but we soon discover that its impact is quite different. It never takes us to that 'beyond', or provides that sense of fading distance; instead, it returns us firmly to the primary site of our experience: the cinema hall. No bird ever chirped as unstoppably as the ones in the film; the 'madman' from Nandan keeps weaving his way back; for no clear reason, we suddenly hear the sound of the muezzin. The effect of this soundtrack is to abolish distance, and to parody, rather than suggest, the notion of 'life'; to create a vast interiority.

During the intermission, I decided that *Chokher Bali* is a 'Raj' film; not so much *Charulata* as *The Jewel in the Crown*. This has not only to do with the mysterious cameo played by an Englishwoman, or with the babbling about tea, or with Binodini's encounters with chocolate, nuns and the English language. Tagore's novel is set in the period of the Raj, and is probably subtly inlaid with the experience of colonialism. But 'Raj', in the sense I mean it, is a cultural temper invented in the 1980s; it is the stirrings of nostalgia, in a newly globalising world, for Indian colonial history as a heritage site. The first half of the film was, I thought, suffused with the pastel shades of that special nostalgia; and both Tagore and nineteenth-century Bengal had become, in the film, elements in a heritage landscape that's no more than a quarter of a century old.

The second half of the film, with its adulterous love bites and scratches (a friend said to me that Ghosh displays, in the film, only a dim idea of heterosexual lovemaking), its separations and personal calamities – the second half is another affair altogether. After watching it, my preferred adjective for the style of the film is 'operatic'. By 'operatic' I mean a unique artistic practice and experience in which both kitsch and the mythic come together. This is probably especially true of early opera, which the young Nietzsche derided as 'bourgeois spectacle'. But it is still a characteristic of much opera; opera is almost the only art form that can make a private sexual scandal the stuff of both overblown entertainment and mythopoeic transport. Something similar happens in Ghosh's *Chokher Bali*; eschewing Tagore's delicate and humane psychologising, it deliberately gives us a spectacle that is larger than life. Those who go to it looking for light and shade, and complexity, are looking for them in the wrong place; light and shade are inimical to the experience I've called 'operatic'.

A few reflections on Aishwarya Rai. People use the word 'beautiful' to describe her, but I'm not sure in which sense they're using a word that has a long and contradictory history. I don't want to load this discussion with the moral and non-utilitarian values the word 'beauty' has had; but I think we need to find a term other than 'beautiful' to describe Rai's very contemporary, and telling, appeal. Perhaps her most ardent admirers are the new beneficiaries of globalisation; the people who covet Jaguar (or is it Jaquar?) bathroom fittings, and dream of their cars metamorphosing into tigers; who like to discover a bit of ancient Rome in their back garden, and Venus de Milo busts in hotel lobbies. She is one of the means by which Ghosh silently transforms Tagore's tale of liminality, interrelationship and social change into a narrative and aesthetic of materialism. Ghosh's film, and film-making, tell us about the rewards and damage that materialism incurs upon itself.

Rai, and the famous collection from Anjali Jewellers, are not the only integers of materialism in the film. There is Ghosh's vision of landscape and of 'reality' itself, in his self-consciously superb visuals. Someone told me who the designer of Ghosh's interiors is; but who, I wondered, designed the outdoors? Here, again, the difference between Ghosh and the Ray he pays frequent homage to is striking: in Ray, reality – whether it comprises a group of Gurkha bagpipers in the distance, or a dog lifting itself up – is provisional, sketch-like. It has the same aura of distance, of suggestiveness, that his soundtracks have. Actual locations, like Darjeeling or Benares, have, like the sets in street theatre, an air of being hastily put together. Location, landscape – in Ghosh's film, they are gilded, finished. The ghats look like expensive furniture; even the sun looks more expensive than anything to be found at Anjali Jewellers. The elusive morning light in Kashi, which Ray went searching for with his camera, is, in *Chokher Bali*, thick with social esteem, like oil paint. There really is no 'outside' in Ghosh's film: everything in its vast, artificial interiority is caught up in a symbolic play of passion, desire and material empowerment.

Chokher Bali has been to contemporary Bengali cinema what the fall of the Berlin Wall was to Europe. It has situated Bengali cinema firmly, almost brutally, in the current of globalisation: flirtations with art-house cinema (as in Ghosh's own early films) and half-baked exhausted commercial movies have been both rendered irrelevant by its release. Ghosh is not an 'international' film-maker, as Ray was; he is a filmmaker of the globalised universe. The absence of a real 'outside' in his new film reflects the fact that there are no foreign countries, no elsewheres, in the world after globalisation. His Tagore, too, is the Tagore of globalisation, quite different from Tagore the 'bishwakabi' or 'world poet'. Something like this was waiting to happen; now that it has, it's brought both celebration and anxiety in its wake. Those who secretly feel at home in the present (whatever their political and cultural predilections are in public) will rejoice at discovering an artist who has understood its language so well. Others, out of joint, might experience unease and bewilderment.

The Truth About Hitler

For a couple of years now, I've been interested to see a book on sale among the pirated editions and originals, among magazines purporting to tell us about careers, astrology, cabinet ministers, sportsmen and film stars, arranged neatly on the pavements in Park Street: *Mein Kampf* by Adolf Hitler. This is a book I've never seen inside a bookshop. Maybe I've never looked for it; but, now that I think about it, I don't recall ever encountering it in the section devoted to autobiography. Now, appositely, I find it on the street, where the careers of most workers of the National Socialist Party began; although the oddity of discovering it on a street in Calcutta isn't easy to ignore.

Why *Mein Kampf*, sitting next to Shobhaa De, Sri Sri Ravi Shankar and *The God of Small Things*, rather than, say, *Capital* or some edition of the *Gitanjali*? I remember noticing, in the early 1970s, *Capital* on the upper shelves of the bookcase in my uncle's house in south Calcutta (that house, sold to contractors, no longer exists). Although I opened the book and puzzled for a while over 'surplus value', and found its first pages, at a glance, dull and unreadable, I knew what I was holding in my hands was potentially incendiary and transgressive. When my uncle rented out the ground floor to tenants, the book moved to a shelf on the second storey, looking as new and untouched as ever. I think *Capital*'s function, in that house, was talismanic – at least for my uncle; its presence was a source of consolation and energy. I grew absorbed in some of the other books in that bookcase; William Shirer's *Rise and Fall of the Third Reich*, which looked forbiddingly boring but was actually an astonishing page-turner, and is probably the longest book, besides *Anna Karenina*, I've ever managed to finish;

and Erich von Däniken's *Chariots of the Gods* – Von Däniken was, in my opinion at the time, a scholar of humbling originality, and opened my twelve- or thirteen-year-old eyes to the indubitable but, till then, largely neglected extraterrestrial origins of human existence.

My uncle, like many Bengali engineers of his generation who trained in Germany about a decade after the war, was sentimental about the Germans; he claimed to speak the language, and refused to call Munich and Hamburg by their English names, referring to them, instead, as München and 'Ham boorg'; he was also, despite his socialist allegiances, somewhat forgiving towards Hitler. 'I'll tell you the truth about Hitler when you grow up,' he said to me – whose vivid proxy life in the Second World War derived from Commando comics and the movies – but more immediate concerns have kept him from making good his promise. Or could it be that I'm imagining he, in his usual excitement, had said those words? A combination of historical circumstances and semi-articulate emotion had come together to give my uncle, like some other Bengalis, his private, tragic vision of Germany – his own loathing for the British, for one; and, for another, Subhas Bose's mistaken trajectory, which used to haunt and trouble Bengalis once as the failings of their fathers trouble and haunt them.

Standing opposite Music World on Park Street, I ask the magazine vendor how *Mein Kampf* is selling. As I said earlier, I've been seeing the book in Park Street at a couple of places (I have a feeling I've seen it well before then without registering the fact); here, near Music World and Flury's, and on the other side of the road, among the magazines on the pavement on the right of Oxford Bookshop. The vendor, handing me the book, as well as Paul Coelho's *The Alchemist*, tells me it sells steadily and well. His younger assistant has little idea of who Hitler was; but both this vendor and the other one across the road not only know of Hitler, but have interestingly similar notions about him – he was a world-famous man; he fought in the 'war' (this from the other vendor, who uses the English word); and he made no bones of his likes and dislikes, and was direct and plain-spoken. They have a point; it's difficult to accuse Hitler of prevarication. Frontal brutality is seen as a kind of honesty. 'Others speak sweetly, but stab you in the back,' says the vendor near Music World. I encountered this fatalistic nostalgia for a more moral form of murder before in Ahmedabad, from the unlikeliest of sources; from a Muslim part-time chauffeur for Communalism Combat, and from a more famous, indeed, a national figure, both of whom loathed Narendra Modi, but admired him, in a shocked way, for his lack of compromise and his clear understanding of his goals. It's the sort of partly ironic praise that victims sometimes deploy to transcend their victimhood.

I tried to imagine who might be picking up *Mein Kampf* from Park Street. Was it someone who wanted to be titillated by the forbidden; was the book purchased as an item of political pornography? Or by some much-bullied person who daydreamed of authoritarianism? Or by someone who was interested in the mythology of the Second World War; or, simply and naïvely, was curious about a monster? Or was it bought (and this possibility was somehow the most difficult to believe in or get under the skin of) by people who had a clear-cut, right-wing interest in the man?

It was in Berlin, after having a Turkish dinner with my German friend and guide, Reini, that I realised that Hitler, as far as most Germans were concerned (and in this matter I think he is fairly representative), was beyond language. I remember how deeply uncomfortable he became when I spoke to him of Bose's flirtation with Hitler, something he already knew about, and the flippant admiration that some Indians had for the Führer. It was as if we'd stumbled on to a taboo subject, and cast aside conventional, socially recognised ways of speaking of it.

I can think of at least two comparable taboos in our own national imaginations. The first surrounds the figures of Godse and Savarkar; they exist just beyond the edge of our rational everyday consciousness, or at the back of it. In recent years, they haven't so much been exhumed and exorcised as turned into theatre – the staging of a private neurosis. Sometimes, the element of theatre has become literal fact; a play, and anxieties around a play. The other taboo is Kashmir; or, more specifically, the idea of, and reasons for, an independent Kashmir. Here, too, the Indian mind stops thinking; it has no language for this problem; it's like a pre-verbal childhood trauma, except that, in this case, the threatened childhood, the trauma at inception, is the nation's; the nation's childhood is woven into our own.

On the whole, though, Indian political life over the last three decades has proved to be far more elastic and accommodating than its counterpart in the West. There, generally, when your political career's finished (often for some trivial, non-political disgrace, some liaison with a secretary), it is, usually, finished; you become a backbencher, or a Lord, or a sports commentator; but you are gently, and forever, removed from the political mainstream. In India, there's always a chance for a comeback. So it is that Indira Gandhi returned to rule us after the Emergency (at the time of her defeat, this was unthinkable); that her son Sanjay returned to active politics, and might be enforcing vasectomies today had he not died in that doomed aeroplane; that her admirers and supporters during the Emergency are lovable members of the establishment today.

So it is that a minor right-wing party with marginal prospects became our ruling party, and might again, not because of the popular vote, but because of 'secular' alliances; that Narendra Modi, who might still, one day, be prime minister, was recently welcomed and celebrated at the Calcutta Club. No one is beyond the pale in India: that is, as long as they have something to offer you and me. Long-term enmities aren't possible; they'd erode our contacts; and networks (a less pretty word than alliances) are the principal political reality of our present. After all, who knows who might be of use to us, and when? The only person beyond the pale is the one who lacks the potential to offer us anything material or concrete towards mutual self-advancement; this person, the most obvious, most common, taboo in our national life.

Cowboys and Indians

When we were children, we played cowboys and Indians sometimes. We rather liked being cowboys; we instructed ourselves that the Indians were 'Red' Indians – the term 'Native American' was still not in currency – not remotely like us, who enacted our make believe in the large basement garages of a building on Malabar Hill in south Bombay. It was while looking for us, we noted, that Columbus had lighted upon America. The enormity of the accident – and the relatively unacknowledged yet not inconsiderable part we'd played in it!

In many places and ways, Bombay echoed, and still echoes, America. This is not to say it is an imitation; its America is to be found *there*, in its streets, and nowhere else. But this echo also sets it apart from every other Indian city; gives it its own melancholy destiny to fulfil.

There is, first of all, the allure of tall buildings. They cluster around Nariman Point – what might probably be called Bombay's 'financial district': the Air India building (where a bomb went off in 1993), the Indian Express building, the Oberoi Towers. This is reclaimed land; I remember when Nariman Point was still a 'point', a strip of land petering out into rocks and the sea. But tall buildings are everywhere in south Bombay. Some of them are as famous as famous people; a few, like some Bombay celebrities, have less than impeccable reputations. Some time in the late 1970s or early 1980s a building called Kanchenjunga, designed by the architect Charles Correa, came up on the hilly incline of Peddar Road, a giant, off-white rectangular box, with large perforations made in it, coloured violently red on the inside (the perforations were the balconies of duplex flats). For a long time, no one occupied those flats. The building had been erected on a disputed site. No matter; the building became a star – if a slightly shunned one – and a part of the skyline of jostling high and low, young and old, structures – the all-night party of the Bombay skyline. Years later, occupants appeared on the balconies; but you are not really meant to see people in the tall Bombay buildings.

There is more than a hint of New York here. The tall buildings are, literally, 'upstarts'; they are mainly post-Independence social climbers; their altitude suggests the precedence of desire over the genteel evasions of the colonial age.

But, in the perpetual sunshine, in the sea, in the palm trees, is also something of California. The pleasures of the body; the body standing in the sun.

And so, all those beaches; in Chowpatty, Juhu, Marve, not to speak of the Governor's private beach, which children from the Cathedral School used to visit once a year. The children taken for pony rides; the men, some of them frauds, racketeers or embezzlers, gambolling on the sand; semi-nude, back to a second infancy. The image crystallises for me Bombay's mixture of the childlike and the grown-up, of naïveté and ruthlessness, a mixture that, as I now know, is also peculiarly American. Childhood fantasy and adult knowingness, innocence and violence, inhabiting the same space, even the same mind and body.

I was introduced to America through the comic book. My parents had taught me no English before I went to school; settled outside Bengal, in Bombay, they had longed to make me intimate with the Bengali language. I was admitted into the school – on what basis, I don't know; I knew no English. The headmistress suggested an unusual two-pronged approach to my mother: to familiarise me with the language by giving me both Ladybird and comic books to read. Through the Ladybird books I was brought to a world of English families and landscapes; this education in English continued with Enid Blyton, whose cocooned universe contained strange cruelties and snobberies as well as buttered scones and picnic hampers.

That world, although close to us historically in many ways, felt remote; but American comic books, which taught me to read, somehow entered our lives in Bombay and became indistinguishable from them; we didn't know where one ended and the other began. The much-thumbed and -perused copy, in the 'circulating library', of the Archie Comics Digest; the thin line separating us from Riverdale. The monthly purchase of Gold Key comics; the 'friendly' ghosts and witches; Richie Rich, that Fitzgeraldian cartoon character, who, with swimming pools, butlers, chauffeurs, was still not completely happy. Superheroes who led dull lives as employees in tall buildings, to whom the simple act of putting on spectacles conferred an impenetrable aura of ordinariness and guaranteed a foolproof disguise; or led reclusive lives as tycoons in opulent mansions with vast underground garages in which a single car was kept; or even, like Elastic Man, turned sad, congenital deformities into a prodigious talent for fighting crime. If Gregor Samsa had been born in America, would his 'metamorphosis' have made him famous, like Spiderman or the Incredible Hulk? In 'The Man-Moth', Elizabeth Bishop's poem, there is a rare early parody of America's lonely and troubled lepidopterous superhumans; this stanza describes the 'man-moth' as he attempts to climb towards the moon:

> Up the façades,
> his shadow dragging like a photographer's cloth behind him
> he climbs fearfully, thinking that this time he will manage
> to push his small head through that round clean opening
> and be forced through, as from a tube, in black scrolls on the light.

Our American childhood in Bombay happened during the Cold War, when one part of the world was under the canopy of Brezhnev's enormous eyebrows. We were in that part of the world. Although India is a democracy, it was certainly a political and strategic ally of Russia; Russia gave us an idea of moral and economic rectitude, while America provided us with a sort of illicit entertainment. As for Soviet entertainment, there were the astonishing films. We went to watch Sovexport films for two reasons. The first was that Russian films emerged from a more consciously artistic tradition of cinema than anything to be found in Hollywood. The other reason was less high-minded: our political friendship led to an odd indulgence on the part of the National Board of Film Censors, and the nudity in bad Sovexport films went largely uncut. The cuts in Hollywood films were clumsily, even insultingly, made – a woman might be unbuttoning her blouse; she seemed to suffer a brief spasm or convulsion; then she was seen to be buttoning her blouse. We, in the 1970s, studied that spasm closely but hopelessly. Nakedness in American movies was kept from us by a wall of propriety harder to penetrate than the Iron Curtain.

Superheroes; but also villains. For a generation, Henry Kissinger was the most hated man in India. In 1975, Sanjay Gandhi would overtake him in loathsomeness; but that bureaucratic suit, those thick glasses and that heavy accent would always make Indians shudder. And Nixon, too, who, with Kissinger, presided over the Bangladesh war; the way the American government always seemed to be on the wrong side of everything. Nevertheless, the young men and women queued up for application forms at the USIS in Marine Lines. The lines were long and exhausting; later, they left for the States. Returning for holidays, the men wore shorts, and T-shirts with the logos of obscure universities. Even their fathers began to wear shorts. On the rear windows of cars in Bombay, they pasted stickers with the names of those unheard-of universities, which others would be obliged to memorise in a traffic jam. What was it that took them there? Was it a desire for success and assimilation that Europe could not offer? And was it the ability, and desire, to merge (but not quite) with those crowds in Manhattan, or settle down in some suburb, or relocate themselves in the vast spaces in between?

A Few Afterthoughts

At a reading a few weeks ago in London, John Berger mentioned two events he'd been witness to recently, presumably in the village in France where he lives. The first involved a procession of wild boars – old as well as young ones – suddenly crossing the road. The second had to do with birds (possibly water hens) taking off from a pond, and Berger noticing the water dripping from their feathers. Both incidents, he said, had to do with what had inadvertently become a theme that evening: the intermittent visibility of what is ordinarily invisible.

Why does this tension between the seen and the unseen move us, almost independently of the value of what's being revealed? I suppose it was a promise of a window opening up, rather than the idea of usefulness, that drew me at first to the Gates Foundation's proposal when they wrote to me about two years ago to contribute to an anthology, with fifteen other writers, about the problem of AIDS in India. The suggestion was that I, like the others, travel to some specific place, with a specific history and constituency in the story of HIV in India. The piece, in effect, would be partly the result of rudimentary fieldwork – interviews and notes – and partly of the traveller's alienated eye. The latter, perhaps even more than the former, would be attentive to the invisible in the visible.

My own sense of the immediacy of the problem of HIV in India came to me without warning five years ago, when I'd gone to Bombay, the city in which I grew up, to take part in a festival of literature and music. Three friends had come to my event; one of them was a friend from school, a former smack addict who now claimed to be 'clean'. At around midnight, we dispersed; my schoolfriend headed to the station to catch a 'local' homeward. The following evening, after several telephone calls, I realised he'd never got back, and pieced together a story: my friend had overdosed on drugs and collapsed in front of the Prince of Wales Museum, an area that was a hub of junky activity; he'd been found unconscious by a constable at 2 a.m., and admitted to GT Hospital.

Where was GT Hospital? The morning after, when I visited my friend in the ICU, I discovered it was in the heart of the city, not far from the route I took to school, or the posh club, the Bombay Gymkhana, where my parents spent mornings in the weekend. The reason I'd never known it is because it is a public hospital: the sort of place that the upper middle class, ordinarily, has so little to do with. In some ways, as my friend's case proved, it served as a dumping ground; and, as a result (or so claims Dr Saple, who was once in charge of the Skin and Venereal Diseases department there), it was one of the first places in Bombay where patients with this new and disquieting disease were 'dumped' by other hospitals. That morning, indeed, the young doctor attending to my friend – who had miraculously survived – told me that a woman was dying of AIDS in an adjoining wing of the ICU; that she'd contracted the disease from her husband, who was a 'migrant labourer'; that 'migrant labourers' themselves pick up the disease from sex workers. The husband, in this instance, was dead. As we know – without the thought ever coming clearly to the surface – the term 'migrant labour' usually describes, in India, itinerant wage earners within the nation, rather than people travelling outside it, generally men without an address who are contributing to building the infrastructure of globalised India. We pass them by repeatedly on roads and construction sites; with homosexuals and intravenous drug users, they, in their lonely nexus and vigil with sex workers, represent one of the main high-risk groups in the story of HIV in India. That morning, standing inside a hospital whose existence I'd only just become conscious of, talking about this woman whom I'd never see, I became aware of, in a new way, the invisible in the visible.

A few years later, I found myself in Bombay again, to write my piece. It was the doctors in public healthcare I chose to speak to (as if I was continuing the conversation I'd had that morning); in spaces and institutions I'd had no interaction with – for reasons I've already hinted at – when I actually lived in that city. There was a new optimism among them; antiretroviral therapy was being offered at subsidised costs, or even free; mortality rates had dropped; importantly, the figures of HIV-infected people in the country had turned out to be exaggerated; more than 5 million at the first reckoning, the estimate was now more than 2 million. The expected epidemic hadn't occurred. On my last afternoon, I met, at my own request, two HIV patients in Dr Alka Deshpande's clinic at JJ Hospital; in the end, I couldn't fit them into the story I went on to write; I already had too much material; oddly – to the unpredictable mind of the author as reviser – they, in a sense the real subject of the piece, seemed irrelevant to its gathering shape and theme. I have, here, an opportunity to revisit them, as well as the words I'd scribbled in my notebook while listening to their answers, with their mixture of transparency and prevarication. The first patient came to me where I'd been seated by a nurse, presuming I was a doctor. He was disabused of this notion, but made to sit and take my questions. He was a generic 'migrant worker', employed at a power loom factory, originally from Uttar Pradesh; but also a generic *Homo sapiens* (literally, 'wise human') of our extraordinary globalised age, patient, anonymous, scratching the scabs on his arm (the only sign, now, of the infection). He'd been cured of the opportunistic tuberculosis infection he'd had; he'd gained weight; his wife and two children were, providentially, HIV-free. He claimed to be ignorant about how he'd got it.

The other person was a Muslim housewife who was also a part-time maidservant, who says she got it four years ago during a blood transfusion during her daughter's birth. She'd been through pneumonia-like symptoms, but was now on the mend. What did her husband do? He drove a tourist taxi. I was struck by the humdrum ordinariness of both people; they might have come here for some free medication for influenza. This ordinariness was immensely moving, somehow an unacknowledged and indispensable part of the planet we live on now and understand relatively little of. They were, of course, living beneficiaries and symbols of the cheap availability today of antiretroviral therapy in public healthcare; but they also reminded me that HIV is not only about dying of, or now living with, the disease, but reimagining the place of the ordinary in our various accounts of contemporariness. The larger story, as the boars and the water hen in Berger's anecdote randomly demonstrate, is the one of survival; intermittently visible, taking us by surprise whenever we become privy to it.

A Season of Betrayals

A month ago, we found ourselves watching Attenborough's *Gandhi* again, with its familiar mixture of earnestness and calculated design – largely because of our eleven-year-old daughter's unexpected interest in nationalist history.

Not that *Gandhi* notices much. It possesses too good a story, composed in a series of neat, revelatory parables, for it not to be a sort of festive offering, a Christmas nativity play. Noticing introduces an element of stillness to a narrative; and almost the only time this happens in *Gandhi* (inadvertently, from the researcher wanting to be true to documentary footage) is in the brief recreations of the Congress Party working committee meetings, the famous leaders situated on a mattress on the floor, their inward restiveness concealed by postures of lassitude. Gandhi's arm is almost always bent at the elbow, as he leans to the left or right; as if either fatigued by the heat or subconsciously aware of an incursion of the erotic into the proceedings, he seems incapable of sitting upright. It's a posture common to certain forms of Indian conversation: Bhupen Khakhar occasionally captured this limpness in Indian, especially Gujarati, men in his paintings, and titled one of them (showing a single such figure) '*Sakhi bhav*' – which might be loosely translated as 'an air of feminine dalliance'. Nehru is too patrician, too angular, to truly possess this languor; but he too, in these meetings, is leaning, trying to ease his slightly resistant body, like an eager, idealistic boy next to his wizened but experienced teacher. Although press photographers were privy to such congregations, they still have an atmosphere of flirtation and intimacy which the public eye can't breach: with one person saying something into another's ear, while the other, head bent, listens – or (if you are watching a newsreel) nods his head. The fact that these people are to be found at floor level, in a place associated in our minds with idleness and childhood, and that these 'leaders' are trying to ignore the heat (the pankha puller is at work; or a fan clatters overhead), gives to our politics a peculiar humidity.

From what I gather from glimpses on news channels, this is the way at least some meetings continue to be conducted today; upon the mattress, with a greater evasiveness of the eyes, accompanied by smiles – somewhat like a family of long lineage hiding its own malaise at a funeral. Someone has died; or possibly something. The progeny are all there: Jairam Ramesh, Chidambaram, Manmohan Singh, Pranab babu, and, at the centre, the matriarch in the beautiful but unostentatious cotton sari, whose status is undeniable but at the same time implicitly uncertain. An old unappeasable grief marks her tranquil expression, mingled with a tenacious faith in power.

Is this, too, how the BJP meetings take place, with the figures arranged almost randomly, but centripetally, converging towards some invisible point of merging? And yet, though languor suggests familiarity and proximity, it also hints at deception and distance. The elbow and shoulder leaning in the direction of the figure on the left, imagine, has leaned tellingly away from the figure on the right. The person whispering into Advani's left ear is a million miles away from the Vajpayee a few inches to his or her left, who, impassive, is ensconced in absolute solitude. The enactment of overweening intimacy also induces trivial but unexpected gulfs. All these working committee meetings, when they are not actually 'working' (which is when, one presumes, the camera records them), have, with their exchange of confidences and their sudden solitudes, an air of *The Last Supper* – of imminent betrayals and disownings. This came to the surface of our consciousness with the emergence of Jaswant Singh in the last few weeks, and the tale of his secret dynamics with Vajpayee and Advani. Singh, you feel, unlike, say, Rajnath or Amar Singh, is not a man to whisper confidences or have them whispered to him;

his aloneness has a gnarled, organic quality; and, unlike Judas, you feel (clearly wrongly), he has no secret discontent. His advocacy of Jinnah, though, is only part of his problem. We'll never know exactly what was going on, or going wrong.

As if in consonance with this theme of disowning (just as Attenborough's film was televised to prime us for Independence Day), another movie, *Gandhi My Father*, appeared on the small screen the other night. I caught it purely by chance, during the obscure beaver-like fidgeting one performs in bed before going to sleep, and which is generally called 'channel-hopping'. I was drawn to it instantly, not because of the film's innate qualities, but because – as if one were suddenly very far away from home – one is irresistibly drawn, late at night, to 'scenes from India' on television: a train drawing into a platform; the glimpse of a field outside.

The film, as it turned out, was about Gandhi's relationship with Harilal, the oldest and most 'difficult' of his sons, who, in intense spurts, did many things during his troubled life: aspired to study law in England; thwarted by his father, turned to other activities, including alcoholism and questionable dealings with businessmen; briefly became a nationalist and a Gandhian, rather than just a Gandhi; later was also, briefly, a Muslim, 'Abdullah Gandhi'; reconverted to Hinduism; died – not long after his father had – of liver disease. It is the story of the prodigal son, except that there's no permanent reconciliation on homecoming. Instead of ever saying to the already loyal, as the father in the parable says to the older brother who never left him, 'Son, thou are ever with me, and all that I have is thine . . . this thy brother was dead, and is alive again; and was lost, and is found', Gandhi apparently confessed, 'I was a slave of my passions when Harilal was conceived.'

Gandhi My Father seems, at first, to have the air and the limita-tions of the Indian biopic, with the values given to this form by Attenborough, Shyam Benegal and Ketan Mehta. Dubbed voices, with the actors speaking their great historical lines in the studio, rather than in the heat and noise and uncertainty of filming, is one of the principal features of the biopic: it gives to it its enclosed, sepulchral, sacred mood. The use of a *lingua franca* is another: English in *Gandhi*; Hindi in the Benegal and Mehta films, and even in *Gandhi My Father*, lifting the politicians from the local languages they actually dwelt, argued and decried in into the high-flown and declamatory. And yet Feroz Abbas Khan, the director, escapes these shackling constraints by making *Gandhi My Father* episodic; by not staying with any event, however significant or traumatic, for very long. History in this film, as a result, begins to lose some of its symbolic fixity, and to take on the characteristics, the emotions, of memory. But I can't believe entirely that Gandhi spoke to Harilal with the controlled puritanical earnestness that he's shown to by Khan. I imagine his manner of undermining his son to be slightly sarcastic; Gandhi had a sense of the acerbic, and used it to counter the English. No man who said Western civilisation is a 'good idea', or could call an unsympathetic study of India 'the gutter inspector's report', would ever let go of irony as a weapon.

At the centre of the film is Akshay Khanna's fascinating performance as Harilal. Here I must interject with a memory which came to me as I was watching the expressions on his face, of vulnerability and resignation. My father used to work in Bombay for a company that owned a cottage on the outskirts of the city, on Marve Beach, to which we'd go on certain weekends. These cottages – called, romantically, 'shacks' – were overseen by a man who looked like a retired Major, who we knew was Vinod Khanna's father-in-law, the father of his first wife, Gitanjali. We also found out that the marriage was coming apart. Partly it was put under strain by Vinod Khanna's conversion to the Rajneesh cult, his move to Pune, where, among other things, he performed menial chores in the commune. Whether this has any bearing on Akshay's execution of his task is doubtful; still, I've never been able to keep the 'Major' doing his rounds, nor my possibly misplaced intuition of a wound, from coming to my consciousness when I see Khanna acting.

This much both Khanna and the film succeed in conveying, as

Attenborough doesn't: that 'any life', as Orwell said in relation to Dalí, 'when viewed from the inside is simply a series of defeats'. It's an observation that probably Jaswant Singh, Advani, Vajpayee and Sonia Gandhi would all agree with. Once admitted, it must lead to a revaluation of history: that the choices we made, and not just others, were often wrong ones. But, remembering Khanna's performance, Orwell's remark on Gandhi's intractable saintliness, made a year after his death, also comes to mind: 'To an ordinary human being, love means nothing if it does not mean loving some people more than others.'

The Key of Dreams

A bout seven years ago, I noticed a longish review in the pages of the *Times Literary Supplement*. What drew my attention to it was not its subject, an obscure French writer called Raymond Roussel, but the author of the book under review, the English poet Mark Ford, whom I knew slightly. Relieved it was a positive review, I was, however, bemused by Roussel, a writer of whom not only I, but, it seemed, many others were not aware. Roussel appeared to be another one of Ford's eccentric, subterranean, un-English preoccupations; for Ford was a devotee of the American poet John Ashbery, whose ironic ludic plangent style was more of a minority taste in Britain than falafel or the *nouveau roman*.

And yet Roussel's reputation had been growing. Born in 1877 into luxury and to a fairly odd mother (who carried a coffin with her on her travels in case she died in transit), more a curiosity who occasionally attracted lavish praise from famous writers than ever the famous writer he himself longed to be, Roussel was taken up, unsurprisingly, as a minor cult by the Surrealists, whose project he, on his part, was not overly taken with. Unsurprising, because there's an intransigent note of numinous solemnity to the bizarrely playful methods Roussel used in his composition – bizarre especially to contemporary French critics – just as his life seems to be a mixture of comic punctiliousness and mysterious unfulfilment. The tranquil poise of impossible juxtapositions: this might be one of the goals of Roussel's life and his writing, as well as the subject of many of the photographs he left behind, starting with the picture of the three-year-old Roussel upon a swan, hands innocently encircling its slender neck, or, a little older, in Turkish costume, 'pretending to smoke,' as Ford's caption reads, 'a pipe'.

Roussel's writing depended, as he put it in *How I Wrote Certain of My Books*, on a 'very special method'. The French word translated here as method is *procédé*, and it's a term that, by now, has come to be associated in certain circles with Roussel's comical-mystical endeavour. 'At the heart of the *procédé* lies the pun,' says Ford. The early stories 'begin and end with phrases that are identical except for a single letter, but where each major word is used in a different sense'. The *procédé* probably came to Roussel with two sentences, '*Les lettres du blanc sur les bandes du vieux billard*' and the near-identical '*Les lettres du blanc sur les bandes du vieux pillard.*' Roussel decided, or, as it were, was directed to, begin a story with the first sentence, which means, 'The letters [of the alphabet] in white chalk on the cushions of the old billiard table' and conclude it with the second, which, with the 'b' in the last word transmogrified into a 'p', means, 'The letters sent by the white man about the hordes of the old plunderer.' One can see why the Surrealists would have liked the *procédé*, emerging straight-faced as it does from the scientism of the nineteenth century, with its complete investment in order and logic, while also undermining that scientism somewhat disreputably. Exactly the same thing, I suppose, could be said about psychoanalysis, its own *procédé* or method, and its relationship to the recognised sciences.

One's also struck by the difference between the Rousselian, even the Surrealist, 'game' or 'method', and the narrative play of much of postmodern writing, which seldom loses its moorings in the histories of the New World and of colonialism. For the Surrealists, the great tension, as in their experiments with 'automatic writing', is between bourgeois artifice and predictability on the one hand, and chance, or even fate, on the other: there's a notable faith in the unknown that the future will inexorably throw up. For Roussel and the Surrealists, chance is the great begetter, and it's to chance – fate's mundane but nevertheless pregnant incarnation – they must attend, and to its disruption of the inevitability that socialisation visits upon us: this is, for instance, what Magritte's painting, *The Key of Dreams*, is 'about'.

The one Indian writer in English I can think of who dabbled intriguingly in a sort of *procédé* in his early work is the bilingual Arun Kolatkar. A *sui generis* song Kolatkar composed in the early 1970s (before he'd embarked on the poem-sequence *Jejuri*, and when he still entertained hopes of being a rock musician) begins with a line which he lifted from a typed message being distributed by an educated beggar on a train: 'I am a poor man from a poor land.' This line clearly suggested to Kolatkar an opening on to a domain whose meaning was quite distinct from the line's original intention: for his song is at once a parody of a Baul devotional, and a sales pitch for Indian rock music to a transcontinental record producer. Then there are the 'Marathi' poems in which Kolatkar began to experiment with Bombay Hindi, often using, as Arvind Krishna Mehrotra pointed out to me, what Marcel Duchamp called 'readymades' or 'found objects'. The line in the beggar's message is a 'found object'; so is the last line of the poem Kolatkar himself translated as 'Biograph', 'Can't you see where you going you motherfucker?', whose original (*'Dikhta nahin maderchod dikhta nahin?'*) Kolatkar must have heard many times, as I have, from the mouths of Bombay's taxi and bus drivers. 'Biograph' is about an unfortunate everyman, 'Mr Nene'; and, at some point, Kolatkar realised that *'Dikhta nahin maderchod . . .'* is an unforgiving philosophical pun, containing both an invective and a vision of existence, and that it could be used both as a summation of a life and the conclusion of a poem: in other words, as a *procédé*. The *procédé*, then, is superficially akin to, but significantly unlike, the Jamesian *donnée*, which, for the novelist, was a banal instant or stimulus that suddenly provided him with an opportunity to explore imaginary narrative terrain. The *procédé* is somewhat different, in that it hints not only at imaginative possibility, but towards a formal one; for Roussel and Kolatkar, the *procédé*, or self-imposed 'method', leads not only to the birth of a new story or poem, but to the necessity of fresh formal construction.

My own interest in Roussel has grown surreptitiously, because, really, I was charmed by the titles of his books, especially *Impressions of Africa* and *New Impressions of Africa*. What held me, in particular, was the fact that Roussel had never been to equatorial Africa, the setting of that first 'novel'; this was instructive, but in what way, I couldn't pinpoint. It reminded me of my late uncle's enthusiasm for *Chander Pahar*; his contradictory satisfaction at the fact that Bibhutibhusan Bandyopadhyay had never seen Africa. Roussel travelled, of course; he even went to Egypt and came to India; but, like the *procédé*, his travels are about the bathos of the idea of onward movement. The staged photographs of Roussel in exotic locations are like Surrealist forerunners of the tourist's experience of foreignness, where people make a studio, a microcosm, of wherever they happen to be, turning a scene into a backdrop for their figures. Often, Roussel visited these places in a *roulette*, a luxurious, caravan-like vehicle, in which he was accompanied and attended to by his staff, and from which he hardly emerged.

Roussel came back to me during my recent trip to the Paris Book Fair; not just because he was from Paris, but because the visit was oddly Rousselian. By the time it ended, it occurred to me that, in Paris after eleven years, I had seen almost nothing of the city. There was the hotel room; then the coach from the hotel to the aerodrome-like building that hosted the fair; then back to the hotel again: all this punctuated by lunches, readings, gossip, dinner. Soon, I realised that there were other writers who'd habituated themselves to, and probably profited from, this peculiar notion of travel. The historian Mushirul Hasan told me he was having a wonderful time in Paris. 'What do you do?' I asked. 'I stay in my hotel room and dictate my new chapter,' he said. In the coach, the Eiffel Tower often followed us about, augmenting the sense of interiority; reduced and reproduced infinitely, it has become a piece of furniture. 'Who is it who said,' observed Ananthamurthy suddenly from the seat in front of me, 'that to escape the Eiffel Tower you have to go inside it?' He ruminated for a few moments, as the lighted geometric shape waited patiently. 'I think it was Barthes,' he said finally, with his sweet sage-like smile.

My Dara Singh Phase

In the late 1960s, when I was six or seven years old, I had a brief passion for wrestling. Of course, since my life itself had been brief till that point, my passion, to my parents, seemed inordinately long-lived, taking an alarming number of months to wane. The death of Dara Singh brought back to me how obliging my parents were during my Dara Singh phase. By this I mean that the death prompted a revaluation of my early life, a retrospection, that took me back to my history, or prehistory, with the man. It was my parents who first introduced me to him. They took me to see his wrestling matches which were mainly world championships. And he played straight into my new-minted worship of strength and power. Although I'd taken an early shine to poems and stories, although I was miserable at school, where the star system was based on athletic prowess – and I detested sports and athletics – and despite the fact that, conveniently, I had a heart murmur which gave me the excuse I needed to be a non-performer during PE, I was a zealous admirer of fighting. I liked writing from an early age, but I also wanted to take part in wars and maintaining order – as an army man or at least a police inspector. I especially looked up to the Calcutta police, for their white uniforms, boots and holsters; I myself had a sizeable collection of pistols. My adulation of strength remained undimmed even when I was thirteen, when, making an exception to my rule about sports, I decided to become a pugilist. By then, I'd long cast aside Dara Singh and was under the spell of Cassius Clay. I, and another tryout, Rupen Arya, attempted to qualify for glory and the school's boxing tournament by gloving up in the presence of the gym teacher and going through the motions – first in the 'shed' near the quad, then in the ring, both of us being interrupted repeatedly by the instructor for raining blows on each other with our eyes closed. He had an air of resignation when breaking the news to us quickly, without unnecessary mollification, that we hadn't made the cut.

The people who worked in our apartment kept me informed, during my first infatuation, of what was responsible for Dara Singh's success: '*Woh nashta mein chhe murgi aur das anda khata hain*' – 'He consumes six chickens and ten eggs for breakfast.' Lunch was equally impressive. It was made even more so by my informant's exactitude with, and relish for, numbers. It was clear Dara Singh had time for little but eating and fighting; eating itself was a heroic feat, rivalling his achievements in wrestling. 'Chicken' or '*murgi*' (both words were used interchangeably for their talismanic virtues) was particularly efficacious – like the magic potion was to Asterix, and spinach to Popeye. No other meat would do. The diet was unvarying, like a sermon – always 'chicken' and '*anda*' – but Dara Singh was ravenous for it in astonishing quantities. When the large billboards came up in front of the NSCI stadium in Worli, exhibiting a giant-sized Dara Singh, exuding goodness and rightness, and a sinister masked opponent, my parents' hearts sank, and they knew it was time for another foray into the world of wrestling. Too late they realised what they'd done in fostering my addiction. The big match would be preceded by endless warm-up bouts in which two thin men were pitted against each other, and which were watched by my parents with dread, because they always ended in a draw – both men, after much circling and manoeuvring, dropping to the ground, while a voice announced – '*Dono barabar ho gaya*' – 'Both have come out equal.' I didn't find this message too disheartening, but for my parents it underlined the growing pointlessness of their evenings.

Dara Singh had a younger brother, Randhawa, a kind of Robin to his Batman, and sometimes they teamed up to eliminate the opposition. He's as good as forgotten to all except the most devoted wrestling fan, and those championship fights themselves became passé. It was just as I was outgrowing my obsession that I encountered Dara Singh in the flesh on a coach taking passengers from Santa Cruz airport to an Indian Airlines plane. My father spontaneously introduced me in English: 'My son is a great admirer of yours.' My respect for physical strength was matched by my shyness; he too, I recall, was pleased but shy. The class divide was clearer then, and just fame not enough to grant you privilege and dominance: a few words of properly enunciated English could quell an opponent.

Death used to be figured as a reaper in medieval Christian iconography, and with good reason – because the scythe topples collectively rather than singly, and in those days people died in clusters; sometimes – if there was a plague – in thousands. I don't know what it is about the modern-day dissemination of the news that makes it seem that the famous also die in small groups at a designated time – a week or fortnight – in the year. It's as if the reaper had taken a leisurely swing at a bygone world. So there was Dara Singh; there was Mrinal Gore; there was Lakshmi Sehgal; and there was the actor Rajesh Khanna, all lopped off more or less coterminously. The political, the historical and the fantastical (what other adjective fits Singh and Khanna?) had been brought together, diminished, and given a brief, orgasmic regeneration or convulsion (such as death can bring) by that swipe.

I was surprised at how moved I was by Rajesh Khanna's passing. No one can tell what kind of emotion the news of a death will lead to: I can't account for the burst of joy I experienced in 1980 on hearing that Sanjay Gandhi had died in a plane crash. Similarly, it's hard to explain the sense of loss I felt on hearing that Rajesh Khanna (who'd once hobnobbed with Sanjay Gandhi) was no more. Enough has already been said about Rajesh Khanna's charm, the way everything around him, including his car, was a magnet for women's kisses, and our susceptibility to his mannerisms (what one commentator described as the 'flirting of his head'), for me to augment that list.

Rajesh Khanna happened on the periphery of my world, where culture was defined by class. In this regard, the barrier separating the well off and the less well off wasn't impermeable, but it was considerable; yet the one between the educated and the less educated was even harder to cross for middle-class families. Nevertheless, Rajesh Khanna made his presence known through the songs he'd moved his lips and 'flirted his head' to: I remember being astonished by the energy and vitality of *'Mere sapnon ki rani'* as it was played on loudspeakers near the Gateway of India in 1970, when I was eight years old, like an anthem proclaiming a new reign. I report this not as a subject in that wonderful kingdom, but as a witness recounting an event. I saw *Aradhana* properly only more than a decade later, in a centre of higher education – Oxford – taping it off British television, and, stricken by nostalgia, studying its charms twice over in quick succession.

By then, Rajesh Khanna was in semi-retirement. All the contiguities that came together to make his films do so well – locations, scripts and especially the music – can be quantified, rated, even analysed for their contribution: but not him. Compared to the songs and the narratives, whose merits we can see, Khanna is a mystery. It's as if he found himself where he was – like the characters he portrayed in films like *Aradhana, Kora Kagaz, Anand* – by chance. Why him? There's no good answer; and, as if reflecting this, the characters he played too possessed an air of bewilderment and incomprehension (*'Yeh kya hua, kaise hua?'* – 'What happened, how did it happen?') – their principal, most attractive characteristic. There's no reason to mourn him more than anyone else – except that the illusions we create are so close and intimate to us.

The Bartholomews

The pictures taken by Richard and Pablo Bartholomew – father and famous photographer son – in the 1960s and 1970s of family, apartment interiors and the Indian art world Richard had natural access to (being an art critic) have now been in circulation for two years. Recently, I saw a substantial display in an art gallery on the third storey of an old house – where the viewers, quickly unmindful of the photos, were behaving with the easeful familiarity – a state of being poised finely between absolute contentment and boredom – that characterised all the figures in the pictures.

Each time I've seen these photos, I've remembered something from my 'other' life in childhood – not the imaginary life I was constructing for myself from the world I knew in Calcutta: my cousins' world of *Shuktara*, Narayan Debnath and Manna De; but the life that was actually my own in Bombay. This life in Bombay, which was my own but utterly distant, which was familiar but devoid of intimacy, had, however, its discontinuities; and it's to these that, for me, the Bartholomews' pictures speak. Occupying one of these discontinuities is a family called the Baruas, and I found myself thinking of them in the gallery.

Jolly Barua was my father's friend, and he was a 'commercial' artist: that is, he worked in advertising in an office on Dadabhai Naoroji Road (roughly, Bombay's Chowringhee), quite a distance from the ground-floor flat he and his family lived in in Khar. To visit him at home was to visit another country: the country captured in the Bartholomews' photographs. Pets – a variety of dogs, but also a cat and, at one point, a rooster – had free range of the flat, including the bits we wouldn't ordinarily access, like the shadowy space beneath the dinner table. Besides dogs, all kinds of filmmakers roamed about the place: I remember the nice bald man simply called 'Sarkar', who was always on the verge of making a feature, and also recall running into Subroto Mitra, Ray's cameraman for *Pather Panchali*. Jolly Barua and his wife's brother, the artist and designer Riten Majumdar, were the first two men I ever saw wearing the short kurta – the type that's now been in vogue for more than a decade because of John Bissell's Fabindia. But I'm speaking of the late 1960s – a time that belongs to the prehistory of the retail outlet – and was struck then by the curious shirts that couldn't be categorised or named, and seemed neither Western nor Indian, antique nor current. All around were other things that estranged me: the coir chairs in abundance; the unnaturally low centre table and divan; the strange, uncanonical visuals that hung from the wall, Jolly kaku's own handiwork (only later would I realise what a gifted innovator he was); the fragile lampshades; the ashtrays that looked like bits of bone or wood till you noticed the lip for placing the cigarette on. All the objects we usually call 'furniture' or 'decorations' were actually the assemblage of a bricoleur. Speaking of cigarettes, Jolly kaku's wife, Chitra, smoked endlessly. She was tall (5' 8"), and grew increasingly large as the years passed – it's possible her constant smoking (and eating) concealed more than one sadness: she'd lost her first son to cancer when he was eleven, and also missed her vocation as a singer (despite cutting a disc soon after coming out of Santiniketan) because of some unfortunate damage to her voice. I remember her dressed in handloom saris and large-bordered Garhwals.

It was here, at the Baruas', then, that I first encountered what Indians called 'ethnic' style. It's taken me about forty years to realise that 'ethnic', in India, is not really a proclamation of identity, but a register of homelessness and displacement. For instance, Chitra Barua née Majumdar and her brother Riten's Bengaliness was as improvised as any of the homespun or assembled things in the drawing room; they'd grown up in Patna. Jolly Barua actually came from 'royal' Assamese lineage. They now lived – and would till they died – in a rented flat in Khar. Charminar cigarettes (Chitra Barua's favourite brand), Kolhapuri chappals, blue jeans (often tailored, since the authentic item wasn't available), cotton or khadi tops, sleeveless jackets with Nehru collars, cloth shoulder bags, a copy of Lorca, an interest in Bergman, a passion for the dhrupad – all or some of these elements, with a few others thrown in, added up to this ensemble of homelessness, of belonging nowhere – an odd, vibrant cosmopolitanism. I should include in the list the saris a certain kind of woman wore – predominantly the cotton tangail, with one or two striking, simple colours – as well as the large bindi (not a stick-on, but actual vermilion) on the forehead. These bold and simple patterns were then replicated on bedspreads, such as the one on which Pablo Bartholomew photographs a pouting child lying, as if the ambition of that generation were urgently to move from identity into abstraction – to become, in themselves, or to at least be woven into, a sort of Rothko painting. So much of that world seems organic, and yet so much of it was design, that it becomes difficult to tell where the apparently natural ends and the created begins.

Naturally, the Baruas had pedigree, but we were only half aware of it at any given time, as were they, apparently: the rather bankrupt obsession today with familial connections – discovering or inventing them – was still nowhere in sight. Chitra kaki's older sister was Sucheta Kriplani, India's first female chief minister; the filmmaker Pramathesh Barua was Jolly kaku's maternal uncle. And so on and so forth. All this – in the vacuousness of present-day India – would be of terrible import; but at that time these facts were worn casually. They were significant, though, as part of the texture of what the sociologist Pierre Bourdieu called, expressively, 'symbolic capital': a domain of artistic and intellectual glamour and power, as distinct from real political power. The bewitching magic of 'symbolic capital' only made itself felt in environments in which there was relatively little capital of the non-symbolic variety: such as the Baruas' rented ground-floor flat, with its beautifully put together bric-a-brac, which risked getting ruined every year when the monsoon flooded the apartment. Similarly, the faces, places and families the Bartholomews photograph: émigrés, artists, men, children, women, whose world possesses the new, idiosyncratic, evocative marks of 'symbolic' wealth – an easel; an ethnic bedspread; a copy of *Thought*; the folds of a printed cotton skirt; a rolled-up joint. This is the sweet, frayed incarnation of the new aristocracy, and it extended – like most of the photos – only to the end of the 1970s. 'Symbolic capital', like light, displaces meaning restlessly: an artist looks like a student and vice versa; an easel becomes a bit of furniture; the exterior of a house is like a giant canvas. The Bartholomews are partly aware of this shifting social texture: that's why they photograph themselves obsessively – not existentially, in anguish, but self-reflexively, to capture the special symbolism they're part of, and which they can't – and don't want to – transcend or escape; to insert themselves into this largely visual 'symbolic' panorama. The Bartholomews' portraits differ, as a result, from Dayanita Singh's great pictures of the affluent of Bombay and Calcutta – photographing the rich requires a shrewd adjustment to the inequality between portraitist and sitter, so that the photographer can make herself invisible, and yet leave an unsettling trace of candour on the portrait. With the Bartholomews, especially Pablo, every picture of the time, every portrait, is also a self-portrait, every self-portrait a picture of the time.

What else can we recall from that peculiar itinerary of habitation and magic in those decades? There are the flecked mosaic floors, like just-begun Pollock paintings, grimy with our footsteps. There's the constant battening of the ceiling fan, which – with the democratic white glow of the tube light, illumining everything from a coaster to a book of poems – once formed the aural and visual prism of these lives. One also notices, from the photos, how lissom Indians are – they will lie and sprawl anywhere; they read (and think) in the oddest of positions mixing languor and total immersion. Nirad Chaudhuri – in another context, that of petit-bourgeois Bengali life – said that the bedroom, not the drawing room, was the main locus of sociability in these homes. Perhaps, with regard to Pablo's pictures, the bed itself:

where people take stock, ponder, make conversation and pacts. And what of sleep? The Bartholomews' portraits of recumbent and, in Richard's photos, sleeping figures are a reminder of their curious, topsy-turvy take on sociability: that one is never not part of a particular social world – itself charged with mysterious meaning, like a dream – even when one is no longer aware of it, or of oneself. How lovely to confront the richness – I use the word in a Bourdieuan sense, without Bourdieu's reductiveness – of the everyday in a country where we struggle to find a language with which to speak of it.

What is an Adventure?

As an angst-ridden teenager, I naturally read a lot of Sartre. And in my memory is buried a comment that has nothing to do with the things that kept me interested at that time - suicide, suffering, the absurdity of existence. It's about the idea of the 'adventure' (quite remote, then, from the preoccupations of a poet manqué). I think Sartre was saying that adventures can't be experienced except in retrospect. That is, you can't embark on one thinking, 'I'm about to have an adventure.' Sartre's discussion takes place, my memory tells me, in his short, cerebral, slightly supercilious memoir, *Words*. I have misplaced my copy. Googling 'Sartre' and 'adventure' brings up brainyquote.com, which, among other aphorisms from the ceaselessly intellectual Frenchman, reproduces the one I think I have in mind: 'For an occurrence to become an adventure, it is necessary and sufficient for one to recount it.'

At sixteen, I'd just graduated from reading what were, in effect, adventure stories (whether these were by Enid Blyton, R.L. Stevenson or, later, by Alistair MacLean and Robert Ludlum) to 'literature'. As a result, I had no intention of thinking about a genre that I associated with childhood. Besides, I was already becoming impatient with the Sartrean generalisation – 'Existence precedes essence'; 'The universe is contingent'; 'Man is a useless passion.' Googling – which, in relation to research, is roughly what casual sex is to passion (that is, it has unexpected results) – brings up something else by Sartre on 'adventure' – in fact, a lovely exchange from *Nausea*: ' "What sort of adventures?" I asked him, astonished. "All sorts, Monsieur. Getting on the wrong train. Stopping in an unknown city. Losing your briefcase, being arrested by mistake, spending the night in prison. Monsieur, I believe the word adventure could be defined: an event out of the ordinary without necessarily being extraordinary." '

Overwhelmed by the universe, I'd read *Nausea* as an adolescent, followed the protagonist's pointless itinerary through the town, and taken in his horror at the gluey texture of existence. My Penguin Modern Classics edition had a simple, powerful design, with Dalí's *The Triangular Hour*, set on a mysterious afternoon, on the cover. I've lost this book too (who'd have thought existentialism would come to this pass!). But I have no memory of the conversation above. In its acknowledgement of accidentality, in its mischief, it shows the myopic Sartre to be closer to the irrepressible Dalí and the Surrealists than one would have suspected.

The word 'adventure' has been coming up lately in the company I keep, especially in England, and in relation to music. A friend of mine, Roger, who's an independent producer for the BBC's Radio 3 and 4, said to me a year and a half ago, 'Would you like me to manage your band? You look as if you could do with some help.' Now, only the commercially viable pop bands can afford managers. 'That would be fantastic. But what, and how, would I pay you?' I asked. 'You can pay me when that becomes a possibility. As for now, I'll do it gratis.' He added, 'It'll be an adventure.' The word is part of his lexicon. His company has the alliterative, optimistic name, Art and Adventure. Besides, I heard him use the term on one or two of our musical excursions. Adam, who plays the guitar with me, uses it frequently. The last time was in November, when I had the two-and-a-half-minute musician's slot on BBC 2's *Review Show*, one of the last extant bits of culture on television in today's Britain. I was allowed one accompanist. In a curious politburo-like move, the BBC had decided from early 2010 that the *Review Show* would be televised live out of Glasgow. The fee offered covered travel costs and the hotel, and left us with a bit in hand; very little, in our case, since we'd neglected to book the Ryanair flight in advance. Adam decided he'd take the train – an eight-hour journey from Norwich, for a two-and-a-half-minute appearance in which he was accompanying the featured artiste. What made him do it? It couldn't have been the money or the fame. During rehearsals in Glasgow, Adam hinted to me what his impetus was: 'It's an adventure.'

Roger and Adam, then, are giving to the word a meaning different from the one Sartre is. 'For an occurrence to become an adventure, it is necessary and sufficient for one to recount it,' says Sartre. The various characters involved in the urgent quest of *Treasure Island* don't know, in other words, that they're in an adventure; neither Tom Sawyer nor Huckleberry Finn is actually aware that the bewildering flow of events they're in the midst of can be classified as 'adventures' – and won't be aware of them as such until, presumably, later. To be in something is to preclude the sense of denouement and narrative that the 'adventure' is all about. Yet Roger and Adam seem to believe it's possible to *decide* to have an adventure; and to be conscious they're having one. The adventure, for them, is not so much about denouement or outcome; in fact, the outcome is already known, and is partly irrelevant. The adventure is the staging of a spontaneous, irresistibly creative impulse. I say 'staging' because there's an element of premeditation here, in deciding, or agreeing, to have an adventure; but premeditation doesn't, paradoxically, rob the act of spontaneity. In contrast to *Treasure Island* and all its offshoots, including the rich tradition of Hollywood heist movies, this kind of adventure is not about the financial reward, the treasure or loot, at the end; the conscious relegation of the financial reward to the realm of secondary interest is precisely what makes it possible for one to identify an action as an adventure and also enjoy it *as it's happening*. Art becomes an adventure – not in the Sartrean retrospective sense, but in this other one, when it exists in the present moment – when chance and creativity gain precedence over outcome and reward.

The free market and corporations – which, in theory, operate on principles of growth and excitement – have done a lot to kill this spirit; and yet there's a strong, persistent undercurrent of it in the West. It was once powerful in India too; *Pather Panchali* must have been made, by Ray and his investors, with some sense of 'having an adventure' in mind. Last year, Dhritiman Chaterji told me how he gravitated towards theatre when he was at the Delhi School of Economics in the 1960s because people then still had an idea of doing things for 'pleasure, rather than for money'. This idea is essential to experiencing an adventure as it takes place.

There is something, however, that we usually grasp and experience after the event, especially in the domain of the arts, and to which, maybe, Sartre's definition applies more accurately: I mean history. A historic epoch, a 'great' or 'golden' age of the arts, is one people often live through without being aware of its uniqueness. I've noticed this when I've spoken with those who heard John Coltrane live in the 1950s, or bought a Jamini Roy original from the painter himself for a few hundred rupees, or listened to Radharani singing before them: they recall what an extraordinary experience it was, but confess they had no idea they were living in an extraordinary time. A great fan of the television series *The Adventures of Sherlock Holmes* told me the other day that David Burke, the actor who'd played Watson, had found the schedule too demanding and, citing family and personal reasons, had withdrawn after the first two series. 'He obviously didn't know he was in a classic, or he wouldn't have done that,' said the fan. *In* a classic! Yes, it's possible to be in a film, a play, a television series, a bar, a concert; but it's only in retrospect we realise we were in a classic, because a classic is a moment and experience transmuted into history. In this sense, history is an adventure in the Sartrean meaning of that word. We can't, it would seem, decide to be part of a historic age.

The Mythologist

A few months ago, I began rereading Roland Barthes. Probably the greatest French critic of the last century, Barthes is associated, in the heads of most undergraduates and dilettantes, with two things. The first is semiotics, or the study of signs; at the end of his life, he even held the impressive sounding Chair in Literary Semiology (a title of his own choosing, apparently) at the Collège de France. The second is his essay 'The Death of the Author', in which he described the author's passing, adding, provocatively, 'The birth of the reader must be at the cost of the death of the author.' Make no mistake: Barthes was not composing an elegy to the author in this essay – he was announcing, with all the peremptory energy of a young capitalist who's taken over a very old franchise, that the author had been sacked.

Let none of this intimidate you. For Barthes was, primarily, a wonderful writer – as great and gifted a writer (sometimes greater) as some of the most well-known poets and novelists of the twentieth century. Trite though this might sound, Barthes is genuinely someone in whom categories such as poet, fiction writer, essayist and critic break down. For all his polemical championing of the reader, Barthes's work is a striking assertion of the fact that, (as Susan Sontag once pointed out), what matters, what is at issue, is writing itself; that generic definitions – novel, short story, essay, poem – are helpful but ultimately constraining.

And, in fact, Barthes is at his most brilliant when attacking genre and its window dressing. In his first book, the brief *Writing Degree Zero* (1957), he took on, among other things, the realist novel and its pervasive conventions, which permeate, particularly, history writing.

By the realist novel', I hasten to add, Barthes wouldn't have meant a genre that's the opposite of, say, the 'fantasy novel' as we understand it now – the latter ranging from Márquez to Tolkien and J.K. Rowling. Barthes would have found in the 'fantasy' genre many of the same tiresome conventions that, for him, made the realist novel such a chore. In *Writing Degree Zero*, Barthes quotes Paul Valéry's shrewd observation that novels always seem to begin with a sentence like 'The Marchioness went out at five o' clock.' The simple past tense (of which that sentence is an example) inaugurates, Barthes says, an 'unreal time' – the time of 'novels, cosmogonies, and histories'. It's a kind of time that suppresses the 'uncertainty of existence' – Gabriel Josipovici, more faithful to the French original, translates the phrase as the 'trembling of existence'. For one who's identified with bringing the word 'text' into currency (along with Jacques Derrida), it's worth recalling that what Barthes desired was liberation, joy and sensation; and that he found these in the 'trembling' and 'uncertainty' of life. And the mode of writing that approaches this 'trembling', this disruption, most closely, is poetry – not, for Barthes, simply a series of words in rhyme and metre, but an ethos of language.

Does this (in case you've persisted in reading until this point) make Barthes sound difficult? I hope not. For, even if he isn't exactly straightforward, he is revelatory – and he gives considerable pleasure. Once you're acquainted with him, you'll find he's less difficult to read than many well-known novels filled either with stories or present-day pieties and preoccupations. You'll find he's more comprehensible than most newspaper reports and book reviews. And you'll see he's easier to understand than almost all the film summaries offered by Tatasky to its viewers (which I, frankly, find indecipherable).

You could start with the book *Mythologies*, where, in short essays originally written for a magazine (one can only marvel at what was once possible in the realm of print media), Barthes proves he's the wittiest observer of popular culture since George Orwell. As you read, you might find that data that had lain beneath the surface of your mind is being excavated by the details Barthes notices. For instance, in 'The Romans in Films', he reminds us that in 'Mankiewicz's *Julius Caesar*, all the characters are wearing fringes. Some have them curly, some straggly, some tufted, some oily, all have them well combed, and the bald are not admitted, although there are plenty to be found in Roman history.' Having established this peculiarity, Barthes wants to know, 'What, then, is associated with these insistent fringes?' He answers immediately, 'Quite simply the label of Roman-ness . . . The frontal lock overwhelms one with evidence, no one can doubt he is in ancient Rome.'

Is the frontal lock or its representation an important historical event – say, in comparison to global warming or the Holocaust? Clearly not. This is where Barthes is an artist: in his ability to translate the banal, even the ridiculous, into the fleetingly seminal. And this is how art differs from sociology: in its absorption with the commonplace, the unpromising, for no extraneous reason. Unlike cultural studies and its ideologues, Barthes is not actually telling us that popular culture is important. It's the frisson between the lack of grandeur, the tackiness, of his subject and the majesty of Barthes's elaborations on it that make for the tone and texture of his art. Susan Sontag points out that it's when his object of study is monumentally meaningless, like the Eiffel Tower, that Barthes's readings are most fecund. Here is his opening gambit in his eponymous essay: 'Maupassant often lunched at the restaurant in the tower, though he didn't care much for the food: *It's the only place in Paris*, he used to say, *where I don't have to see it.*' Like Walter Benjamin – but largely devoid of Benjamin's melancholy – Barthes is an epicure of the inversion; meaningless things are important to him, important things (the realist novel; the author; the subject) meaningless.

It would be a mistake to continue to view Barthes through the prism of semiotics. Despite his professional chair and his academic legacy, Barthes is no more a jobbing semiotician than Christ was a devout Christian. Semiotics is a necessary scaffolding for Barthes, and a creative point of entry into material otherwise banal or resistant: just as Greek mythology is for the modernist novelists and poets, for Joyce, Rilke, Pound and Lawrence. Like semiotics, mythology is a carefully coded system with correspondences to other, unlikely systems; it allows Joyce, for instance, to write about the tiniest detail of contemporary Dublin. I would reiterate that, despite his chair, Barthes is no more an authority on semiotics than Joyce a scholar of Greek myth; semiotics is not a separate domain of professional knowledge for Barthes, but a component integral to affirming the primacy, and alchemy, of writing.

And what of the ubiquitous 'The Death of the Author'? Don't we sense that its proclamations are at least partly tongue in cheek, because irony is often the most effective means of making, and deflecting, a point? One also has to keep in mind Barthes's innate playfulness. It's best to place this essay in the company of mock essays, like Borges's 'Pierre Menard, Author of the Quixote', where, outrageously, the narrator suggests that the translation of a text might well be more authentic than the original. Barthes perpetrates comparably outrageous inversions: Proust didn't write autobiographical fiction, he claims, but 'made of his very life a work for which his own book was the model'. Similarly, Count Robert de Montesquieu, on whom Proust based the character the Baron de Charlus, is 'apparently no more than a secondary fragment, derived from Charlus'. The humour of these inversions moves Barthes beyond Benjamin towards Borges and, even earlier, Oscar Wilde, with his constant rebuttal of sincerity. Here, in a similar vein in 'The Decay of Lying', is Wilde: 'Where, if not from the Impressionists, do we get those wonderful brown fogs that come creeping down our streets, blurring the gas lamps . . .?' It's in that over the top, teasing, grandiloquent Wildean gesture that we need to place Barthes's most outrageous pronouncement, concerning the author's demise.

One should also bear in mind that the idea of the author's death must have been in circulation for a while before Barthes wrote his piece; Foucault would present his own variation on the theme a few years later in 'What is an Author?' So it's perhaps best not to look at Barthes (or Foucault, for that matter) as the originator of the idea, a *thinker*, but as a performer who's in play with a notion, a bricoleur; like Borges in his little essay on the fictional Pierre Menard, Barthes is adopting a tone, a style, a form, that makes play possible. Ideas, as Borges shows us, and as Barthes knows, already exist; it's writing that comes periodically to life.

If you've read this far, you've probably already read Barthes. Yet I'd urge you to read him again, as a writer.

As Good as None

My gradual realisation about what a one-off and distinctive institution Ujjala Chanachur is came to me when I began to notice its queues. I don't mean that I was impressed by the number of people who lined up to purchase the product – that number varies from two to ten – but the fact that a queue was enforced by the proprietor or vendor at all. This makes the tiny shop exceptional in its dealings with customers. We all know how one of the ubiquitous innovations of contemporary India is the horizontal queue, stretching from left to right or right to left, whichever way you choose to see it, instead of front to back, as is the convention; this horizontal line can be added to at any time, by simple joining, in a stealthy act of mock political solidarity, the others who are already waiting, and adding your voice to theirs. The vendor's strategy in this regard is to keep his head bowed and finish working on whatever he's rustling up, and then question the next person he arbitrarily glances at about what he wants. Whatever his inner feelings – and they can't, despite his apparently contained air, be calm – the person in the horizontal line experiences a roller coaster of emotion. Ujjala Chanachur abhors this kind of drama. I've seen people try to slip in sideways, adhering to an existing customer like an unobtrusive rib, and then make a careless interjection in the vein of '*Achha dada, araisho deben*' – 'Two fifty grams, dada' – only to be sternly gestured by the vendor (they're eagle-eyed and miss nothing, the Ujjala staff, immersed though they might seem in their task) to go and stand behind the other customers. So there's no milling in front of the shop; the queue, when there is one, stretches to its right. In this way, everyone is ensured that they'll get the manna of the *chanachur* without having to spectate as someone gets theirs out of turn. And so customers here exude an unusual confidence, and are noticeably silent, patient and not worked up in comparison to their counterparts elsewhere, even allowing themselves the luxury of thinking of other things as they wait: all this arising not only from trusting the product, but from trusting the system by which they'll eventually procure it. It's an exemplary ritual of civilised buying and selling which you might well miss if you pass by the shop in a hurry, or haven't visited it a couple of times.

For me, this is familiar territory, since it's not far from where my maternal uncle has lived for about half a century. Yet such claims have to be qualified by irony – I never heard of Ujjala Chanachur when I used to visit my uncle's family every year (though I knew of Ujjala Cinema, and probably even went there to watch a film with the extended family); now that I hardly visit my uncle's house (though we finally live in the same city), the main reason for my sojourns to this terrain is the *chanachur* shop. And it's because Ujjala Chanachur is in my thoughts that I mention it to my cousin, this very maternal uncle's daughter, who's come here from America, on holiday with her two children; I learn for the first time that my uncle has not only tasted it but is, in his unmistakable manner, a champion: 'He claims it's not just good, it's the best *chanachur* anywhere,' my cousin informs me, slightly indulgent towards her father's habitual extravagances: for him, things belong to two categories, 'the best' and 'the worst'. But I do agree – though my experience and comparitivist knowledge in *chanachur* is limited. Ujjala's variety I came to know of after my marriage, through my wife, a Calcuttan born and bred. Earlier, I wasn't terribly conscious of *chanachur* as a worthwhile snack or even a pastime. Unlike many people who measure their humanity and others' through how addicted they are to, say, *phuchka*, my passion for Indian junk food burns with only a low-grade intensity. From graduating to a consciousness that Ujjala Chanachur exists, I now have an irregular but foreseeably permanent relationship with it. Along with this relationship has come an appraisal that this *chanachur* is probably, in its own way, famous, at least among a freemasonry of connoisseurs.

The shop, with its superior fare and its superior view of queues, is remarkable partly because it's so unprepossessing. It's actually not quite a shop as we understand that word today; but it's more than a stall. Primarily, it is a small room – divided by a wall into the shop in the foreground, that gleams because of its stone and glass surfaces, and the workplace at the back, largely invisible except for the giant black *karhai* whose one end juts out into the customer's line of vision, and the blackened, medieval walls. The owner seems to think it's perfectly appropriate for the customer to understand that *chanachur* is created in a timeless furnace before it travels just a few feet into the petit-bourgeois propriety of the front part of the shop, with its smart, blue-tinged weighing scale; here it acquires the air of having been manufactured by a form of immaculate conception, with no connection to oil, grime and smoke. This front part has large mirrors, a mandatory likeness of Ganesh on the left, a mother goddess in the background before the mirror, and a large, minatory Kali on the right. On shelves are edibles in cellophane packages: the sort of thing that few people come to Ujjala in search of, and for which they can go to Haldiram Bhujiawala. The shop, which is all floor, always has two people in it, and often three; these people are never seen standing. Mostly, it's the proprietor who sits like a *munshi* on the left, relaying the customer's preferred permutation to the vendor on the right, who's usually too busy rustling up these very specific, nuanced orders to be mindful of the existence of the customer themselves; the latter just might, occasionally, leave without being looked at even once by the man who's prepared their mix. The proprietor or his substitute receives the money, hands over the parcel and, in keeping with Ujjala's generally enlightened outlook, is businesslike and isn't insistent about customers handing in exact change. The shrine-like *bhakti* or devotion imparted to the interior by its three or four deities is reflected in the quiet, methodical zeal with which the vendor concocts the *chanachur*. Not far above him hovers an orb-like clock, alerting us to the fact that this narrow, busy scene is slightly reminiscent of Bhupen Khakhar's *Janata Watch Repairing*, in which, too, someone, in a constricted space of which he's the centre, is painstakingly handling bead-like objects

– the parts of a watch. Both in Khakhar's painting and at Ujjala Chanachur we're asked to understand that time is work, that it's precious, and that it's a barely graspable aspect of eternity.

In fact, not much else is happening in this environment: the Ujjala Cinema itself, after which the chanachur is named, is long gone, replaced by a seven-year-old glass-fronted edifice that looks, oddly, like it's still expecting occupation. Walking in the opposite direction, you find that Basusree is barely extant, with idlers gathered on a sofa by the entrance, waiting for Jism 2 to end and the audience for Muktodhara to arrive; the cinema largely forgotten by the bustling, carefree middle class (itself now so remote as to be a fiction) that climbed up its stairs only thirty years ago. Back at Ujjala's, I must remember to instruct, like many other customers, that I want 'naam matro' peanuts in my mix – that is, as good as none – and an abundance of the papri that's made of some variety of besan and/or flour, and resembles more closely than its equivalents in other kinds of chanachur the curled petals after which it is named. The man nods dourly, distributes a percentage of each ingredient into a brown paper bag, grudgingly adding a few peanuts for the sake of form, sprinkles the mixture with a brown dust that may be rock salt or chaat masala, and shakes it temperately. Turning my back to the shop with the precious parcel, I see, diagonally across the road, one of the city's most magnificent monuments, the Greek Orthodox Church, which I used to pass as a child going down the wide avenue that's SP Mukherjee Road but haven't yet investigated. Such grandeur in proximity to the small-scale domesticity of my uncle's house was something I could never get used to. I'm still a bit overwhelmed by its portals. I have little to do with this Calcutta any more though; getting back into the car, I encounter it each time as a transient while relishing the ebbing warmth of the papri in the brown paper bag.

Ways to Unwind

For me, the best way to unwind is, inevitably, to watch TV, and the best TV where unwinding is concerned is crime TV. I don't mean documentaries – such as are shown regularly on Fox History. Fox has long taken a view that the idea of 'history' is capable of accommodating Nancy Reagan and trashy murders. Now, as if in response to my tastes, and in a kind of evolutionary development, Tatasky has dispensed with Fox History altogether and given us Fox Crime. But I don't like reality crime either, of which *Cops* is presumably one example: 'Television cameras follow real life enforcement officers as they perform their daily duty to "serve and protect" the public.' So says the prolific author of Tatasky's information panel. No, for me, unwinding means a story and, most of all, immersion in a particular world: a film, if possible, or, in lieu of a film, a series about fictional characters who have a propensity for solving crime.

Most of the new fare is unsatisfactory. Good films about homicide or even about violence in general are rare. When I say 'good', I'm not referring to thoughtful and unsparing psychological studies of killers and killing such as *Dead Man Walking* and *Mystic River* undoubtedly are. I mean a film that captures the anomalous and inexplicable magic that's imparted to an environment by the occurrence of a murder. Of this magic, Hitchcock was maybe the sole purveyor – but, in making such a generalisation, you miss mentioning *Double Indemnity*, or the musically clinical *Anatomy of a Murder*, whose enigmatic formalistic preoccupations begin with the poster by Saul Bass, with its Matisse-like collage of the dead man's outline in the foreground, the background comprising a simple Rothko-like scheme of two vivid rectangular

166

patches of colour. In Hitchcock's hands, and in Billy Wilder's and
Otto Preminger's respectively, sudden death is an uplifting experience
that leaves us curiously light and happy – not uplifting, then, in
some Aristotelian cathartic sense, but in the way it generates the
sort of sensuous experience that's peculiar to art, in response to art's
exactitude, its embodiment of a kind of perfection. These movies
aren't intended to instruct and delight – for instruction, we return to
Dead Man Walking. These – *Strangers on a Train*, *The Man Who Knew Too
Much* and, especially, *Shadow of a Doubt* – are meant for delight alone.

As an aesthetic achievement, surpassing all crime on television – in
fact, most stuff on TV – is the early series of *Columbo*, with Peter Falk
(who always looks Irish to me, but is of European Jewish ancestry)
playing the shambling, irritating, middle-class detective for whom the
sites of homicide are the immense houses of the tanned Californian
rich of the early 1970s. Each episode begins, famously, with us being
a party to the carefully planned murder; and then we're invited to
witness how the superior or even genteel type who's committed it
becomes the disorganised detective's unlikely quarry. Columbo is
almost the only person here who belongs to the real world, such as you
and I do, a fact underlined by his uxurious references to his wife and
his infrequent mentions of his children, a real world given veracity by
the fact that we never once see either it or the wife and children. The
series takes us, in episode after episode, on a limited, idiosyncratic,
picaresque tour of the houses, rooms and recreational spaces of the
Los Angeles nouveau riche. It is one of the few instances on film –
besides the relatively recent *Collateral*, which has similarly picaresque
and voyeuristic impulses – when the sterile stretches of Los Angeles
look inexplicably alive. Or maybe LA was an interesting city once? But
the main pleasure of *Columbo* derives from its contradictory love of
colour: the hedonistic, Fauvist hues of the sunlit California in which
the murderer lives and kills. I say contradictory because Peter Falk
himself is drably clad in a mackintosh, and his often stubbly cheeks
are grey: despite being of Italian stock, the detective is an Anglo-
Saxon Puritan. Not so, clearly, the murderer.

What *Columbo* and other great crime offerings on screen give us is a closed world, defined by the murder, the killer's delusions, the hunter's constantly interrupted pursuit and the details that comprise the scene of crime. The larger world is kept out; and this makes the murder movie akin to a parable or allegory, a formal kinship that's in tension with its deep realism – in fact, the detective, with his unnatural eye, is a fetishist and connoisseur of the real. For the great crime movie, both political history and psychological inwardness are secondary; the kind of physicality that can be apprehended by the senses is everything. Being inside a closed world means that we experience, in a crime movie, what it's like to be a child again. The scene of murder is a sort of ersatz home, at once intimate and indefatigably explorable. To be at home, to be vulnerable to a self-invented but plausible danger, and to be also happy is to approximate the condition of being a child. But the child at play in this way must have an implicit faith in a benign patriarchy, even if the father is remote or invisible. This is why the great crime stories and movies emerge in the time of imperialism or when the bourgeoisie is predominant, when the closed world denies, on one level, everything outside it, but is both protected and shaped by that invisible, nurturing authority. (In Bengal, this comforting microcosm of mysterious death and retribution, presided over by the *bhadralok's* distant but watchful gaze, culminates and ends, like a brief seasonal holiday, with the Feluda movies.)

The various crime series on TV today – *Silent Witness*, *Wallander*, *Waking the Dead*, *Criminal Minds*, *Dexter* – are, in this regard, more grown up, in that they reflect the total erosion of faith in the paternalistic. This doesn't necessarily make for better television or cinema, or better crime. The English crime dramas are now more and more indistinguishable from soap operas, because they're mainly about the betrayal of trust – arising from adultery, and bullied and sexually abused children who have become adults. No one transcends this blighted social fabric: policeman, victim and murderer are all obedient to Philip Larkin's dictum: 'They fuck you up, your mum and dad. / They may not mean to, but they do.' Given their soap opera-like longueurs and ambitions, English murder mysteries like *The Midsomer Murders* and *Inspector Lynley* lack the compression and economy of the earlier classics; they drift, and are inordinately long, which is the preferred manner when the scriptwriter and director, rather than the murderer, have a long, tortured confession to make. The American franchises, such as *Criminal Minds*, are uneasily quasi-religious: the deluded murderer – usually a man trapped in an arid working- or middle-class suburb – is awaiting the Second Coming. As a result, the focus of *Criminal Minds* is not detail, worldliness or physicality (what used to be charming about murder was the way it engendered a taste for minutiae), but apocalypse and the refulgent birth of new worlds.

I watch these various series largely because there's nothing else. I have my own kind of relationship with them, which involves bemusement and incomprehension. Most of the time, I don't understand what's happening in them, and have to turn to my wife for clarification. Part of the reason for this is that the sheer badness of, say, *Criminal Minds*, makes my mind work associatively rather than receptively. Instead of listening to what somebody's saying, for instance, I am, without premeditation, wondering whom their face reminds me of. As a result, about fifteen minutes into the episode, I've identified the murderer, and convey my hunch to my wife; five minutes later, I might correct myself and find a new candidate. Whatever the case, years of unconscious training – in reading expressions, in familiarity with filmic and murder mystery conventions – ensure my intuition about the killer is correct a startling 80 per cent of the time. OK, maybe 70 per cent. In other words, I now view the murder mystery not as an object of pleasure, but as a crystal ball on which to test, to my wife's chagrin, my psychic abilities. My drifting incomprehension, my hit and miss guesses, are apposite to the post-patriarchal world, in which none of us – viewer, murderer, victim, director – is any longer sure where we are.

Close-ups in Hindi Films

B y close-ups in Hindi cinema, I don't mean movies today (though these aren't necessarily excluded), but primarily those of the 1950s, 1960s and 1970s. In other words, films made in the midst of, marked by and contributing to the music renaissance, the golden age of film songs. Many of us know that the close-up is not one of film-making's respectable undertakings, and is looked on with almost as much disdain by trained filmmakers as the zoom shot is. Yet why did it possess such transcendental beauty in Hindi movies?

Part of it has to do with the untranslatable quality of the Indian face, particularly the Indian head, and its range of expressions and gestures, both fleeting and recurrent. I use the catch-all term 'Indian' because Hindi cinema, located as it is in Bombay, occupies the borderline of north and south, of Karnataka and the land further below, but also of Gujarat in the west and then further north into Punjab – not to speak of the impact of migrant Bengalis. And so one notices a gamut of cranial movements in Hindi films – not pan-Indian movements, but a collage of shakes and nods from different parts of the country – that may be richer than its counterpart in other parts of India, however compelling popular cinema (and its faces) in, say, 1950s Bengal might have been.

There's no denying the complexity of the codes that inform moving the head from side to side in this country. The arc or swivel from left to right, or right to left, or left to right to left to right, have all sorts of registers here, and only one of them means 'No'. I recall standing early one morning in Gloucester Green, the central bus station in Oxford, waiting with my wife and mother for the bus to

Heathrow. As usual, my mother found herself in the middle of a conversation with a young woman, a Japanese student, who, like her, was also going to India, although she'd be visiting it for the first time. She was very soft-spoken, but at one point, amused by some thought, she started laughing, and leaned forward, at the same time, to explain to my mother, who began to smile too. When I asked my mother later about what had caused laughter, she said, 'She is a bit nervous about going to India, because she isn't sure she'll understand what people are saying. She has heard that Indians say yes by shaking their head from side to side.'

It's undeniable that the straightforward nod exists in India, an urgent, vigorous indicator of agreement. Urgent, vigorous – but frugally used; because other head movements are employed more commonly to signal agreement, but in a more emollient, tender manner. There is the sideways shake of the head, which in other countries means no; confusingly, in India it means no too, but one can also, in the right context, infer absolute, unqualified agreement from it. Then there is – often seen in Bengal but perhaps not exclusive to it, and especially used by Bengali girls – the tilting of the head to one side. This gesture, in England, would be accompanied by the eyes following the same direction the head is tilted towards, to suggest 'Look at that.' In Bengal, the head is tilted gently, but the eye contact with the interlocutor is immovable; the tilt is the most ingenuous gesture available to imply agreement, assent, even complicity – 'All right' ('thhik achhe') or 'Yes, I'll do it' ('hain, korbo'). Further south, people are apt to make doll-like movements with their head: not a shake of the head, but quick tilts on either side; almost, but not quite, a cranial rotation. Again, this, notwithstanding its wobbliness, is essentially a genteel, unintrusive gesture, meant to convey agreement and camaraderie without starkly emphasising and reducing these to a single unambiguous movement, as a simple nod does. That the nod and the shake of the head, with their conventional global significances – of agreement and disagreement respectively – are also a part of this vocabulary of gestures, brings home to us the sweet contradictoriness of Indian emotive life.

This emotive life and its gradations and paradoxes are nowhere as clearly on display as in the life of the face and the head of both the listener and the artiste during a north Indian classical music performance. The most reliable integer of a listener being touched or moved by a phrase that the singer has just rendered is the movement of the head from side to side – what in most contexts means denial or disagreement. Here it means astonishment, delight and also, incongruously, stoic resignation. All three – astonishment, delight and resignation – are components of wonder, the wonder that accompanies revelation. But why resignation – denoted so fully, to the brim, by that shake of the head? Is it at the fact that what might have seemed implausibly beautiful has somehow been made possible, without us quite knowing why or how? Is it because, given the partly improvisational nature of Indian classical music, that the moment will not return again, in a future performance – unlike a piece of Western music, where it can be reproduced almost verbatim? Is it just that a vague crystallisation of the fact that life is at once mundane and sublime that occurs at that instant, leading to that bewildered shake of the head? Sometimes, a simple, predictable component of a raga – like, for instance, the downward glissando from the upper tonic to the flat *ni* (or, in Western notation, *ti*) in Khamaj, will produce that gesture; a chromatic sequence there, including both the normal and flat *ni*, will only exacerbate and intensify that emotion.

Much of the time the head, during the performance, is relatively still (punctuated by occasional oscillations from side to side), especially in comparison to its behaviour in African-American music, although, in contrast to a Western classical music aficionado, the expression might be less focused than far away – on both the singer's and listener's part. This is because both singer (or instrumentalist) and audience are listening; listening, even more than performance, and certainly more than composition, is the principal raison d'être and gravitational field of Indian music. Long ago, I remember a piece of research was reported in a British newspaper saying that Western classical music was conducive to workers, and functioned well as a prompting to action; while Indian music had the opposite effect, of slowing down work, seducing the worker's attention and retarding his regime. It's the old story of the Lotus Eaters, of which there are several variations in Western culture; it's instructive that Indians have no comparable parables, since that slowness appears to be so integral, historically, to our response to the classical arts.

There are other reasons why the head is relatively still during a music concert in India, to do with the fact that our enjoyment of rhythm (unlike the Afro-Caribbean's) is uniquely cerebral, despite, or because of, our time signatures being so difficult, and Indian rhythmic improvisation so sophisticated. But now I must come to those close-ups, which, during a film song, reproduce the experience of listening as no other tradition of cinema does. The close-up during a song is an arrested moment; the effects are minimal – backlighting; a breeze unsettling the hair. The breeze, as in Kalidasa, is a metaphor for the far away and the invisible, and its sudden closeness: 'The breezes from the snowy peaks have just burst open the leaf buds of deodar trees and, redolent of their oozing resin, blow southward. I embrace those breezes, fondly imagining they have lately touched your form, O perfect one!' – a metaphor for sound and melody, then, which are always invisible, and arrive from elsewhere. The song, and the close-up, are a hiatus, during which the story is set aside and the universe revolves around the head or the face, which is singing, or listening, or doing both simultaneously. The actors who 'sing' the best songs – Dev Anand and Rajesh Khanna – will make potentially silly movements with their head to convey the uncontainable emotion they feel on hearing themselves (or the playback singer, who is them, but in a transient, disembodied sense). The beloved, who might be singing too, will stop in a duet to listen to her partner; as Sadhana does in *Abhi na jao chhodkar*, with a curious expression, which in another kind of cinema would signify sex or love, but here denotes the listener's peculiar ecstasy. In Hollywood, the close-up attends to visual clichés of fear, the orgasm, pain and feel-good denouements to do with winning – a race or a fight with cancer – and is, as a result, properly discredited. In India, the close-up frames the pleasure, the surprise, of registering the loveliness of melody – Waheeda Rehman woken up from sleep by Guru Dutt singing in *Chaudhvin Ka Chand*, her expressions ameliorating from startlement to surrender; the husband stealthily creeping up on his wife at the piano in *Anupama*, singing *'Dheere dheere machal'*. His charged, almost bewildered, face records the discovery of an unlooked-for surplus.

Hovering Above

Indian cities, when they're attempting to give themselves a facelift, and to send out a message that they're reinventing themselves, inevitably have recourse to constructing flyovers. Yes, shopping malls, multiplexes and especially international airports increasingly perform the same function: of heralding the fact that the city is prospering, or is expecting an imminent boom. But, traditionally, the sudden elevation created by a new flyover is a message that the economy is similarly spiking.

Flyovers are never entirely uncontroversial in our cities: mainly because they're associated with kickbacks. A new one indicates that a deal has been made, that bribery is clearly involved, and someone's pocket is suddenly heavier. The other reason for their being greeted with resentment is that they often run through not suburban spaces, but congested areas that are an organic combination of shops, residential houses and office buildings: neighbourhoods with an identity that the flyover will now intrude on. It's because these areas are congested that the flyover is built in the first place – what you're 'flying over' is the resistance of the city. But the consequence of these constructions is that they alter a known topography permanently. As if in response to this, there's a deep disengagement among Indian city dwellers from the flyover as a part of the city's evolution; it's as if it's literally fallen from above, and, long term though it may be, is seen to be perennially extraneous to the thoroughfares and junctions it looms above. It is parasitic in some paradoxical, privileged way; of the city, but foreign to it. This might explain why city photographers in Calcutta, say, seem to have recorded so relatively little of the change that the emergence of a flyover brings about.

Calcutta, of course, has been famous for being a place where nothing, generally, happens. Yet, in the last two decades, construction has quickened, in a sort of mimicry of change. There are, now, as we well know, malls, multiplexes, an immense new international airport which, until recently, was always to open *next* month – but, before all these, in the early 2000s, there were two flyovers. They suggested that, even in a city in which nothing happens, things *will* happen in the time of globalisation.

The second one, which I somehow think of as the first new flyover, came up in 2003 above a long stretch of Lower Circular Road, connecting the Park Circus roundabout in the south-east to the racecourse in the south-west. Everyone was impressed by how easily they could now escape the traffic, but, gradually, people began to puzzle over why anyone should want to journey urgently from Park Circus to the racecourse. A conspiracy theory came up – involving the government, inevitably. The ex-Chief Minister Buddhadeb Bhattacharya lives on Broad Street, south of Park Circus; and the government offices are in the Writers Building, north of the racecourse. According to the theory, the flyover was built for the convenience of Bhattacharya's morning and evening travel. Nevertheless, the long, horizontal, hovering structure brought a new weather to Lower Circular Road, sunless, faux cloudy, not undesirable in a hot city. On the flyover itself, the road below was an irrelevance. The city could now be viewed in a succession of vantage points that, from Park Circus to the racecourse, related you to it in an odd unspooling of distance and proximity.

As a result, domes of colonial buildings and balustrades and cornices of rooftops that you hadn't noticed in the thick of things below are now suddenly near, if momentary; Lansdowne and SP Mukherjee Roads, which cut across Lower Circular Road at right angles, become clarified for the populous vistas they are. Calcutta, from the flyover, has the remote, retrospective air of the historic 'old town' section of a metropolis: at once palatable and superannuated. In the reverse direction, you first swoop up till you're almost contiguous to and parallel with the dark angel on top of Victoria Memorial in the distance, then shoot past the top of Rabindra Sadan, with buildings that must have seemed unnervingly contemporary in the 1970s, then the art cinema, Nandan, with the merged Bengali letters of the name floating like a single hieroglyph just below eye level, then an indescribably brown office building probably from the 1970s, a sign proclaiming LA MARTINIERE SCHOOL FOR GIRLS, an old people's home with a Madonna bent over nobody apparently, her mercy only meant for your brief passage, then the watered expanses of Minto Park before the Belle Vue Hospital, my daughter's birthplace – all these instances of the city's frozen decline and obstinate fresh beginnings, of your own splintered memories and the city's terminated histories, its provenances, its multiplicity of faiths and vocations, rulers and subjects, present themselves fleetingly, interspersed with cameos of dailiness: the houses with verandas, grilles and flower pots. Never have you floated so close to these existences, and never will, until you take the route again.

The other flyover, running over Gariahat and its teeming avenue by the market since 2002, and descending in front of the surreal and impeccably painted Ramakrishna Mission and the statue of Swami Vivekananda, is shorter in distance and duration. Underneath, like curious varieties of life that either embrace the shade or flower only against the glow of artificial light, a multiplicity of settlements, from fractious destitute families surrounded by all their belongings to men absorbed, each evening, in carom or chess, transpire and congregate at different points of what was the old road, both invisible and in some fundamental sense unknowable to those passing above. Those gathered below are vaguely but constantly aware of the people zipping by on the flyover, as one might be subconsciously sensible of the weather; but those on the flyover are unconscious of any life except what they glimpse and piece together from fragments. As with the one above Lower Circular Road, the Gariahat flyover provides that sense of brief transit through a wave of lives unfolding discreetly (potted plants, curved art deco balconies), the unexpectedly abandoned decades (a tall building, unpainted and unoccupied, many of its glass panes shattered), and shops long heard of but never visited except by aunts and mothers, whose giant signs (TRADERS ASSEMBLY) rush past you like symbols whose individual elements mean nothing, fading quickly. There is no equivalent you know for this elsewhere in the world, or in other epochs – the trams that pass within a hair's breadth of people voraciously eating pasta at tables in Rome, in the narrow neighbourhoods of Fellini's *Roma* and *Amarcord*, are analogous, but not exactly. You can't stop or tarry on a flyover to admire the vistas or to double check your location in relation to the older criss-crossings of roads and junctions below; I once tried, and almost precipitated a traffic disaster. Instead, you must idly watch these half-known scenes flash repeatedly, till, one day, you (temporarily) stop noticing them.

Two:
The Personal and the Political

Partition as Exile

In school in Bombay, we were taught a certain narrative about modern Indian history. Like all constructed narratives, it told a story of key moments, and thus it had an almost mnemonic quality that made it impossible to forget. Some of these key moments were, for instance, the inception of the Indian National Congress in Bombay, Gandhi's Dandi march against the salt tax, the Quit India Movement, Partition, Independence. At this point the narrative stopped, as if history had ceased to exist with Partition and Independence; but it had not ceased; it had probably become ourselves.

We, in the classroom, came to accept Partition as an event, more importantly a concept, that fundamentally defined our country's history as well as our own; this, in spite of the fact that we were living in a place, Bombay, that had little to do directly with Partition and its aftermath, and that most of the pupils in the class were Parsi, Maharashtrian, south Indian, whose parents came from parts of India relatively unaffected by Partition. I was an exception, because my parents were born and grew up in East Bengal, and lost their homes and property in 1947.

Yet the historical narrative we were taught in school, with its emphasis on Partition and freedom, did not accentuate or define, in my mind, my parents' experiences and lives, and my own place as a child of people displaced from their homeland; if anything, it suppressed such formulations. Even now, I find it hard to connect the two. Partition, as a concept taught in the classroom, as part of a narrative taught to middle-class Indians as the *Mahabharat* and *Ramayan* were once disseminated in feudal Hindu India, served to define ourselves as members of this middle class looking back upon the creation of our new nation, and suggesting, implicitly, the part we would play in totalising and interpreting it. Every time this historical narrative would be repeated by us in the future, it would be a way of revealing we had once belonged to that classroom, and restating the role we had been assigned then, as members of the middle class, as the only ones who had grasped the idea of the nation as a narrative, a totality, and our responsibility to control and interpret it.

Partition as it existed in my parents' memories, however, and in the memories of other members of my extended family, was another matter altogether; its presence seemed to be, as it were, fragmentary and poetic rather than narrative and total. Its part in my life is profound but its entire meaning still unclear. It had no fixed identity, as the Partition in the textbook did; it meant different things at different times; at times it meant nothing at all. It was disruptive rather than definitive; and it was part of a story that involved personal history, memory, family lore and the vernacular; it had no overarching, decisive key role to play, but nor had its meaning ever stopped unravelling. Its relation to the Partition described in the school textbook, and described again and again even now in reports, films and recent novels in English, many of which are fictionalised versions of the official historical narrative of India, was the relation that the semi-conscious and half-remembered have to the waking world.

During the time of freedom and Partition, my father, already having lost his homeland in Sylhet, a student in Calcutta in Scottish Church College, was thinking of going to England. In 1947, my mother was worrying about who would marry her, a daughter of a family without a father, once well to do, but long struggling since her father's death; in 1948, she accepted my father's proposal, but no sooner had this unexpected stroke of good fortune occurred than she had to reconcile herself to a prolonged engagement and to the marriage being postponed as my father went to England as a student. The movement from Sylhet to Shillong after the referendum and Partition, although startling, was not wholly new to her or her family, as their life had anyway been a series of movements from one house to another since their father's death, and then from one town to another, Sylhet, Naugang and Shillong. It might be said that freedom and Partition, which would affect my parents' lives profoundly, were met by them with a certain degree of incomprehension and even indifference; for key moments, unlike their representations later in texts, do not really have clear outlines, and might not even be perceived as having really happened; just as it's impossible to accept as real, on a non-rational, physical, fundamental level, the absolute absence of a loved person when that person has died. Often, one does not mourn until much later, and then, possibly, at the provocation of some seemingly irrelevant stimulus. The human reaction to change, whether personal or in the form of historical events, is extremely complex; a complexity, a hiatus of the mystery or incomprehension of a response, not allowed for in official versions of history.

Partition in Bengal is central to the filmmaker Ritwik Ghatak's work – not the moment of Partition itself, or its place and representation in the nationalist historical narrative, but its human, almost elemental, story of displacement and resettlement. In Ghatak (who was of East Bengali origin, and was married to an East Bengali), Partition becomes a metaphor for migration, resettlement and exile, among the most profound preoccupations of twentieth-century creative artists everywhere; for the twentieth century is an age of great and continuing displacement.

Let me dwell briefly on certain characteristic images in Ghatak's films that make his work, for me, a visionary meditation on the kind of movement and trajectory that marked the lives of my parents and others from their background. For the West Bengali, the Partition of Bengal represented an undesired truncation of the land; but, for the East Bengali, Partition signified the complete loss of the old world and the sudden, violent recreation of a new one. Ghatak's images of Partition, thus, are the elemental ones of land, water and sky, suggesting the composition of the universe in its original form, and belonging to a mythology of creation. It's not so much history-book Partition we have here as the world as an immigrant or exile or newcomer would see it, starting from scratch and reconstructing his life and his environment from nothing. Air, water and sky recur, the properties available to the first man and to the homeless; *Meghe Dhaka Tara*, a film about lower-middle-class East Bengali refugees struggling to start life again in Calcutta, begins with a scene in which we see only land and water, as we hear the voice of an unseen onlooker reflecting on the process of loss and resettlement; the river, which is probably the Padma, separating West Bengal from what then was East Pakistan, looks more like a sea: water and horizon. The elements, configuring the process of the world in creation, recur in other films; *Titash Ekti Nadir Naam* is dominated throughout, for instance, by images of deltas of sand emerging from the water – prehistoric images of erosion and creation, as it were – turning the film into a metaphor for the process of displacement and renewal, although its story concerns the life of a community by a river.

In *Subarnarekha*, the title of the film is the name of a river never actually seen in it. Most of the story unfolds in Ghatshila, a mining area; the protagonist, an East Bengali refugee, with his daughter, a child of six or seven, and a boy from the refugee camp whom he has adopted, arrives at the mine at which he has been appointed foreman. The backdrop against which the tragic story of lost identity and orphanhood mainly takes place is the stark white rocks of Ghatshila; not the lush greenness associated with Gangetic Bengal, but this dream image of prehistory, as if the rocks had just cooled and world were new. It is through these images suggesting the original creation of the universe that Ghatak makes material the inner world of Partition, of apocalypse and rebirth. This serene background, where the historical and the natural seem to be as good as identified with each other, frames, almost indifferently, the small drama of the story's human characters. Partition, according to this vision, which conflates the natural, the geographic and the political, is seen as almost pre-determined, and exile, displacement and movement conditions of human existence.

Movement, exile and displacement, as those which occurred in my parents' lives and others of their milieu and generation, have been a part of life in India from the beginning of the twentieth century, and certainly before; during Partition, movement and exile simply took place on a mass scale, and with sudden and violent intensity and coercion. But the story of Partition is not the story of a moment, because it does not stop in 1947, but the story of exile, movement and resettlement, the agonised transition from old to new, and also the search for happiness in one's 'own' country that was also a 'foreign' country, India.

Event, Metaphor, Memory

Reading Mukul Kesavan's response to my article ('Partition as Exile'), I was reminded once more of the following, familiar question: to what extent is the discourse we call 'history' a representation of the truth, and to what extent is it a construction, informing us as much of its authors and the conditions in which it was written as of the events and people it describes? Certainly Mukul Kesavan's article tells us as much about Mukul Kesavan as it does about Partition, history and my piece; and it does this not through what it says explicitly, but by elision, and by taking a few liberties with interpretation.

Kesavan says something similar about my essay midway through his article: 'But Chaudhuri's essay isn't really about the events of 1947. It tells us more about his narrative strategies for writing fiction than it does about narratives of Partition, public or private.' This is true; although I would extend the second sentence somewhat to say the piece is also about the way Partition affected the lives and consciousnesses of those who lived through it, and the consciousness of the generation born later; or, at times, significantly for me, failed to affect them in just the way one might have expected. I don't think I make any claims that I approach the issue as a historian, or any bones about the fact that I am a writer whose interest lies in individual memory and consciousness and the way they may be related to narrative, creative expression, and to history. It is interesting, though, that Kesavan, who says he comes to my article, and writes his, as a teacher of history, fails to mention, or even imply, anywhere that he himself is the author of a novel about Partition, *Looking Through*

Glass, and that he may be more interested in the relation between narrative strategy and history than he would have us believe; that, at the heart of his response to my article, might be a difference of viewpoint about the way fiction works in relation to history.

Towards the beginning, Kesavan points out that, 'for him [that is, me] the reports, films and novels that speak of Partition, rehearse a nationalist script that the authors first learned in their schoolrooms'. Going back to my piece, I find I make a slightly more qualified statement, a statement made in the context of the experiences of a middle-class, post-Independence generation, such as the one to which people like Kesavan and myself, separated by a few years, belong, a generation that did not experience Partition or Independence at first hand, learning about their history, necessarily, in the classroom, or through oral sources like maternal memory, which Kesavan, later in his piece, derides. The novels I refer to in my essay, however, are specifically 'recent novels in English', and not all novels. That I do not refer to all films is evident from my final section on Ghatak.

The novel Kesavan offers as an exemplary instance of the literature of Partition is Amitav Ghosh's *The Shadow Lines*; oddly, he doesn't speak of the greatest fiction to come out of the experience of Partition, written by people who were directly traumatised by it, Qurratulain Hyder's novel *Aag Ka Dariya*, her novella *Building Society* or the stories of Saadat Hasan Manto. I am not making a value judgement here; I'm not saying a writer has to witness an event in order to write about it. But I'm led from this observation to what I think is a fundamental paradox in Kesavan's position.

Kesavan, in his response, is a spokesman for the irreducible authenticity of Partition as a historical event, for its ontological given-ness, and its colossal, unignorable immediacy; it is unquestionable in its immutable presence, rather like a frieze on an urn that never changes. He takes issue with me for locating an event that brooks no argument in my own subjectivity, for challenging its centrality by giving it ambiguity, for calling it a 'metaphor'. (I should point out that, in my piece, I speak of Partition being 'disruptive rather than definitive' not as a general, prescriptive statement, as Kesavan leads his readers to believe, but in relation to my own life, prefacing the statement with, 'Its part in my life is profound but its meaning still unclear.' Further, Kesavan's repeated assertions that I claim Partition was not a historical event are baffling; I can find it nowhere in my piece, and must conclude he had a bad dream after reading it.)

Kesavan doesn't explain anywhere, however, why Partition should be so unambiguous and central to his imagination, and to those of other writers of his generation, some of whom began to write about Partition about forty years after it occurred, none of whom had any memory or experience of the event, for none of whom, indeed, had Partition *been* an event. If there is anyone for whom Partition is a central, founding trope, or signifier, or metaphor, rather than event, it is surely Kesavan and others of his generation. It is not a paradox Kesavan attends to, but it would surely enrich our understanding, not of Partition, but of the intellectual life of a generation that grew up in post-Independence India, if it *were* attended to. How is it, in other words, that Partition came to be a central signifier in, and component of, the cultural life of English-speaking, urban India, even of its elite diaspora, in the 1980s and 1990s?

Certainly, in the 1970s, Partition and the national narrative were still not principal themes of the major Indian writers in English, as they would become a decade later (Khushwant Singh's romance of Partition, *Train to Pakistan*, is the sole, though not very demanding, exception). Narayan had his own fictional universe to chart; Ramanujan spoke of bilingualism; Arvind Krishna Mehrotra, who was born in 1947, and himself displaced by Partition as an infant, carried in a train from Lahore to Dehradun at the time, hardly writes about Partition in his relatively few but outstanding poems: does that mean that the event means less to him than it means to Kesavan, or that, simply, the event, as a trope, has less significance or centrality for him than it does for the latter? How much, then, does Kesavan's interest, as an individual, historian and novelist, in Partition owe to the actual event itself, and how much to his privileging of a national narrative with which he identifies as a member of the post-Independence middle class; and how much, too, to the fictional strategies of Rushdie, who, early in the 1980s, opened up horizons for writers like Kesavan and others, prompting them to appropriate, through the lens or glass of postmodernism, that narrative for their fiction? Partition, then, hardly forms part of Kesavan's intellectual landscape as an immediate and unmediated presence, but as a complex trope embedded in a number of discourses, historical and fictional, that have grown in importance since the 1980s. To consider these questions is surely not to diminish a writer such as Kesavan, but to arrive at a more nuanced engagement with the cultural moment he represents than he himself seems to allow for.

Kesavan concludes with a few snide allusions to my fiction, noting, not very originally, that I'm content to relegate major historical and political events to the background, and to loll about observing the domestic bric-a-brac of middle-class lives. There has long been a tone of moral puritanism in much of what passes in India for criticism, and Kesavan is not entirely free of it. He would have me attend to major events with suitable awe and reverence; he would have made a good, but probably not excellent, court poet (the greatest court poet, Kalidas, composed seemingly apolitical poems and plays, and a rather ambivalent national narrative, *Sakuntala*). Abandoning the rigorous adherence to truth that a historian might have, he becomes, unannounced, a novelist, fictionalising my response to the Bengal Famine, implying I would say, '*Was the Bengal famine an event? Hard to tell . . . People experienced hunger in such different and complex ways.*'

Would that Kesavan would find other ways of writing fiction than putting words into people's mouths. His comment reminds me of the case of Satyajit Ray, who lived during the Famine, but for a long time resisted, in spite of pressure, making a film about the important political and historical events he was living through, saying they were too remote from the purview of his experience for him to address. He once admitted that the Famine did not make as much of an immediate impression upon him as one might expect; Kesavan would probably find this remark as incomprehensible as my statement that Partition meant different things to different people, and sometimes meant nothing at all.

Ray's last truly great film, *Aranyer Din Ratri*, was accused, by Bengali critics and contemporaries, of being about the silly foibles of a self-indulgent middle class. Ray's subsequent attempts to deal with more 'important' events witnessed the beginning of his decline; his first unsatisfactory film was *Ashani Sanket*, about the Famine. It seems, now, that the films that contemporary critics considered the least responsive to history, like *Aranyer Din Ratri*, were actually most so, while those that seem to engage with history directly, like *Ganashatru*, are least responsive to it.

Kesavan, in his conclusion, makes the mistake of thinking that writing about a political event in a fictional work is a sign of engagement, while ignoring it one of aesthetic remoteness. History tells us otherwise. The dream world of Kafka certainly seems, now, far more responsive to history and culture than do, for instance, the many European social realist fictions that would follow, or, in India, much of the writing of the Progressive Writers Movement. The impoverished peasants and young idealists in the latter now seem as aesthetically removed and perfected as any figure etched upon a Wedgwood plate in a curio shop; hopefully, Partition and modern Indian history, too, will not be made to enter that great curio shop of historical writing.

Living in the Mohulla

Soon after the towers collapsed, those minarets of the 'free' world, other stories began to drift in; of survivors, deaths and of Indians. Among these first stories was one about a Sikh man, on his way to work in Lower Manhattan, probably in the financial district, who disembarked from the underground to confront a disaster of frightening proportions. He found he was being stared at in a less than friendly way (all those who have been to America and experienced its prelapsarian charm, with passers-by throwing smiles and how-are-yous at you before they vanish, will have to contend with a new knowingness about strangers). The Sikh kept his calm; he retreated into a shop, took off his turban and borrowed a hairband from someone; he came out after tying his hair in a ponytail and merged with the crowd.

A week later, I saw him on television. He was sitting in a café; he repeated his tale – the ponytail had been an inspired temporary measure, but he didn't, he said, intend cutting his hair or abandoning his turban. Afterwards, we saw the man, properly turbaned, disappear into one of New York's 'avenues'. A Sikh's kes, his unshorn hair, is an astonishing thing; I saw it in Bombay twenty-seven years ago, and haven't forgotten it – I had gone to the house of a Sikh friend and surprised him after a bath. He was drying his hair; it was an image of unsettling tenderness.

The story about the Sikh in New York, its potential comedy pervaded by its harrowing context, has brought to my mind a short story by Sadat Hassan Manto called 'Mozel'. Its protagonist is Tirlochen Singh, a young Sikh (I have read the story in Tahira Naqvi's translation); its setting, Manto's beloved Bombay, which he left forever in 1947; and Partition the historical moment in which its action takes place. The story takes us into the heart of the lives of working-class people, with their religious adherences, political affiliations and emotional ties, amidst whom, most often, political violence erupts, and who always face the brunt of that violence.

Manto's Bombay, even under duress, is an extraordinary city; long before Rushdie, Manto turned Bombay into a chameleon-like metaphor that was capable of being many things to many people. Now, in this period of unrest, Tirlochen's brother Narenjan reassures him, 'Yaar, you worry needlessly. I've seen many such disturbances here; this is not Amritsar or Lahore, this is Bombay . . .' Or, as they once said, this is New York. The narrator intervenes: 'What did Narenjan think Bombay was? He probably figured this was a city where disturbances, if they did develop, would disappear of their own accord, by magic.'

The story opens in this time of 'disturbances'; Tirlochen is 'looking at the sky' from 'the terrace at Adwani Chambers', where he lives, 'so that he could think rationally in the open air'. He is engaged to a 'small and delicate' woman, Kirpal Kaur, who has recently moved to Bombay from a village with her parents. She lives in a *mohulla*, a neighbourhood, 'dominated by staunch Muslims. Several houses had already been burned down and a great many lives had been lost . . . there were Muslims everywhere, and surrounded by these dangerous Muslims, Tirlochen felt helpless. In addition to that there was news pouring in from Punjab of the widespread killing of Muslims by Sikhs.'

'These dangerous Muslims' – the terrible irony of the phrase! Was Manto himself a 'dangerous Muslim'? Only perhaps to the Progressive Writers Movement, which found his very individual allegiance to his craft a nuisance and a threat. The story unfolds: it turns out that Tirlochen's first love was Mozel, who used to live in a flat in Adwani Chambers, a Jewish woman of striking physical beauty and of easy virtue; Manto describes her in an image that conflates the artifice of feminine beauty and a ghastly premonition of death: 'Short brown hair covered her head; her querulous lips were covered with red lipstick which was badly chapped and cakey and reminded him of dried blood.'

Mozel, the promiscuous woman, has a distaste for underwear, as she does for religion; indeed, clothing is equated with religion, and nakedness with liberation, in the story, in the way these are equated, in Western art, with culture and innocence respectively. In one of the story's great comic moments, Tirlochen and Mozel first meet by colliding with each other, in a parody of the violence to come, and falling on to the floor: 'When Tirlochen attempted to pull himself together, he realised that Mozel was sprawled over him in such a way that her legs, naked now that her dress was pulled up all the way, were spread on either side of his body.'

Tirlochen falls in love with Mozel; she reciprocates parsimoniously, with kisses and barbs: '. . . she raised her heavy-lidded Jewish eyes, batted her thick eyelids and said, "I cannot love a Sikh." ' They have an argument during one of these interchanges; and Mozel utters a damning condemnation: 'If you shave off your beard and leave your hair down, you'll have boys running after you, I promise; you're beautiful.' Tirlochen shouts angrily at Mozel, but she is unruffled; thus, 'deflated', he sits 'quietly . . . on the sofa', and Mozel approaches him. In a scene worthy of one of Bonnard's paintings, or one of those episodes in *kathak* dance in which Radha is adorning herself, the narrator describes how 'Mozel came and sat beside him and began unravelling his beard, taking out the pins one by one and holding them between her teeth'.

The narrator observes, 'Tirlochen was beautiful. When he was younger, before the hair on his face appeared, he had often been mistaken for a girl when he was seen with his kes down. But now the heavy bulk of hair concealed his features.' Manto, here, is talking about the androgyny that the warring tribe of men, wherever they come from, suppress in times of conflict, the softness which is concealed like 'some infinitely gentle / Infinitely suffering thing'. He is also talking about disguise and mistaken identity; the disguises which, as we have learned from news reports in the last fortnight, make people appear different from what they are, and the misprision due to which communities must have their identity taken away from them, and suffer for what they are not.

To woo Mozel, Tirlochen cuts his hair. He becomes, then, according to his religion, a 'patit', a renegade; like Mozel, an outcaste. But Mozel vanishes without leaving an explanation; and Tirlochen is engaged to Kirpal, the 'delicate' girl from the village. We return to the present moment of the story; Tirlochen is contemplating going into the *mohulla* to rescue his fiancée, when Mozel appears in the semi-darkness of the terrace. She offers to help him; they enter the *mohulla* together, where, in the silence, 'a Marwari's shop was being systematically looted'. They find the building Tirlochen is looking for and run up the stair to Kirpal's flat; as they hear men approaching, Mozel strips Kirpal Kaur of her salwar kameez, and slips her own dress over her – for clothes denote community – while she herself is 'completely naked'.

In the panic and tussle that follow, Mozel falls down the stairs and, fatally hurt, begins to bleed to death; but Kirpal and her parents have escaped. It is a 'filmi' moment; Manto worked for years in the Hindi film industry. Tirlochen covers her naked body with a turban; Mozel pushes it away, saying, 'Take away . . . this religion of yours'; then she dies. Her remark is less a secular rejection than a deeply religious protest, emerging from a long tradition of heretical spirituality; her nakedness is a preparation for meeting with her maker in such a way that nothing, not even religion, should come between them when they meet. In a way, her mission, to save Kirpal, is a suicide mission, or at least a suicidal one, and, disturbingly, she would have probably shared with the Arab terrorists of 11 September the conviction that 'we come from our maker and to Him we return'.

Two words in the story have, with great tact, been left untranslated by the translator. The first is 'kes', that untranslatable expanse of male hair, a trope for a softness concealed, 'some infinitely gentle / Infinitely suffering thing'. The other is *'mohulla'*, whose approximate meaning is 'neighbourhood'. Since Manto wrote his story, the entire world has become a '*mohulla*'; but the life of the *mohulla* is contingent upon compromise, understanding and interdependence between all neighbours and cohabitants. In the global *mohulla*, nation-states are still to acquire the capacity for sacrifice and compassion that human beings have; instead, they – whether they are Pakistan or India, Afghanistan or America – are governed by a primeval self-interest that must eventually contribute to the destruction of the *mohulla*. The undemocratic functioning of the global order ensures that nations are at battle with each other long before a single shot has been fired. Then comes a turning point, as we had two weeks ago: and the courage that ordinary human beings – like Mozel, like Tirlochen – are capable of is betrayed by their nations in the name of war.

Planetary Configurations

Returning from a literary festival in Delhi, I was thinking to myself, on the plane, about what these festivals achieved. You say yes upon being invited, thinking you'll revisit a city and meet a group of people, and are thrown into a situation that's neither city nor gathering; at some point those 'black existential moods', as Yasmin Alibhai Brown described them to me, descend upon you and you wonder what you're doing here.

The eating and imbibing, the listening and declaiming are meant as much to numb those 'black moods' as they are to illuminate or nourish. But probably the most instructive part of the festival was, for me, the experience of coming into contact with writers from other countries – Britain, of course, but Pakistan as well – and those who seem to come from (I say this without disrespect, to convey my genuine astonishment at certain world views) other planets. Among the latter, the most prominent but accessible was William Dalrymple. I admire Dalrymple for his many achievements and his bustling friendliness. Unlike some of the other participants, who could be alternately voluble and reticent about their culture, Dalrymple is never stingy about giving us news of his planet. It is, by all accounts, an alluring place, because things that are muddled on my planet are, in Dalrymple's, humblingly clear. In many ways, Dalrymple's planet is exactly like mine; and, in many ways, I realised with a start during the festival, it is utterly foreign and different.

For instance, on Dalrymple's planet, as on mine, there's a paucity, in Indian writing, of compelling non-fiction in comparison to fiction – or so it seems at first glance. On my planet, a less emotional examination shows that influential travelogues, essays and histories have existed in India for a hundred and fifty years, especially in the Indian languages; it's a question of intermittently visible forms we're dealing with, then, as well as our own ignorance, rather than non-appearance. On my planet, I also find that the blinding excellence of Indian fiction in English is a shibboleth; that much of it is, unsurprisingly, second rate. The contrast between popular and academic histories is also less clear on my planet than on Dalrymple's; where I live, breathe and write, popular histories aren't magically more urgent, less boring, than their academic counterparts – in fact, they can be extremely badly written and dull. Also, on my planet, non-academic historiography is a more frustratingly heterogeneous affair than on Dalrymple's: it comprises serious non-academic historians of various political persuasions and world views of various degrees of difficulty, as well as retrograde thinkers and popularisers. All kinds gather under the rubric 'popular history', making it problematic as a concept; which is obviously not the case where Dalrymple lives.

As with history, the matter of Indian writing in English has been decided once and for all on Dalrymple's planet. The scenario there is simple: Indian writers who live in the West write better, more 'exciting' stuff than those who live in India. The criterion for coming to this conclusion is simple too, as is everything where Dalrymple lives: success in the West. On Dalrymple's planet, not only is the West an uncomplicatedly absolute repository of value, with an absolute right to define what's 'exciting' and what's not; it's a static conceit, no different today from what it was before, unaffected, in its reading and publishing practices, by political change, or the all-encompassing advent of the free market. This ahistorical idea of the West, as a setting for the reception for Indian literature, is strange, coming, especially, from a historian; but perhaps historians work differently where Dalrymple lives. Anyway, I'm not disputing the facts; Dalrymple lives on a different planet, and what he says of it must be true, though it's hardly true of mine. What I find surprising is that people on Dalrymple's planet actually find this mode of analysis an enriching means towards enlarging their understanding of the role of, the very need for, literature today.

Returning to Calcutta, I carried *Fulcrum* with me on the flight: a poetry journal from America. Half of this issue was devoted to anthologising Indian poetry in English, and I was reading this section (excluding my own poems, which I'd read before) with deep pleasure. What interested me was that a different idea of cross-cultural contact was at work in the journal from the one we're indoctrinated with today, to do with globalisation and diaspora. Here, an older internationalism, which culminated in America in figures like Robert Bly, in India in Buddhadeva Bose and, later, Arun Kolatkar, was the operative paradigm. Internationalism became significant because it brought different literatures together, and addressed, in a new way, the primacy of literature; texts travelled, not necessarily authors; unlike today, when it's globalisation that's primarily being celebrated, and literature, like sports or information technology, is an offshoot that's remarkable inasmuch as it reflects the marvel of the global. Reading the anthology, I became aware of what should be obvious: that some of the best writing in English in India is being done by poets. How are we to speak of these writers, attend to their craft as well as the historical change they embody? And where is this discussion possible? Neither my planet nor Dalrymple's appears to have much space for it.

Diary

We have read all about Hindu revivalism in newspapers, and seen the pictures on television; one's personal feelings about it cannot be separated from the information the media give us. When I returned to Calcutta for two months in mid-January, I listened to all the arguments given by people one had always thought of as 'liberal', a category as vague as 'normal', for and against Hindu fundamentalism. I listened to the various ways, small and big, in which middle-class Hindus had been infuriated by Muslims – the recitation of prayers five times a day on loudspeakers; the Shah Bano case, where a Muslim woman pleaded to be divorced under civil rather than Muslim law (her plea was upheld by the Supreme Court, but overruled by the Rajiv Gandhi government in the face of widespread Muslim protest, and against the advice of 'secular' Indians, both Muslims and Hindus); the way in which Muslims supposedly support Pakistan at cricket matches. Hindu fundamentalism was only an extreme reaction to years of 'pampering' Muslims, I heard; but then I heard about its disturbing consequences as well: many innocent people were killed, mainly in the slums, during the riots in Bombay, the city where I grew up; militant Marathi Hindus – the Shiv Sena – even invaded the exclusive, inviolate upper-middle-class areas where my parents and I had once lived.

Visiting a building in Cuffe Parade where we had lived before my father's retirement, I noticed that the metal nameplates on the ground floor, on one of which my father's name had once been inscribed, now were all blank – this had been done, apparently, to protect the Muslims living in the building. Small, accidental sensations, too small to be called incidents, told me I was now living in a slightly altered world, where certain signs and words had changed imperceptibly in meaning. Taking a stroll down a quiet lane near where my parents live in Calcutta, I noticed the usual political graffiti on the walls, and among other things the symbol of the north Indian Hindu revivalist party, the BJP – the lotus. Yet the sign, or the emotions I registered on seeing it, had changed in some way from two months ago; it inhabited a new world, and I would have to find new words to describe it. Similarly, people had changed, and I mean the everyday, recognisable people who form one's friends and family. Everyone speaking for and against the Muslims, and sometimes doing both at once, seemed to have discovered a faculty or talent that they did not know they had had before.

In Calcutta, news came to us of what was then happening in Bombay from the National Programme – although these days even Calcutta has satellite television, with stations like Star TV and Zee TV and the greatly revered BBC Asia. Satellite dishes multiply on terraces where clothes used to dry and servants bathed, and still do. A small industry has spontaneously grown up around them; boys who were bad at studies but good at 'fixing things', and who once would have become motor mechanics, have now become fixers of antennae and tuners of satellite frequencies. When Star TV first came to our building, the picture our set received was very poor. It soon got better, though the general consensus on the quality of its programmes was that, as a Third World country, we had been cheated again – not only were banned drugs and obsolete guns being dumped on us, but also, now, a huge mountain of television programmes that the Americans no longer wanted to watch. However, BBC Asia – in fact, anything with the letters 'BBC' appended to it – continues to be trusted, as something natural and whole, in the way that preservative-free orange juice is trusted these days in the West; as something that has the ring or the flavour of that old-world thing 'truth' about it. And it was BBC Asia that had first flashed the news, to Indian audiences, of the demolition of the Babri Masjid. Yet during my visit, I often found myself seized by a great nostalgia to return to that forgotten giant, the National Programme, to watch its numbing series of documentaries, news programmes, historical dramas. Compared with the liberating and anarchic fun of Star TV, the governmental, bureaucratic world of the National Programme served as an anodyne to the muted panic of what was happening now in India; it muffled, numbed, took me back to my grumbling adolescence, when we hated television, politicians, the Hindi language, longed to see adult films without the crude cuts, but took for granted the immortality of our parents and the existence of the nation.

The National Programme showed us thousands of people crowding the Victoria Terminus railway station in Bombay, nearly all of them from the working classes, anxious to leave the city. Not only Muslims, but Tamils, Bengalis, Gujaratis had been attacked or threatened; and I remembered the servants we had had, people who had arrived in Bombay from different parts of the country and quickly been absorbed into its world of part-time jobs as cooks or bearers, people from villages in Kerala or flood-hit Midnapore who learned how to make a perfect cheese toast or twist napkins into flowery shapes and put them in tumblers. I remembered James, an honest, ebony-coloured Keralite, who called himself 'butler', and who had a weakness for only one thing – coconut oil. One day, more than twenty years ago, my mother found the lid off a tin of coconut oil in her bathroom – and in the afternoon, she found James, bathed and fresh and smelling of it. He was the one who told me that the Marathis wanted the Madrasis (as all south Indians were then collectively called) out. In much of the next two decades, however, Marathi chauvinism went underground and remained hidden, only to resurface a few years ago in Bombay as Hindu fundamentalism. James retired and went back to his village long before that happened; his life as a 'butler' had been a distinguished and unendangered one; and we received letters from him, one of them asking for money for, as his letter writer put it, 'the affection of his body', until we heard from him no more.

And I remembered the Shiv Sena as well, vague images from a protected childhood. One day, in the mid-1960s, I first became conscious of them, in the strange new way that I was then becoming conscious of things, as a shadowy but noisy procession of men that caused our car to become immobile for forty-five minutes in Breach Candy one evening when we were returning home from the suburbs. Who were they? My own life had its certain and fixed coordinates: soon my mother would get off at Breach Candy and buy a few hot 'patties' from a hugely popular confectioner's, Bombelli's; these men had no place in that life. On my visit to Bombay in mid-February, I noticed, while taking the taxi from the airport, hundreds of small orange flags flying on the roofs of slum settlements on the outskirts, denoting the Shiv Sena's power if not necessarily its popularity. Those flags suddenly had a brightness and a presence: to the Muslim, they signified a certain kind of disquiet about the present and unease about the future; to the non-Marathi, another kind; to the lower-caste Hindu, yet another; and yet another to the representative of the middle class, whose life had generally held no terrors, except nightmares about promotion and his children's school admissions and higher taxes, and to whom, if anyone, India had made sense as a nation and a democracy.

The Shiv Sena – its figurehead, and the derivation of its name – is not to be confused with Shiv, the Hindu god. For, although Shiv is, aptly, the destroyer of the universe, ridding it of civilisations and human beings when they become too corrupt and too many, he is generally a god who spends most of his time alone, meditating and smoking charas (cannabis). The politics of power sharing, which most of the other Hindu gods are always indulging in, and by which characteristic they so faithfully allegorise Indian politicians, is of no interest to Shiv. No, the Shiv in Shiv Sena refers to Shivaji, a brave Marathi ruler who used brilliant guerrilla tactics to strike terror into the hearts of fierce Muslim kings – or so we learned from history books, and more vividly from Amar Chitra Katha comics, the Indian version of Classics Illustrated. (Amar Chitra Katha means 'Immortal

Picture Stories'.) There, Shivaji was shown as a lean man with a pointed beard who smuggled himself into enemy camps in sweet baskets and neatly chopped off villainous heads.

Bombay, in the 1960s and 1970s, had a utopian air about it: it was the only city in India in which everyone was potentially upwardly mobile. We who were born at the beginning of the 1960s, and whose fathers belonged to that corporate class whose activities constituted the commercial life of this seafront town, grew up with Tintin, Archie and Jughead, Richie Rich, with war films like *Where Eagles Dare* and Westerns like *McKenna's Gold*, with Coke and Gold Spot and later with rock music. The comic-book idyll of 1950s America, of California, with palm trees, swimming pools, sunny promenades, sodas and jukeboxes, persisted in that Bombay. Half the life of a human being, they say, is made up of dreams; living in Bombay then, one would have known that half the life of a colonial or postcolonial is made up of dreams of the West.

In the 1970s, Bombay began to change. Increased growth accompanied continued deprivation. The number of homeless people, living in makeshift 'bastis' or shanties, multiplied; at the same time, property prices rivalled those of Tokyo. Young film stars, usually the sons of older 'veterans', kept guns in their houses; there were Mercedes-Benzes on the roads and 'bastis' along the sides, some of them selling 'smack'. The aura of the colonial city had disappeared from Bombay, replaced by the feverishness and electric radiance and wealth and destitution of a Latin American town, the contradictions of a Third World city. Seventeen-year-olds drove Marutis – a new lightweight car made with Japanese collaboration, symbolising the buoyancy and lift of upward mobility and money – that had been given to them by their fathers; often they had no licence; often they ran over and killed or crippled people sleeping on pavements. My old friends – the comic-book generation – either got into drugs or into business management (a degree in business management was a symbol of prestige for this generation, just as a degree in science was for the previous one) or they left for the real America which they had always dreamt about. It was in this context, strangely, but perhaps logically, that the Shiv Sena had its rebirth.

In mid-February, when I was there, Bombay seemed to have recovered from the riots that had taken place more than a month before. Half of the upper-middle-class population seemed to gather each day at the Bombay Gymkhana, to eat from the hot buffet, and children from the Cathedral School, which was nearby, and where I had once studied, kept coming in and sitting in groups, or alone, to study for exams during the lunch break, while bearers brought them sandwiches. The members of the club seemed addicted to its atmosphere, to its cricket grounds, its swimming pool, its Chinese soups, its dining room, and the long veranda, on which everyone sat in wicker sofas; many of them would not leave till it was night. Members kept coming in, waving to each other, looking at each other's clothes; the middle-aged men were like boys, wearing jeans and eating ice creams, or wearing shorts and swinging tennis racquets. Everyone, in an oppressive but childlike way, enjoyed being on display. Beyond the cricket green to the right, one could see a steady stream of anonymous commuters hurrying to catch trains, either at the Churchgate station which lay on one side, or the Victoria Terminus on the other. When the bombs went off three weeks later, I was back in Calcutta. Once more, it was BBC Asia that first told us about it. I thought, then, about the commuters, for one of the bombs had gone off at the Victoria Terminus, and I also wondered if the members of the Bombay Gymkhana were still able to gather inside it as before, or whether the veranda was more or less empty now. I could not imagine it, though: in my mind, I saw the dream-addicted members still finding their way through the war-torn city to the club in order to recreate their world.

Hitchens and the Mother

A mong the welter of images and mythologies that constitute the middle-class Bengali's consciousness – P3 and Ganesh underwear, the Communist hammer and sickle, Lenin's face, fish and vegetable chops outside the Academy, wedding and funeral invitation cards, the films of Satyajit Ray, the loud horns of speeding state transport buses, Murshidabadi and Tangail saris, the daily *Ananda Bazar Patrika*, the songs of Tagore, the destitute outside Grand Hotel, Boroline Antiseptic cream, Madhyamik school examinations (to name just a few of the constituents) – Mother Teresa, too, is present. Not only is she undeniably a part of the contemporary history of Calcutta, but she is, to the ordinary middle-class Bengali, only a segment in a reality that is complex and constantly changing, and is composed impartially of the trivial and the profound. In contrast, to the average middle-class European or American Mother Teresa *is* Calcutta, or certainly its most life-affirming face. The rest of Calcutta is impossibly 'other', romantically destitute and silent; the 'black hole', unsayable. It is interesting that the poor whom Mother Teresa attends never speak. They have no social backgrounds or histories, although it is precisely history and social background, and the shifts within them, that create the poor. Instead of speaking, the poor in the photographs look up at her silently, touch her hand, are fed by a spoon. The 'black hole' of Calcutta, figuring as it does an open, silent mouth, no longer refers to the historical event that took place in the eighteenth century in which English men, women and children were trapped by Indian soldiers in a small, suffocating cell in the city. It refers to the unsayable that lay, and still often lies, at the heart of the colonial encounter, the breakdown in the Western observer's language when he or she attempts to describe a different culture, the mouth open but the words unable to take form. In Western literature, the unsayable is represented by 'The horror! the horror!' in Conrad's *Heart of Darkness*, and 'ou boom', the meaningless echo in the Marabar Caves in Forster's *A Passage to India*, the complexity of both Africa and India reduced to hushed, disyllabic sounds. In history and the popular imagination, another two syllables, 'black hole', have come to express the idea that, for the Westerner, Calcutta is still beyond perception and language.

Silence is a strange attribute to ascribe to the noisiest and most talkative Indian city. Calcutta, capital of India and second city of the Empire for 138 years, until 1911, was the crucible of Indian nationalist politics, and the home of its chief instrument, the Indian National Congress – and of modern Indian liberal consciousness itself. Nehru thought that if, in a sort of metaphorical laboratory, you were to mix, in a metaphorical beaker, an equal amount of Western rationalism and science on the one hand, and ancient Eastern values (a vague and largely unexamined ingredient in the experiment) on the other, you would produce a new compound that was the modern Indian personality – an idea that was actually prefigured by the beliefs and works of people such as Raja Rammohun Roy in Bengal in the early nineteenth century and Henry Louis Vivian Derozio, the Anglo-Portuguese poet and lecturer at the Hindu College, Calcutta, and his fervent Bengali followers. The metaphorical laboratory turned out to be the Indian middle classes.

Bengal had the earliest printing presses in India; during the nineteenth and early twentieth centuries more books were produced in Calcutta, the capital, than in almost any other city in the world. This was not surprising given that Bengal was the site of perhaps the most profound response to the colonial encounter; and in the middle of the nineteenth century began what is sometimes called the Bengal, and sometimes the Indian, Renaissance: an aspect of it being the flowering of one of the richest modern literatures – Bengali – in the world.

Bengal's history has also been one of political unrest and even tragedy. In particular, there were the famines, the last of which, in 1943, was not caused by a real food shortage at all. It was partly created by the unscrupulousness of local traders and by the diversion of staple foods, such as rice, to the British Army; the largest share of the blame must be apportioned to British rule. With the famines came an influx into Calcutta of the rural poor, who arrived in the city to die. Many of the poor to whom Mother Teresa would have ministered when she opened her first slum school in Calcutta on 21 December 1948 (she had been teaching geography in a missionary school in the city from 1929) would have been victims of the famine or their children. The number of poor people in Bengal is always being added to, and in 1948 Mother Teresa would also have encountered a huge insurgence of homeless refugees from East Pakistan, newly created after the 'stupid' (to use Hitchens's adjective) partitioning of Bengal by the British at the time of Independence. Partition would permanently alter, even disfigure, Bengal (or West Bengal, as it had now become) and its capital. The backbone of Bengal's heavy industry would be broken and a huge homeless, rootless population of East Bengalis would be added to the population of Calcutta. Leave alone the poor, even the middle-class or upper-middle-class Bengali, bereft of ancestral property, has had to struggle to make a home in the city. (One of my mother's closest friends from her childhood in Sylhet, Bangladesh, a retired schoolteacher, still lives with her older sister in north Calcutta in a small rented flat. My father's ancestral house languishes in Bangladesh and is at last, we hear, to be torn down; but he has been luckier than most other 'refugees' – he rose to a high position in the company he worked for, and bought his own flat in Calcutta in his middle age.) After Partition, the constitution and nature of the Bengali middle or *bhadralok* (literally 'civilised person') class changed significantly: once associated with privilege, education and genteel values, it now became increasingly beleaguered, both culturally and economically.

In 1971, millions of refugees – a large number of Muslims among them – began to flee from East Pakistan to Calcutta. The reason for this was a political impasse between East and West Pakistan, resulting in the genocide of the largely Muslim East Bengali population by (West) Pakistani troops, a project backed by American and Chinese diplomacy and arms. India intervened and went to war with Pakistan; East Pakistan was liberated and a new country, Bangladesh, created; but, in Calcutta, the number of the poor and homeless increased substantially. Areas like the Esplanade and Gariahat in central and south Calcutta respectively were to change forever; colourful pavement stalls selling T-shirts, woollens, trousers, kabaab rolls, sprang up in these parts to provide a livelihood for the new jobless and homeless. Families began to live in abandoned bus stops and under partially constructed bridges; the smell of rice being cooked in a pot would occasionally surprise the passer-by. Add to this the daily migration from villages in Bengal and the neighbouring states of Orissa and Bihar (for Calcutta continues to be the major metropolis in eastern India), not to speak of the continued migrations from poverty-stricken Bangladesh, and one begins to get some idea of where the destitute that Mother Teresa lifts up from the pavements come from. Two facts should be mentioned in this context. First, there have been no more famines in West Bengal since Independence. Second, in contrast to other, richer cities like Bombay, and even certain Western cities, Calcutta, despite unique pressures, has been free of fascist or right-wing politics. The only chauvinist party, Amra Bangali – 'We are Bengalis' – has almost been laughed out of existence. A Marxist government has ruled the state for the last twenty years (which has brought about a special set of problems associated with long-running governments, as well as a constant neglect of the state by central government, where the Congress Party has almost always been in power).

My own mixed feelings about Mother Teresa were born some time in the early 1980s, when I was an undergraduate in London. There was a film about her on television (not Malcolm Muggeridge's *Something Beautiful for God*, which apparently first turned Mother Teresa into an internationally known figure, and about which Hitchens writes extensively in his book); the only things I recall about the film are the large number of affluent, admiring British people in it in close proximity to Mother Teresa, and the latter smiling and saying, more than once to the camera, 'We must sell Love.' Both these memories irritated me for some time; I couldn't see in what way, except the most superficial, these affluent and photogenic Europeans had anything to do with the poor in Calcutta. Nor could I see how 'selling Love' was going to help the poor.

One of the things that has struck me ever since about the publicity concerning Mother Teresa is that it has less to do with the poor than with Mother Teresa. The poor are shown in a timeless, even pastoral, light: Muggeridge even claims that the interior of the Home for the Dying appeared in his film in spite of insufficient light because of a 'miraculous light' that emanated from Mother Teresa. Hitchens and the cameraman Ken Macmillan believe that it was the new improved Kodak film that did it. Whatever really happened, the 'miraculous' light seems to be a metaphor for the ahistorical; it fixes the Bengali destitute in a timeless vacuum; it further uproots from community, background and identity those who have already been uprooted from community, background and identity. In blocking out history, the 'miraculous light' also blocks out one's proper empathy with, and understanding of, the poor. While it may be true that the poor are people like you and me because we were all created by God, it is only through an understanding of a country's history, and the history of the poor, that we can begin to appreciate that, indeed, the poor *were* people like you and me before something happened to them. Mother Teresa herself, too, is always represented out of context, as an angel of mercy who descended on Calcutta to pick the dying off the streets. If Muggeridge's film made Mother Teresa a 'star', as Hitchens puts it, in 1971 (the year of the Bangladesh war, of which Muggeridge seemed blissfully unaware), it still leaves unaccounted for the immense stretch of time between 1948 and 1971, during which her Order must have established and entrenched itself in Calcutta. This was a time when there were no Reagans, Clintons, Thatchers,

Queen Elizabeths or Duvaliers to give her their largesse or approval. Could she have worked, then, during this most crucial time, without the support of the local people or local government? After all, she was working, not in a desert, but in a major city which provides a context and parameters for everything working within it, including organisations that do social work, among which Mother Teresa's is only one. (For instance, the Ramakrishna Mission and the Bharat Sevasram Sangh are only two of the most active and well-known organisations doing social and charity work here for the poor.) If Mother Teresa worked for the poor in Calcutta, then it goes without saying that this work was made possible in fundamental ways by the support of Bengali people and the West Bengal government. And in the flood of publicity and photo opportunities that have followed Mother Teresa's celebrity, in which various world leaders have basked in the reflected light of her virtue (and her gratitude), it would seem that only the people of Calcutta and the West Bengal government have missed out, even been blanked out, to be represented only by the solitary destitute at the Mother's hand. This is somewhat unfortunate because the Marxist West Bengal government, whatever its other limitations, has done more work in land reform and land redistribution than almost any other Indian state, immensely benefiting the poor and less privileged in rural areas. The positive aspects of this on the alleviation of poverty would certainly be more profound than the work done even by the most well-intentioned charity.

And yet, whatever reservations one might have about the media projections of Mother Teresa and her work (done with her tacit endorsement or not), however banal her occasional utterances might be (several examples are provided by Hitchens, including her exhortation, 'Forgive, forgive, forgive' after the Union Carbide disaster in Bhopal), not even the stupidest banality can cancel the importance of real action and real work done for the poor. And so far, this much seems to have been undeniable: that Mother Teresa and her Sisters *do* pick up the poor from the pavements of Calcutta, give them shelter, food to eat and, if need be, the possibility of a dignified death. Hitchens has much to say about this aspect of her work in his book (which is really an extended essay of about 25,000 words), giving information that would be new and even shocking to most readers. If there is a slight Eurocentric quality about *The Missionary Position* this is because Mother Teresa and her reputation in the West, the workings of the Western media and Mother Teresa the Roman Catholic proponent of anti-abortion dogma are central to Hitchens; Calcutta and its history and people are mentioned sympathetically, intelligently, but briefly, and remain in the background.

Hitchens's Introduction examines, with the acuity of a literary critic, a portfolio of photographs, printed in the middle of the book, each showing Mother Teresa with a dubious character – either with people known to enrich themselves at the cost of others and to terrorise the powerless, like Michèle Duvalier, wife of Jean-Claude Duvalier of Haiti, or big-time crooks like cult leader 'John Roger', 'a fraud of Chaucerian proportions'. These people have donated money, at one time or another, to Mother Teresa's organisation. Indeed, there is something Chaucerian about the world explored in this short book, with its range of tricksters and frauds and their close proximity to the holy and to absolution. Two-thirds of the way through the book, we come across Charles Keating, who is 'now serving a ten-year sentence for his part in the Savings and Loan scandal – undoubtedly one of the greatest frauds in American history'.

At the height of his success as a thief, Keating made donations (not out of his own pocket, of course) to Mother Teresa in the sum of one and a quarter million dollars. He also granted her the use of his private jet. In return, Mother Teresa allowed Keating to make use of her prestige on several important occasions and gave him a personalised crucifix which he took everywhere with him.

During the course of Keating's trial, Hitchens adds, 'Mother Teresa wrote to the court seeking clemency for Mr Keating.' Her letter elicited a response from a Deputy District Attorney for Los Angeles, Paul Turley, who pointed out that, in all fairness, the stolen money Keating had donated to her Order should be returned to its original owners. Turley has still not heard from Mother Teresa.

For all that, there is no evidence in *The Missionary Position* to suggest that Mother Teresa has used any money from donations for her personal material benefit – in this much, at least, she stands apart from most modern godmen and television evangelists, as well as from Chaucer's Pardoner. Money might have helped her operations in Calcutta to expand into a 'missionary multinational', but conditions in her 'homes' are hardly opulent – indeed, if anything, they are unnecessarily austere. This is precisely Hitchens's point – much of the money she receives remains unspent and unaccounted for. Hitchens's contention is that Mother Teresa's ambitions aren't material at all, in the ordinary sense of that term; her aim is to establish a cult of austerity and suffering. The most disturbing section of the book, the first part of the chapter entitled 'Good Works and Heroic Virtues', does something to support this contention. Among the testimony of others (former nuns, social workers), we are given an account by Robin Fox, editor of the *Lancet*, written after a visit to Mother Teresa's 'operation' in Calcutta. Dr Fox, although favourably disposed towards Mother Teresa's work, found that medical facilities for the ill and the dying were not only woefully inadequate, but even prohibited or deliberately circumscribed beyond a certain point. Sterilised syringes, antibiotics and chloroquine for malaria were unavailable. Blood tests were seldom permitted. According to Fox, 'Such systematic approaches are alien to the ethos of the home. Mother Teresa prefers providence to planning; rules are designed to prevent any drift towards materialism.' Moreover, 'How competent are the sisters at managing pain? On a short visit, I could not judge the power of the spiritual approach, but I was disturbed to learn that the formulary includes no strong analgesics.' Hitchens comments:

> Mother Teresa has been working in Calcutta for four and a half decades, and for nearly three of them she has been favoured with immense quantities of money and material. Her 'Home

for the Dying', which was part of her dominion visited by Dr Fox, is in no straitened condition. It is as he describes it because that is how Mother Teresa wishes it to be. The neglect of what is commonly understood as proper medicine is not a superficial contradiction. It is the essence of the endeavour, the same essence that is evident in a cheerful sign which has been filmed on the wall of Mother Teresa's morgue. It reads: 'I am going to heaven today.'

The charge of deliberately curtailing medical care, of promulgating 'a cult based on death and suffering and subjection', is a serious and substantiated one, and it cannot be ignored. Surprisingly, although Hitchens gets his information from authoritative sources – such as Dr Fox, among others – the facts about Mother Teresa's neglect of the poor are not widely known: certainly not in Calcutta. Most Bengalis have viewed Mother Teresa's work with admiration (there seems to be little doubt in most people's minds that she *does* do valuable work for the poor), although rumours that her main aim is the conversion of the poor to Christianity have circulated from time to time. Not long ago, she was embroiled in something of a controversy, when the BJP, the Indian right-wing nationalist party, accused her of demanding job reservations for Dalit (low-caste) Christians. It is not unusual for caste structures to persist among Indian Christians, Sikhs, and even Muslims, bringing all kinds of problems to the already problem-ridden matter of 'quotas' and 'reservations' – for jobs, and places in schools and colleges – kept aside by the government for the 'backward classes'. This time, unusually for her, Mother Teresa decided to answer her detractors. At a press conference at the headquarters on AJC Bose Road, she denied not only the BJP's allegations but also, it seems, Hitchens's accusations. According to *The Statesman* of 25 November, 'she said she would like her detractors to come to the Missionaries' home for the sick and dying in Kalighat and see how "the sisters serve the suffering humanity irrespective of their religion, nationality, caste or colour".' Moreover, 'she also admitted that in her mission for the "salvation of the poorest of poor" . . . she would not mind taking charity from "dictators and corrupt people. Everyone should be given the chance to show his compassion – even a beggar on the street," she said.' (It has to be said here that Hitchens's book, which is now being sold and reviewed in India, and from which an extract was published recently in a Calcutta newspaper, seems to have been generally received in this country without rancour and with equanimity.)

In the climate of tremendous political and popular support for Mother Teresa, especially in the West, it is obvious that Hitchens's investigations have been a solitary and courageous endeavour. The book is extremely well written, with a sanity and sympathy that tempers its irony. In spite of this, Mother Teresa remains an enigma even after we have finished reading it. According to Hitchens, she is 'a religious fundamentalist, a political operative, a primitive sermoniser and an accomplice of worldly, secular powers'. She might be all these, and yet one feels that there is more to the complex personality of the Albanian Agnes Bojaxhiu, who arrived in Calcutta from Yugoslavia one day in 1928. Hitchens's Mother Teresa, at times, is in danger of assuming the one-dimensionality of the Mother Teresa of her admirers. As drawn by him, she becomes something of a wizened but powerful machine of single-minded intentionality. Hitchens quotes Freud towards the beginning of the book, and as a reader of Freud he would know that the genesis of, and reasons for, actions are never clearly revealed to the protagonists themselves, let alone to others.

The Tailor of Gujarat

One day in August 2003, I heard that Qutubuddin Ansari was moving to Calcutta. This man, whose photograph had been reproduced a thousand times in newspapers and magazines, had, reluctantly, become a national figure. He was a tailor. In the photograph, now as famous in its way as the picture of the naked Vietnamese girl fleeing from napalm, he was imploring, his palms joined together, somebody either to forgive or protect him; his eyes were blurred with tears; his shirt was slightly torn, and only recently did I notice, after seeing an enlarged version of the photo, the bloodspots spattered on it.

Nobody knew very much about him. To be unknown, of course, is the lot of most people: a happy lot, some would say, and I think Ansari would agree. There are hundreds of millions of people like Ansari in India; paradoxically, they don't exist. Then, once in five years, sometimes fewer, their presence becomes tangible during the elections; like spirits given leave to visit the earth for a limited duration, they queue up to drop their ballot paper in the ballot box (this time, in a slow symphonic swell, voting took place electronically throughout the nation) and have the tiny black stain imprinted upon one finger, the spot which will be indelible for a few days. It's at this time that everyone says – by 'everyone' I mean the educated and economically empowered middle class – that the 'man on the street' has a proven maturity that we don't always credit him for; after the elections are over, the moment passes and we talk of other things. Ansari is a part of the national fabric inasmuch as he possesses this awesome, if underused, privilege granted him by the Indian constitution: the right to vote. He also has, as I discovered later, a family: a wife and two children; a mother; a brother and sister-in-law; two or three close friends.

Ansari became famous shortly after the riots in Gujarat at the end of February and early March 2002. About two thousand Muslims were killed to avenge the sixty or so Hindu activists who were burned alive in a train in Godhra; the violence was both tacitly and openly supported by the right-wing Bharatiya Janata Party state government and its police force. (Muslims in Gujarat comprise about 9 per cent of the population, slightly lower than the national figure, 12 per cent.) Qutubuddin Ansari's photo was circulated everywhere in India as the face of an endangered minority asking someone – an army officer; policemen; the nation-state; the constitution; the reader who was now holding the periodical in his or her hands – for protection and justice.

This was the story I heard about Qutubuddin Ansari moving to Calcutta: that, after the picture had catapulted him to national fame, the tailor had received a great deal of unwanted attention – from the media, from friends and acquaintances, from passers-by and strangers. His old life had become difficult to sustain. He feared some sort of reprisal from Hindu militants in Gujarat, some form of harassment to him and his family. Others feared reprisals too; his employer, a well-meaning Hindu who was now understandably nervous, had politely asked him to leave his job.

Then a piece about Ansari appeared in a magazine called *Communalism Combat*; the magazine's agenda is self-evident. The article had been brought to the notice of Mohammed Salim, the Minister for Youth in West Bengal; enquiries had been initiated into whether Ansari could be moved to Bengal, specifically, to Calcutta. The idea of a man seeking, or, being offered, political asylum in another part of his own country was unprecedented. Ansari had already tried, unsuccessfully, to move to Mumbai, where his sister lives. Had he succeeded in relocating himself there he'd perhaps have been less disoriented than I found him in Calcutta, for the distance between Ahmedabad and Mumbai is much smaller, both in miles and in culture. Mumbai abounds with Gujaratis, Gujarati Muslims and Gujarati tailors. But there are other similarities he might have felt less at ease with; the sporadic but recurrent production of right-wing violence, the subterranean antipathy towards the Muslim.

Calcutta was an altogether more surprising destination. Ahmedabad and Calcutta lie at the extremes of east and west in India, with a thousand miles between them. And Calcutta is a city to which no one moves if they can help it; members of the middle class have been leaving Calcutta for decades now. The big companies began their exodus in the 1960s. More than twenty-five years of Left Front rule – the Left Front, at whose helm is the CPI(M), the Communist Party of India (Marxist) – has turned West Bengal, according to the government's critics, into an industrial graveyard. The government, under its new chief minister, Buddhadev Bhattacharya, translator of Gabriel García Márquez and other Latin American writers into Bengali, has for some time now been making siren-like noises to attract investment; but investors, suspicious of a recalcitrant labour force long abetted by the Left Front, have been slow to respond. In the midst of all this, Qutubuddin Ansari's arrival seemed like an astonishing event, a political migration to a place no one wanted to migrate to (I say this despite the daily influx of unskilled and semi-skilled labour from villages and neighbouring, poorer states).

Bengalis were reminded at this point, as they were meant to be, of what is arguably the Left Front's greatest achievement after the rural reforms of the 1970s: the creation in West Bengal, and its capital Calcutta, of a secular, non-sectarian civic space. Here's the paradox: the institutions and infrastructure that sustain civilised living are often damaged or ruined in this city – sewers, buses; life, particularly for the poor, hard; and yet, for all that, people of different communities and religions have found a way of living peacefully with each other.

When Ansari reached Howrah station, there were photographers and TV cameramen waiting for him. In the picture in the *Hindustan Times* the next morning, the tailor looked harried and unhappy; he'd expected his arrival to be a quiet affair. It was said that Ansari suspected the Left Front government had tipped off the press; something it strenuously denied. According to another story, Ansari had been spotted at one of the stops on the way, and the information had travelled quickly to newspapers in the city.

I felt a curious urge to meet him. I say 'curious' because I've never wanted to meet celebrities or famous people before. Of course, Ansari is a savage parody of the notion of celebrity; he brings to it an unacknowledged humanity, an anxiety, a shabbiness, inadmissible to our current idea of fame. Nor is he, in spite of his suffering, a Christ-figure, a miracle worker; he is not blessed with a great gift; he was only a famous photograph.

I couldn't just go and knock on Ansari's door. For one thing, I didn't know what his new address was. Besides, the government would have taken measures to make him inaccessible to the prying, the plain curious and the hostile; and especially to journalists – although, vainly, I saw myself as a cut above the paparazzi.

I decided to follow up on a remark someone had once made to me, that Somnath Chatterjee likes my writing. Usually fans try and get in touch with the object of their enthusiasm, surreptitiously procuring telephone numbers and addresses; in this case, I tried to get in touch with my admirer. Somnath Chatterjee is one of the CPI(M)'s most senior and respected leaders, and its most effective parliamentarian; he's recently been made speaker in the Lok Sabha, the national parliament. I obtained his number from the Bengal Club, of which both he and I are members. The Bengal Club, one of the oldest clubs in the world, once a bastion of the British Raj, is, admittedly, an odd place for either a writer or a Marxist to frequent. For both Chatterjee and myself, it is, I suppose, part of our fathers' legacy. Somnath Chatterjee's father, N.C. Chatterjee, was one of the most successful barristers of his day; my father, who lost his ancestral property with Partition, was a successful business executive. My profession and Chatterjee's suggest an uncomfortable relationship with our fathers' world, but the Bengal Club implicates us both in a continuity with it.

When I finally got through to Somnath Chatterjee, he was most cordial. 'Let me talk to Mohammed Salim, our Minister of Youth,' he said. And it was Mohammed Salim who met me in one of those large cars that have recently become popular in India – Sumo, Qualis – which are called SUVs in the West. He was waiting for me, as he'd promised, in Park Circus, near the Don Bosco school. He had a smallish contingent with him, including someone called Mohammed *bhai*, who was a sort of minder of Ansari's. I got out of my car and joined them, and asked my driver to follow, so he'd remember the route. Mr Salim, the Minister for Youth, is an understatedly debonair man in his mid-forties; he wore steel-framed spectacles and was in white, in kurta and aligarhi pyjamas. 'I've impressed upon him,' he said, 'that you're not a journalist, but a different kind of writer. Understandably, he's nervous about journalists.' I'd wanted this matter to be made clear – that I wasn't writing for a newspaper. I was worried Ansari wouldn't talk to me if he thought I was. I had two copies of *Granta* to show him. 'I don't think you need take those,' said the minister. 'They might confuse him.'

Tiljala, Ansari's address, is not far from Ballygunge, where I live. But a universe separates the two localities. When I'd told my family I was off to Tiljala, my elderly parents had baulked, as if I'd announced I was going to the Gaza Strip. One of the surprises of this part of south Calcutta, in fact, is how the demography and population change fluently and seamlessly within the span of a few miles. Ballygunge is one of the two most affluent districts of Calcutta – the domain of old money – and, increasingly, of new money as well. The conquest of old money by the new is evident from the number of multi-storey buildings that have come up here in the last twenty years; in the lanes, the decaying mansions that indeterminately await destruction slightly outnumber, or at least rival, the mansions owned by families that can afford to maintain them, and throw the occasional garden party. In a quarter of a mile, beyond Mayfair, the locale begins to change. The first sign of this is the mosque a little distance from the Modern High School. Then, in the interiors of by-lanes, tailors' shops, more mosques and butchers' shops begin to appear. The cluster of mosques, tailors, traders and skewers on open fires culminates in Beck Bagan market; and, at the other end, after the interruption of Ballygunge Road, continues into Shamsul Huda Haq Road, a long street whose inhabitants are almost entirely Muslim. This street is no more than a fifteen or twenty minutes' walk from where I live in Sunny Park, but visiting it, in my mind, is like being in a street in Cairo or Lahore, although I have no idea what either city is actually like. There's a sense of huddled community here, of festivities at Eid and fasting before Mohurrum, of a different auditory life with the muezzins' call at dawn. This area, and beyond it, is no longer Ballygunge, but is collectively called Park Circus.

Beyond Park Circus, accessed by a narrow lane, is Tiljala. That day it looked less remarkable to my eye than its reputation as a place of shelter, in the past, for itinerant terrorists had suggested; a congested and somewhat down-at-heel Muslim enclave awaiting the gentrification that's been coming to other parts of Calcutta. The traffic was mainly scooters, cycles and people lounging about in the middle of the street; and then the lane straightened. We got off busily in front of a beedi stall and a parked scooter. There was a narrow driveway on our left, alongside a building.

Here, on the ground floor, were a packers' shop, a carpenter's shed and a small yard in which it seemed there was a makeshift workshop where spare parts were made; and, next to these, a flight of stairs. Ansari's flat was on the third, the topmost, storey. One or two children looked at us curiously as we went up. Then, finally, the flat: before you entered it, you had to climb up a slope, and then enter a tiny room which was the sitting area. The door was already open.

Ansari was as I'd seen him in the photograph, but a little smaller than the photo suggested. He is a dark, pleasant-looking man, about five feet six inches tall, with light brown eyes. He was wearing a grey shirt, the sleeves of which were rolled up at the wrists, and dark trousers – the way I always saw him dressed, and the way he appears in the photograph. He smiled, but was a bit anxious; not so much about meeting me, but about life in general: about being where he was. He had the ill-at-ease air of a recent migrant; and little of the air of relief and release you imagine an asylum seeker who's reached his destination might have.

There was a single bed on the left, and two white plastic chairs before it. We sat down and Mohammed Salim introduced me briefly: I was a writer, well known outside India, I was not a reporter, I'd been curious about Ansari and wanted to meet him, to listen to his story, I wanted to write about him. Salim spoke in Hindi interspersed with elaborate Urdu words I didn't always understand, perhaps to emphasise to Ansari their common Muslim lineage; perhaps because he didn't get a chance to speak in Urdu too often. Ansari nodded, attentive to the minister, and smiled at me absent-mindedly and a little dismissively. He knew the minister was an important man; but what sort of creature was a 'writer'? He knew, though, that this little occasion had been rustled up at my request. Different emotions flitted over his face as he listened. 'But nothing will be written that will bring harm to my family?' he asked no one in particular. The language he used was an ordinary street Hindi inflected with a faint Gujarati intonation. His tone was polite but firm. By 'family' – *parivar* – he meant, I think, the family he'd left behind in Ahmedabad: his mother, his brother, his brother's wife, their children.

I hastened to reassure him that I didn't intend to write that kind of piece. I was not writing for a newspaper, I continued; the place in which the piece would eventually come out was a magazine which was, in fact, something like a book; its aims were not sensational, and it was published in England; it was unlikely anyone in Ahmedabad would see it. I blabbered this to him solemnly, and he looked unconvinced, probably taking it for the nonsense it was.

He turned back to Mohammed Salim. I was a diversion, almost a waste of time; it was the minister he was interested in. By this time, Qutubuddin had been in Calcutta for about a month. The West Bengal government had promised to set up a tailoring business for him. Nothing had happened so far; and Qutubuddin was feeling nervous. He received an allowance, he told me later, that covered his family's daily costs and the rent; but he was uneasy living on government charity; he felt lost not working.

He went a few times a week to a tailor's factory in Dum Dum, to learn the local cutting methods, the local requirements. (Earlier, Mohammed Salim had said he was also receiving psychiatric counselling.) This was probationary work, Mohammed Salim explained, necessary to his initiation into the business. The machine with which Qutubuddin's operations would begin was still to arrive.

'It'll be here any day now,' said Salim, rising swiftly and patting him on the shoulder. 'I'll phone you. Now why don't you talk to each other – we'll leave you.' And he and his contingent were gone.

'This won't affect my family in any way, will it?' Qutubuddin asked again. Reassuring him, I turned briefly to other subjects.

'What is this "cutting" you have to learn? What kind of things do you make?'

'I make ready-made shirts. That is what I'm trained to do.'

'My mother's tailor is called Qutubuddin too,' I said. 'He's an expert at making blouses and salwar kameezes.'

The other Qutubuddin has a shop in a lane off Beck Bagan, behind a tube well; his charges are steep and his behaviour erratic. Sometimes he will take more than a month to finish a blouse or salwar kameez. This Qutubuddin – the famous one – smiled; he seemed pleased to discover a namesake.

On 27 February 2002 – it was a Wednesday – Ansari was in his factory when, after lunch, he and his fellow workers saw on TV that a train at Godhra station carrying vociferous and rowdy Hindu activists had been set alight by a Muslim mob. After a couple of hours, the apprehensive Hindu factory-owner (a good man, said Qutubuddin) asked the workers to go home. (Qutubuddin was almost always understanding of the fears of his Hindu employers or neighbours.) They usually left the factory at seven or eight o'clock; that day, they went home at five.

'There was tension in the air. We knew something would happen. My friends Sunil and Chandrakant and I got on to the bus, and I said goodbye to them when they got off at their stops. My stop was further on.'

The next day, a *bandh* – total closure – was declared in the city. This was not unusual, since there had been disruptions already after the train burning the previous day: buses had been attacked in Ahmedabad. An auto-rickshaw driver from Qutubuddin's *mohulla* – his locality – had been beaten up that day, and his auto burned. Still, Qutubuddin and his family couldn't have expected the ferocity of the reprisals to come: after three hours of rioting in 1992, he said, the police had acted swiftly and things were brought under control. His mother was nervous; watching the news that night, she said, speaking of the incident at Godhra, the words Atal Behari Vajpayee and his second-in-command, Lai Krishna Advani, had so wanted to hear from the Muslims: 'They shouldn't have done what they did.' But her words were meant for her family and not the nation. Despite her nervousness, and theirs, they did not move, as they'd had to during riots in the past: their Hindu neighbours, whose settlements faced theirs from the other side of the national highway that divided the Muslim and Hindu *mohullas*, assured them there would be no violence on their part.

Qutubuddin now came to the heart of his story: 'On the morning of the 28th, Sairaj Bano, who lived in the front part of the *mohulla*, came running to us to tell us of disturbances on the road. Ten or eleven of us rushed towards the road, me and my friend Aslam included. We went out and found people standing with pipes and rods in their hands, telling shopkeepers to pull down their shutters. The elder of the *mohulla* waved the younger men in; then elders from both communities went on to the highway and spoke to each other. This was between 10.30 and 11.00 a.m.

'At about 11.45 a.m., six or seven jeeps full of policemen arrived on the scene to dissuade the public from going any further towards the *mohulla*.' 'Public', I noticed, is the English word Qutubuddin uses when he means 'mob'. 'We in the *mohulla* were too far away to hear what was said. Later, at six or seven o'clock in the evening, the police returned and aimed tear gas shells towards our *basti* – this was the first sign that the police were not with us. And now the public began attacking and burning the shops. There are 700 shops in this area, and the public were throwing stones at them, while we retreated into our *basti*. This went on for about four hours.

'At 1 a.m., jeeps gathered outside the *mohulla* with their headlights turned on, and blew their horns continuously. Children and women were shouting; people couldn't decide what to do. One camp thought of vacating the *basti*; the other, because the stone-throwing had by now stopped, thought the main troubles were over. On Friday morning, we woke up to find we had no fresh provisions, no vegetables, or milk; we drank black tea for breakfast.'

At this point, Qutubuddin interrupted himself to say two things. The first, as it turned out, was a commonplace among most Gujaratis, and has become one in all political conversation in India – that the reason the BJP returns to power in Gujarat is because it orchestrates riots and creates panic, a false sense of endangerment which makes its reign seem necessary. The other thing was that it was only then that it dawned on Qutubuddin and the others in the *mohulla* that the police had turned against them – for the police had helped, apparently, during the earthquake in 2001, in which thousands had died or been left homeless.

'As the stone-throwing and violence began once more, we regretted not leaving during the night. The men fought back a little: we leaned over the partition of the *mohulla* and threw stones at the public, while the women packed. My brother took the children to a safe place. Meanwhile, even the gate to the Hindu *mohulla* had been forced open, and the house of the head of the society looted.'

It was our first meeting; it was late; neither of us had eaten.

Qutubuddin, who'd been hesitant about speaking to me, was now gripped by his own tale. 'Qutubuddin *bhai*,' I said, 'I'm keeping you. I should come back in a couple of days.'

When I visited him a week later he looked unhappy. 'My business hasn't started yet. It's been more than a month. How will I support my family? My daughter's going to school.'

'They give you money, don't they?'

'They do, but how long can you live on an allowance? I want to start work.' Then he said, 'This flat is too big. I have to pay a lot of rent for it.' The flat was tiny.

'Too big?'

'Yes, in Ahmedabad we used to live in a room.' Later, he told me what its size was – twelve feet by twenty feet.

He resumed his story. 'On Friday the 1st, we began to evacuate the *mohulla* in trucks. People moved to Bapunagar, half a kilometre away – lots of Muslims live there.

'My friend Aslam, and his brothers Arif and Liaqat – all married men – were urged to leave by their mother. Aslam lived with his family in a room on the first floor of a building facing the main road. I treated it like a second home; I used to spend a lot of time there. This room, which still had some valuables, some jewellery and possessions in it, was now locked up by Aslam's mother. When we were inside the car, we realised that Ruhanna, Aslam's wife, was not with us: there was panic. Had Ruhanna stayed back in the room by mistake? Aslam and I took the keys and returned to the house; the room's ground floor was being vandalised by six or seven boys. They had a look of enjoyment on their faces: *Oh, I can slap anyone I feel like now.* We ran upstairs. Ruhanna was in the room; she'd been sitting silently, so as not to draw attention to herself – she'd lingered on because of the valuables. The boys were downstairs. But by this time the soldiers had arrived; there was a *sardarji* before me, a Sikh from the Rapid Action Force. I turned to him for help – please do something. The press had reached the scene too; and someone, at that moment, took the photograph of me.

'By 2.30 p.m., our families had left, but Aslam, Farooq and I remained. Prayers were offered at one of the three mosques in our locality; the two others had been set alight. A godown full of plastics was also on fire, and the fire spread. We were helping the fire to grow by adding things to it, because we felt it created a barrier which kept us safe.

'At five or six o'clock in the evening, the Border Police and a unit from the army came to the *mohulla*; the soldiers were from Kerala.' This last detail wasn't offered perfunctorily; Qutubuddin knew that a complete failure on the state police's part had forced someone in the government to bring in soldiers from outside. Who had taken that decision? 'Amit *bhai*, the colonel in charge wept at what he saw. An army driver wanted water, and Farooq went back to the building on the main road to fetch two bottles of water from the fridge; from the balcony he saw the public running; the army were firing into the air. By 6.30, the public had disappeared.

'The army positioned themselves in the locality in the following days. People were transferred to another *mohulla*; a relief camp was set up; my own *mohulla* became a museum for people to look at.

'On 2 March, my photo appeared in the papers; I knew nothing about it. On the 10th, I was chatting with friends when a group of Europeans who'd seen my photo and were looking for me finally found me. They showed me the paper, and I saw my own image in print. I was very anxious.'

Ansari's infant son toddled in. He was born after the riots, Qutubuddin tells me.

'Other reporters came and took down notes like you. Once they got what they wanted, I never heard from them again.'

He is suffering from a constant sense of betrayal and abandonment. His story is done; he probably thinks I'm about to lose interest. He knows the BJP and the government in Gujarat for what they are. It's those who'd make him a secular mascot that he's disappointed by; he knows that, in his post-riot life of supporters, well-wishers, empathisers and protectors, he has made no real friends. Uprooted from his habitat, he misses the friends he left behind: Aslam, Farooq.

I met Farooq in December last year. It was my first visit to Ahmedabad. I took the taxi from the Ellis Bridge Gymkhana, where I was staying, across one of the bridges over the River Sabarmati that connected the Hindu and more prosperous part of Ahmedabad to the less affluent and mainly Muslim areas of the city. Farooq was waiting for me in his small shop, behind the glass doors. I had not expected a man at once portly and dapper, a dark friendly man dressed impeccably in white.

His shop, which sells 'electronic goods', is air-conditioned. In fact, it might be the only air-conditioned shop in the area. 'Please have a cold drink,' he said.

We deferred the cold drink and got into my car. The *mohulla* in which Qutubuddin lived was not far away—only a few minutes' drive from the shop. Farooq pointed out personal landmarks from the riots ('They came down here'; 'They burned that shop') as if we were retracing some ancient historical journey.

'Wait, wait,' said Farooq to the driver. He had noticed Qutubuddin's elder brother, Siraj, and wanted to introduce him to me. I wasn't sure if this was a good idea. Before I left Calcutta, Qutubuddin had asked me not to look up his family. But it was too late; Farooq had already got out of the car, he was walking towards where Siraj was standing next to his scooter.

Siraj is quite different to look at from his younger brother – stocky, moustached – and he also seems unlike Qutubuddin in temperament. Rais Khan, Communalism Combat's Ahmedabad representative, had told me, only the day before, that Siraj is more *hoshiyar* – more a man of the world – than his brother is.

I liked Siraj instantly; I liked his warmth, his openness. He'd heard about me from Qutubuddin; he, too, wanted me to have a cold drink. We went inside a restaurant, climbed up the stairs to the first floor, sat solemnly at a table with a soft drink before me, and discussed Qutubuddin's welfare and the present state of the *mohulla*. The only other people besides us – it was four o'clock in the afternoon, after all – were a thin young man and a woman in a red sari. Most of the shops along this line of buildings had been burned on 28 February and 1 March.

And that was our small meeting, Siraj's and mine; I don't know when I'll see him again, but we behaved as if it might not be before too long – we embraced – and he rode off on his scooter. Here, in front of the tiny 'hotel', Farooq and I stood facing the featureless national highway number 8, which led, in the direction opposite to the one Siraj had taken, to Bombay. We proceeded towards Qutubuddin's former home in Rehmatnagar. Everything here had the look and air of a working-class settlement in an industrial suburb: the Muslim *mohulla* on this side, and the Hindu *mohulla* on the other side of the highway. Almost two years after the event, I tried to sniff the smell of burning in the air; but inhaled only gasoline fumes and dust. No one had been prosecuted.

We came, at last, to the gate of the *mohulla* where, on its right, was the building on whose first floor Ruhanna had been hiding while hoodlums were on the rampage; Qutubuddin had stood on the balcony, the palms of his hands joined together, when his photograph was taken.

Beyond, a narrow dust road led to the interconnected rows of houses and other paths. Children, goats and men loitered at various spots as Farooq gestured towards a path and said, 'We escaped down there.'

'Can I have a look at Qutubuddin's house? I won't disturb anyone inside it,' I said.

Farooq seemed unsure of what to do; then he seemed to think it could do no harm, and he nodded. The house was absurdly near where we were; we turned right, and then left. Farooq pointed out a small one-storey house on the left, after a couple of other houses, and retreated. A woman emerged from the door of Qutubuddin's house; it must have been his sister-in-law. I turned back and retraced my steps.

This, then, was Qutubuddin's world – his *mohulla*. This interlocking network of houses, of human beings and animals, which bear few marks of the conflagration that had once engulfed it, is the home from which he is in exile.

From here Farooq took me to the man Qutubuddin had urged me to meet, the maulana who ran the madrasa nearby. The madrasa was a three- or four-storey building which still bore, on its upper wall, the imprints of the bullets that were aimed at it on the 28th. The maulana, Mehboob Alam Qasmi, the light-eyed, very gentle man of religion who peered at us from behind the gates, guided me and Farooq into the building through a throng of buffaloes standing in the courtyard. He took us to his room on the first floor; next door, children were rocking back and forth and memorising verses from the Qur'an. The maulana offered me coffee; I was grateful at the prospect of caffeine. He told me how this room we were sitting in, and the classroom next to us, were burned till they were unrecognisable. 'This room was not like this,' he said, looking around him. He retrieved a photo album; it is an important document. The heavy and innocent tome, meant for wedding or holiday snapshots, was full of photographs of the debris, the aftermath, of the event: the madrasa's transformation. I browsed through them to the accompaniment of the maulana's soft-voiced commentary. 'This is the classroom,' he said. 'This is this room, where we are now. And this is the photo of the burnt Qur'an.'

The maulana was an articulate and exceptionally intelligent man; his tone was entirely devoid of anger or grievance or moral righteousness. In spite of having been attacked and terrorised – he showed me, from his window, the vegetable patch and field at the back where rioters exploded oxygen and cooking-gas cylinders – in spite of all this, he knew the problem he faced was primarily a political one: a calculated chafing of old wounds, rather than a spontaneous outburst of hatred. The BJP Chief Minister, Narendra Modi, and his party had a landslide victory in the assembly elections that had been brought forward and held soon after the riots. 'During the elections they displayed cardboard cut-outs of Musharraf and warned people that

Gujarat would become Pakistan unless they voted for the BJP. Tell me, what does Gujarat have to do with Pakistan?'

As I left, he showed me where the attackers, that day, wrote JAI SHRI RAM on the wall in large letters – 'Victory to Lord Ram' – and improvised a Hanuman temple underneath a switchboard.

It was Rais Khan of Communalism Combat – a gentle, burly man with faintly hennaed hair – who'd introduced Qutubuddin to the organisation's most prominent activist, Teesta Setelvad, who, in turn, had first discussed with the West Bengal government the matter of Qutubuddin moving to Calcutta. In his office in Ahmedabad, Khan told me more about Qutubuddin's background.

The family were migrants from Uttar Pradesh, and Qutubuddin belonged to the third generation in Ahmedabad. They lived in the old mill area, Gomtipur, where the majority of workers – 80 per cent – were from Uttar Pradesh. On the way to Rehmatnagar, I'd noticed the abandoned textile mills for which Gujarat had once been famous, the tall chimneys like sentinels. Qutubuddin's grandfather worked in a clothes mill, a daily wage earner, as Qutubuddin was.

I had assumed, wrongly, that he'd at least had fixed employment at the factory he'd worked for; I'd thought of him simply as a tailor, like that other Qutubuddin, my mother's tailor, who, indeed, was fortunate by Qutubuddin Ansari's standards, and had his own small business in Beck Bagan. But, as Rais Khan said, a daily wage earner gets no bonus, no leave, and risks forfeiting his job to another man if he falls ill. The daily wage earner has no future – such was the existence of Qutubuddin Ansari before he was photographed.

Many Gujaratis who've gone abroad have an ideal Gujarat in their heads: *braj dham*. This is the mythic zone in which Radha and Krishna dally with each other eternally, in which the child Krishna, in his haste and greed, steals curds from a pot in his mother's kitchen, in which he loiters as a cowherd, his flute mesmerising those who listen. *Braj dham* exists in song and artistic representation and the imagination, an endlessly fertile playground.

Of course, there are neither Muslims nor textile mills in *braj dham* – how could there be? But the great nineteenth-century Muslim ruler of Awadh, Wajid Ali Shah, whose province was wrested from him by the British in 1856, had been enthralled – hypnotised – by the possibility of its existence. Composer of several semi-classical love songs about Radha and Krishna in the form called the *thumri*, and one of the great patrons of *kathak*, the classical dance whose narrative content is entirely to do with the same erotic subject, he is part of the shadowy, unacknowledged, but substantial Muslim authorship of *braj dham*.

On my last evening in Ahmedabad, I went to a restaurant called Vishala to eat authentic Gujarati food. Vishala is a restaurant that's built, very charmingly and successfully, as a heritage site; it showcases folk arts and folk dancers, puppet shows which enact particularly violent family quarrels, and the place itself is a series of thatched huts in which you sit on the floor or on a very low stool, and are served by men in traditional costume. I thought I was in *braj dham*. Here and there, men and women wandered about in groups, speaking English in accents from Leicester and London.

Six months have passed since that visit. The great, exhilarating surprise of the national election results in May is already history; so is, at least for now, the BJP government. I happened to be in Delhi at the time of the formal investiture of the new Congress government, to give a reading at the India International Centre, where I was being put up by the Sahitya Akademi, the Indian government's literature wing.

As I sat at lunch, I saw around me, in the dining hall, members of a class that has, in the last twenty years, hardened and congealed into India's post-Independence ruling elite. It was an uncomfortable sight, watching these people greet each other, eat soup, raise their cutlery, whisper to a waiter. I could spot, among them, members and supporters of both the new and the superannuated regime: secretaries, under-secretaries, hawkish editors who'd once reasoned on behalf of the BJP's nuclear programme. In a corner by one of the large windows sat Maneka Gandhi, Sanjay Gandhi's widow, who had joined the BJP some years ago, and had just been re-elected as an MP although her party had been thrown out of power. As I sat in the hubbub in the dining hall – everyone was talking – I was startled and chastened by the self-absorption of this ruling class, and by the way they had betrayed the world outside this room – a world that, for twenty-five years or more now, they had been too busy with their own negotiations and gains and losses to notice.

This sense of disconnection, I think, gave rise to the disgust I sensed in Qutubuddin when I spoke to him before I left for England. Before and during the elections, I rang him at his new shop which the West Bengal government had set up for him with two machines and two workers. He was not there; he'd gone back to Ahmedabad with his family, to be with his mother and brother during the elections. I presumed it was because the period leading to the elections is seen to be a difficult time in Ahmedabad, a time when, as the maulana had said, violence is orchestrated to inflame and influence the electoral process. But the main reason Qutubuddin had made the journey, he said later, was because it was his daughter's vacation time; besides, he was homesick.

Then, a week before I flew out, he called me; he was back. 'Amit bhai,' he said, 'many people have written about me for their own purposes and gone away and I've never seen them again. But with you I felt there was something different.' I concluded this was a mixture of goodness on his part, and of wishful thinking; the longing for, more than the discovery of, trust.

I visited his flat in Tiljala three days later. It would be easy to give this piece a happy ending in the sense that my writing it has coincided with an electoral outcome that, for me and many others, is as satisfying as it was startling. Even in Gujarat, to Narendra Modi's discomfiture, the BJP fared worse than expected. Far from Tiljala, a new government was in place; and here in Tiljala itself, and its contiguous neighbourhoods, there was a new MP; Mohammed Salim, the Minister for Youth, had been elected to the Lok Sabha.

I asked Qutubuddin if he was happy with the election results. But, for him, there was no simple answer to this simplistic question. Continuity was what he valued most, and even, intriguingly, a return to his old life. That was going to be difficult, though; Qutubuddin had become part of the anti-BJP campaign in various parts of India, including his own street, where, later, he showed me posters with his face in the centre bearing the slogan in Urdu: DO YOU WANT YOUR LOCALITY TO BECOME ANOTHER GUJARAT? He then picked up an Urdu newspaper – there, on the pages in the middle, was his own picture alongside Atal Behari Vajpayee's, surrounded by Urdu text.

'Won't people think that I am responsible for this? People made use of me, and forgot me. They put my banner up everywhere during the elections. My photograph is everywhere again.' 'Banner' is the English word he uses for 'poster'. 'Amit *bhai*, big men have security and Black Cat commandos. I am not a big man. I fear for my life and my family's.' And he began to weep; I saw before me the man as he was in the photograph, frightened, his eyes full of tears.

It is true. Qutubuddin is India's first celebrity who is also anonymous and poor; the fame has left him no better off, but robbed him of the protection of being no one. Every month almost, some nameless man somewhere in India will try to insert himself into history, usually via the *Guinness Book of World Records*, by growing his nails two feet long, or by spending a night in a room full of poisonous snakes, or by eating crushed glass. Qutubuddin really has passed into history, one of the first 'ordinary' men in independent India to do so, and he's resistant to it.

He was desperate for the photograph to cease to exist: as if the man in the photo and he are competing for the same oxygen. We discussed the possibility of litigation, of invoking some privacy law that will banish the photo once and for all; and also whether this will have the opposite effect, of drawing to him more attention than he already has.

Finally, we realised it's impossible: history can't be changed or undone – not the burning train, the razed shops and houses and mosques, the dead that Qutubuddin says he saw lying by highway number 8, the landslide victory for Modi in the assembly elections after the riots, the advent of a new Congress government in parliament in May 2004.

'But, Qutubuddin *bhai*,' I said to him after a minute, 'the photo will stay where it is. You will have moved on; you'll have your own life. People will cease to connect the two. That Qutubuddin will be associated in people's minds with a moment in history; you'll be elsewhere – people will stop confusing you with the photo.'

He stared at me – it was impossible to know if he believed me.

Our Awful Record

Despite being the world's largest democracy, India's embarrassingly awful record on freedom of expression is plain to see. Salman Rushdie was the first celebrated casualty of the Indian state's repressiveness (in the end, the Indian state must take responsibility for what elapses within its borders), of its refusal to abide by the tenets of its own constitution; as I write this, he's also its latest casualty. Meanwhile, the Indian state and others who speak in its name have been proactive abroad, complaining to the BBC of insults in *Top Gear*, to NBC of insults on the *Jay Leno Show*: complaints that were briskly, and rightly, ignored. It would be nice if the Indian state could deal with complaints arriving at its own doorstep with the same decisiveness and clarity.

Both decisiveness and clarity were lacking all round in connection with Rushdie's abortive Jaipur Literature Festival visit; and they're lacking when it comes to the matter of free speech. There has to be a law pertaining to this question, of the freedom to say and write things which may be offensive to others, and this law and the right it protects is fundamental to the political system called democracy, since that system works on the idea of government and opposition, of elections and change of government, of the provisionality and impermanence of world views: no absolute view is tenable in a democracy, except the context of democracy itself, in which we've all chosen to live, and where we have the peaceful right to disagreement and even to be disagreeable. Being disagreeable is fundamental to a democracy, and so it's admissible for Rushdie to be disagreeable in *The Satanic Verses*, for his critics to be disagreeable about him, and for his Islamic detractors too, if they so wish; but it's inadmissible under the law for any of these parties to use violence or coercion. The transgressor, on many counts, has clearly been the state, which, in acts of coercion, banned Rushdie's novel, ensured M.F. Hussain had no safe haven here, made Taslima Nasreen's life difficult, and now wants to censor Facebook; the state, and all who (the Bajrang Dal, the Darul Uloom, and others) initiated, abetted and participated in coercion and violence.

So it was right of the four writers who read from *The Satanic Verses* at the JLF to have done what they did, in the face of state-supported coercion. There was a nuance that people may have missed; that one of the readers was Amitava Kumar, who has, in the past, been harshly critical of Rushdie's work. This detail is pertinent to the nature of both democracy and literature; that upholding them passionately doesn't preclude disagreement. However, public readings from *The Satanic Verses* can't stop, now they've begun. This is easier said than done, but our secular middle class – in which I include myself – needs to learn that free speech can't be arrived at via a well-mannered compromise with its enemies. Yet free speech can be peaceably pursued.

So much for our record on free speech; what about India's record on literature and the arts, since they seem to be at stake in most of the examples I've cited? With regard to both the state and the secular middle class now clamouring for free speech, the answer is: abysmal. Not just the rise of the sciences and rationality, the role of the arts in the emergence of the secular is crucial. The paradox of secular modernity is that it treats certain literary texts, even very profane and irreverent ones, like *Ulysses*, with a reverence accorded once only to sacred texts. And it treats certain sacred texts purely as literary texts; thus, Matthew Arnold's view that the Bible was literature, and also the *Bhagavad Gita*; thus, Gandhi's remark that the *Gita* was allegory; thus, Michael Madhusudan Dutt, in a letter to a friend, distinguishes between the secular/literary and religious dimensions of Hindu tradition as he embarks on his own modern poem based on the *Ramayana*: 'I hate Rama and all his rabble . . . I love the grand mythology of my ancestors, it is full of poetry.' Secular modernity is precisely about accommodating this curious mix of love and hate towards the textual and the mythical, this uneasy but liberating combination of disregard and reverence.

In India, though, I get the feeling that the liberal middle class is only dimly aware of the importance of the arts, and how integral they are to the secular imagination, except in a time of media-inflated crisis, when they become a 'free speech' issue. Indians know how to talk about writers, but not about writing; in India, famous writers aren't writers who happen to be famous, but famous people who happen to be writers. This means we don't have a persuasive idea of the value of the writer we're upholding volubly at certain moments. *The Satanic Verses* needs to be defended from censors even if it's a bad book; but very few people in India seem to be able to speak of its virtues or, for that matter, Rushdie's, in anything but the most self-serving clichés. So with A.K. Ramanujan's essay: it's clear that not many people had read Ramanujan, except after the ban, and that few can tell us why he's such an important writer. About Hussain, I don't know which was more tragic: the fact that he was exiled by a cowardly government, or that he belonged to a country that called him its greatest painter without seeming to have the slightest inkling why. When he died, there was piety and self-flagellation in the papers, but no illumination as to which – in contrast to, say, Picasso, to whom he was mysteriously compared – his great paintings or phases of creativity were. In India, with its robust democratic tradition, one often senses that neither detractor nor supporter has any penetrating case for or against the arraigned writer or artist's achievement. Argumentative Indians indeed!

Part of the failure of the 'free speech' issue in India has to do with the nature of our so-called secular intelligentsia, which has been busy, in the last twenty years, building its own fiefdoms. This was visible to anyone who followed the Rushdie debate on television. That liberals are complacent in their power and their class, and the right wing generally confused, unpleasant, poor and desperate, is a paradox we can't entirely ignore. From the glimpses of the JLF on television, one noticed, despite the tears, rage and anxiety, a sense of unassailability and centrality, rather than marginality, in the liberals, notwithstanding their defeat, shored up as they are not just by a common belief in free speech and literature, but by networks of mutual support and interest. Liberalism is not just a matter of solidarity, but of an openness to people, even strangers, of disparate social backgrounds, who haven't necessarily been domesticated into the mainstream, and who come together out of a shared respect for the realm of ideas. One has to admit that this isn't the case in India; that our liberals are too over-familiar with one another, and comfortably so. An idea of freedom that emerges out of a closed world, from a sense of entitlement rather than from constant intellectual striving, can experience its crises with only so much urgency.

Three:
Listening, Writing, Planning

Interlude

In 1984, my parents moved to a small, appealing flat in St Cyril Road, Bandra. My father had retired from his corporate position – as the head of a company – the previous year: the year I'd gone to England as an undergraduate. At the time of retirement, we moved out of the 4,000-square-foot four-bedroom flat on the twenty-fifth storey of Maker Towers 'B' on Cuffe Parade, and briefly occupied the company guest flat at 'Brighton' in Nepean Sea Road, overlooking the sea (I had lived, from when I was about nine years old, in buildings that had an unobstructed view of the sea). From there we moved to the first flat my father actually owned in Bombay, a two-bedroom apartment in a building in Worli called Sea Glimpse, whose lift had a sign saying 'Use Lift at Your Own Risk'. The sea, from here, was a blur. But buildings in Bombay have their own biographies and destinies, and are named, at birth, with presumably the same mixture of wishful thinking and superstition as our children are.

My father had bought this flat from the company years ago, for a sum he could afford. It took us by surprise; it was the sort of building we had seldom visited, let alone lived in. The ramshackle lift, with its dark lift shaft like the inside of a toilet in a small town, and the message on the top of the door, made my mother and me smile resignedly at the sort of life that was in store for us after my father's retirement. But, property prices in Bombay being what they are, even this flat, with its view of the dirty blur of the sea, the back of the Aarey Milk Colony, and the distant figures, at twilight, of a line of defecating squatters by the promenade on the sea face – even this flat was not worth little. The blur which constituted the sea – like a smear on the

241

glass which a duster had failed to wipe away – would itself have raised its price by a few hundred thousand. Almost as soon as we occupied this flat, we decided to sell it. The difference from those company flats, where all those parties used to be thrown so unthinkingly every one or two weeks, was too much to contemplate for too long. People – prospective buyers, of whom there is a rich supply in Bombay – came in to survey the flat; our faithful maidservant, Bai, distracted their attention away from the rats who had come to inspect the kitchen from the neighbouring flat, towards the drawing room and the veranda.

From this view of the sea, separated from me by glass, and with the flat yet unsold, I left for England; the untrustworthy lift, one last time, took me and my bags downstairs. In England, in the anonymity of my life in London, I kept hearing of my parents' attempts to locate a suitable new flat, and to find buyers for their own. Their search took them to Bandra, a part of the city we used to once take outings to, two or three times a month, but which was now proliferating with 'developments' and new buildings that would be more affordable than anything in the southern parts of the city. St Cyril Road was one of the lanes off Turner Road where I remembered seeing a building coming up, still incomplete, on one of our tours around that area, and others, before I went to England. I had recalled liking it then, though it was still an unfinished series of rooms, with labourers moving in and out of them; liking it for the lane it was situated in and into whose life it was sketchily emerging. But my memory of it is as fragmentary, as ridden with gaps, as the structure itself. Besides, we had been told then by an estate agent that its rate per square foot made the flats slightly beyond our reach.

Suddenly, one day, I heard the flat in Worli had been sold and the one in St Cyril Road purchased, the exchange of money and the simultaneous relinquishing and exchange of properties taking place almost overnight. The Worli flat had been sold to a family called Ambo for thirteen lakhs; the new flat in the Eden of St Cyril Road had been bought for fifteen. The difference had been made up with my mother going to Calcutta to sell some of her gold jewellery. The remaining one lakh my father had borrowed from the HDFC. The jewellery had been sold for two reasons; although my father had been a finance director, then a managing director, of a multinational company, his income had had a huge tax imposed upon it – 75 per cent – and a stringent ceiling – it could rise no higher than 10,000 rupees – under Indira Gandhi, and the ceiling and the tax would substantially remain unchanged until a long time later, when the country entered (too late for my father) the era of 'liberalisation'. The other reason, of course, was that my parents came from East Bengal; they had no ancestral property, no hinterland, no inheritance, to fall back on; they had started their lives from scratch after 1947.

'Yes, it's happened,' said my mother on the phone to me, recounting how Mr Ambo, in the end, had paid my father 10,000 less than thirteen lakhs, how he'd been distressed because his own father was unwell, and pleaded that my father accept the twelve lakh 90,000, which he did. I have never seen Mr Ambo and never will, but his name is enough for me to feel the proximity of his presence; I see him, and his family, enter the new flat, with the blurred view of the sea from the balcony, close the door behind them, and then I don't have to think about them again. There had been a moment of panic, my mother told me – it was all interesting in hindsight – when my parents realised they had given Mr Ambo the key to the flat before they had taken the money from him. She was now speaking to me from the flat in Bandra, where she would be ensconced for a few years to come.

I arrived at the flat, I think, in the summer of 1984. It was after midnight; most flights from London to Bombay landed in the small hours of the morning. The door was opened by a man I didn't recognise; a corridor led to the phone at the end, and on the left were three rooms – the sitting room; my room; and my parents'. The kitchen and the guest room, which had been converted into the dining room, were on my right. At 2 a.m., awake with what felt like a heightened caffeine-induced awareness, but what was the deceitful alertness of jet lag, I couldn't have taken in these details. I sat in my parents' room, excited, surrounded by bags and silence, and talked in a way it is possible to at such moments, when the rest of the world is asleep. Later, I went to my room to lie down, like an interloper who's been put in his place.

I should have slept the next morning till ten, but was woken up by half past six or seven. There was an eerie chorus about me, disorienting and frightening, urgent enough not to be confused with the final moments of a nightmare; it was birdcall. For more than fifteen years I'd lived in tall buildings; I had forgotten how violent this sound could be, how it could drown out everything else.

It's hard to let go of your old life. But that is what I did when I moved here. Gone, those four-bedroom apartments and that sea view, the perspective of the Marine Drive – those precipitous visions, first from the twelfth storey on Malabar Hill, then the twenty-fifth storey on Cuffe Parade. But those flats were on lease; they were company flats, they did not belong to my father. And yet the years there, and the memories I inherited from them, did belong to me.

Now I was here. While this lane was called St Cyril Road, all the lanes that ran parallel to it were also named after saints, most of them as obscure as St Cyril. Mentioned together, those names became a fading, if absurd, hallelujah to a way of life.

A balcony joined my room to my parents'; opposite, there was a three-storey house, and, on eye level, a flat in which an ageing Parsi couple lived. This couple absorbed me at certain moments; the way they sat face to face with each other, at either end of the veranda, the old man never actually looking at his wife, but at something else, while the wife regarded him sullenly through her spectacles. She had a loud voice, and reprimanded him with it; I could hear her angry Gujarati words. He never answered back, but kept staring at that mysterious object.

This couple became part of my new life, my new sensibility; for them I exchanged the view of the Arabian Sea, of Bombay's mercantile and civic power – the land that inexorably advances upon the sea, so that there are apartment and office buildings, even auditoriums and theatres, today, where there had been only water yesterday; the thirty-five-storey Oberoi Towers and the Air India building, with its logo shining at the top; the pale dome of the old Taj in the midst of other buildings.

I must have been lonely in that old life; sometimes I was conscious of that loneliness, and sometimes I mistook it for a sort of unease. But I can find no other explanation for my welcoming of St Cyril Road into my life. It wasn't that the flat was the first one my father properly owned in Bombay. It was the discovery of a community – made up, predominantly, of Goan Christians – and of the lanes and by-lanes in which that community existed. What I had missed in my childhood, without knowing it, was community; we had camped – our nuclear family; my father, my mother, and myself – in company apartments; I had surveyed, from windows and balconies, the expanse of the city, and, through binoculars, the windows and balconies of other multi-storey buildings. I had not suspected the need, in myself, for physical contact, the need to be close to ground level, within earshot of my surroundings, to be taken out of myself, randomly, into the lives of others.

Like a shadow moving first in one direction, then another, itinerants came and went. The lane changed with seasons; there was a gulmohur tree facing our veranda, which shed its blossoms during the monsoons, and, by summer, was again orange with flowers. I found these little changes marvellous.

The birds that had woken me the first morning after my arrival became a part of our daytime lives, as we did theirs; their excrement hardened into green scabs, every day, on the balcony's banister. In the mornings, they fought upon the air conditioners, and I could hear their claws scraping against metal. Each morning, their twenty-minute bout started afresh. Opening the bathroom window, I could see the air conditioner protruding outward; occasionally, a pigeon or crow set up home on it, and would fight off intruders. If I saw a pigeon alighting on the veranda with a twig in its beak, I knew a home was in the making somewhere, either on the branches of the jackfruit tree that stood next to our balcony with a kind of awareness, or on one of the air conditioners, our compulsory accomplices in middle-class comfort.

Our building itself stood in the place of a cottage that had once belonged to a Christian family. I had heard the family lived in the ground-floor apartment, but I had never seen them. Perhaps they rented the flat out, or had paying guests; because employees of Air India came and went from it at odd times of the day, including a beautiful girl, infrequently glimpsed from my veranda, who was supposed to be an air hostess. And there were other cottages and houses in the lane, I'd noticed, that seemed to be going in the direction that the house that had once stood here had gone, towards disappearance and non-existence.

This was the place I returned to in the summer, and for the short break in the winter. The rest of the year I lived in England. It was my ambition to be a poet; the ambition had taken me to England.

I was doing nothing much in London; I hardly had any friends. I hardly attended lectures at University College. But I was writing poems; these poems were like little closed rooms, like the rooms I lived in in England; they were closed to everything but literary influence. No door or window was left open to let in the real world, or to admit the self that lived in that world; in the closed room of the poem, I tried on yet another literary voice, or a style I had recently found interesting. I speak of this in architectural terms because that is what would strike me most when I returned to Bombay, to St Cyril Road, for my holidays: the continual proximity of the outside world; a window left open; the way the outside – manifested as noise, as light – both withheld itself and became a part of the interior life.

I wrote a poem in 1985, while living in the studio apartment on Warren Street. It was called 'St Cyril Road, Bombay', and I must have written it between avoiding lectures, looking despondently out of the window, and eating lunch at half past three. From where, at the time, St Cyril Road came back to me, I don't know; here, though, is the poem.

Every city has its minority, with its ironical, tiny village
fortressed against the barbarians, the giant ransacks and the pillage
of the larger faith. In England, for instance, the 'Asians' cling to their
    ways
as they never do in their own land. On the other hand, the
    Englishman strays
from his time-worn English beliefs. Go to an 'Asian' street
in London, and you will find a ritual of life that refuses to compete
with the unschooled world outside. In Bombay, it's the Christian
    minority that clings
like ivy to its own branches of faith. The Christian boy with the
    guitar sings
more sincerely than the Hindu boy. And in St Cyril Road, you're
    familiar
with cottages hung with flora, and fainting, drooping bougainvillaea,
where the noon is a charged battery, and evening's a visionary gloom
in which insects make secret noises, and men inside their single
    rooms
sing quaint Portuguese love songs – here you forget, at last, to
    remember
that the rest of Bombay has drifted away, truant, and dismembered
from the old Bombay. There, rootless, garish, and widely
    cosmopolitan,
where every executive is an executive, and every other man a Caliban
in two toned shoes, and each building a brooding tyrant that towers
over streets ogling with fat lights . . . Give me the bougainvillaea
    flowers
and a room where I can hear birds arguing. I won't live in a pillar of
    stone,

as ants and spiders live in the cracks of walls, searching for food
    alone
in the sun-forgotten darkness. That's why I've come to St Cyril Road
to lose myself among the Christians, and feel Bombay like a huge
    load
off my long suffering chest. Woken up at six o' clock in the morning,
by half-wit birds who are excited in the knowledge that day is
    dawning
on the sleeping lane – that's what I want. The new day enters my
    head
like a new fragrance. I rise, dignified, like Lazarus from the dead.

'I like the parody of Yeats,' said a friend after reading it. 'Yeats?' I said disbelievingly; I hadn't been thinking of Yeats. 'Yes, silly,' she said, smiling, and pointed out my own lines to me: 'where the noon is a charged battery, and evening's a visionary gloom/ in which insects make secret noises, and men inside their single rooms/ sing quaint Portuguese love songs . . .' I saw now that, unknowingly, I'd tried to transform St Cyril Road into Innisfree; to trace a similar journey of desire. 'There midnight's all a glimmer, and noon a purple glow/ And evening full of the linnet's wings,' Yeats had said. I replaced the linnet's wings with the nocturnal sound of crickets I'd heard each day after sunset.

The view from the room I lived in on Warren Street was very different from St Cyril Road. There was a restaurant opposite, Tandoor Mahal; it was one of the three or four Indian restaurants, all of which seemed fairly successful, English people hunched inside them mornings and afternoons, except this one. It looked like the family of the man who owned it – a balding Sylheti Muslim in a suit with a round face and compassionate eyes – were in and out of the restaurant all day; but almost no one else. I can remember seeing the two daughters, who would have been in their early teens, and the energetic little boy, their younger brother, many, many times, but never a single customer.

I was not quite sure if this was England, or somewhere else; I was never sure how to characterise or categorise this place. It certainly did not approximate any idea of England I previously might have had. Next to the restaurant was another three-storey house, like the one I lived in, in whose attic lived a tall Englishman who I presumed was a painter. I thought this because he often went about carrying large canvases. A friend came to see him frequently; a shorter stockier man who had moustaches, whom I used to call 'Lal' because he resembled a man of the same name who used to be a director in the company my father had retired from. There was a graceful bonhomie in their meetings, which mainly took place on the pavement before the black door to the house, near a parking meter, and it was always interesting to note, in passing, the angularity of the taller man juxtaposed with, and almost reaching towards, the settled centre of gravity of the stockier companion. The tall man seemed in danger of being blown away by a wind. Lal, the stocky man, sometimes had a dog with him. There was a strange loneliness, or aloneness, about them; they seemed impervious to the passers-by making their way towards the Warren Street tube on the right.

What was I doing here? It was a question I often asked myself. I had come to England to become, eventually, a famous poet. The ambition left me lonely. I hardly went to college or attended lectures. Instead, I sleepwalked through that area around Fitzroy Square, Grafton Street and Tottenham Court Road, stepping in and out of newsagents', surreptitiously visiting grocers' and cornershops, while I waited to become famous. Knowing my attachment to Larkin, my mother bought me his new book of selected prose, *Required Writing*, for my twenty-second birthday. There were two interviews in it. Larkin was a reluctant interviewee; he was always politely admonishing the interviewer for his stupidity. When asked by Robert Phillips of the *Paris Review*, 'Was it your intention, then, to be a novelist only?' because of Larkin's two early novels, Larkin said, in his unfriendly but interesting way, 'I wanted to "be a novelist" in a way I never wanted to "be a poet", yes,' as if 'wanting to be' was a necessary but misleading part of a writer's life. As for myself, I wanted to 'be' a poet; I had never thought of 'being' a novelist. It was towards this end that I'd come to England; and sent out my poems to the National Poetry Competition, as advertised in the *Poetry Review*, a pound the entry fee for each poem submitted.

Those first years of living in London made me acutely aware of light, and space, and weather, and how they influence ways of life. And it was partly this, I suppose, that made me see St Cyril Road in a new way, that made me, in Warren Street, write the poem, and allowed, for the first time, a 'real' place, a real locality, to enter my writing. At that time, I didn't know anything unusual had happened. I was pleased enough with the poem; but I was pleased with almost every poem I wrote. Later, that poem would become my first publication in England; it would appear in the *London Review of Books*, its long lines clustered at the bottom of a page, in 1987.

By the time the poem was published, we were already thinking of leaving of St Cyril Road. The flat that had been bought with such excitement three years ago – the small three-bedroom flat with its perspective of the lane – was up for sale. On long walks down St Cyril and St Leo roads, my parents had discussed the matter with me, and we had come to the same conclusion. For a variety of reasons, my father was under financial pressure; and the debt of one lakh rupees from HDFC had still not been quite resolved. We would move to Calcutta; my father had bought a flat there in a government-erected block in 1975. My father, at that point of time, could not afford, we decided, the luxury of two flats in two cities; and his plan, anyway, had always been to retire to Calcutta.

I didn't mind the idea of moving to Calcutta; I encouraged it. All my life, I'd been vociferous about my dislike of, my impatience with, Bombay, and the fact that Calcutta was my spiritual home. And the money, once the flat was sold, would be a comfortable investment for my father. In the meanwhile, I continued to explore the area, and

the explorations continued to result in poems. In 1986, when I took
a year's break between graduating from University College, London,
and leaving for Oxford, I wrote 'The Bandra Medical Store':

When I first moved here, I had no idea whatsoever
where the Bandra Medical Store really was. But someone

in the house was ill. So I ventured out, let my legs
meander to a chosen path, articulate their own distances.

I guess my going out for medicine, even the illness, were just
excuses for me to make that uninsisting journey

to a place I hadn't seen. Two roads followed each other
like long absences. The air smelled of something not there. Branches

purled and knitted shadows. There was a field, with a little landslide
of rubble, and a little craggy outline of stone.

I drifted past heliotropic rubbish heaps, elderly
white houses. An aircraft hummed overhead. And did

the houses look like rows of slender barley from the pilot's
window, row pursuing row, held in a milieu of

whiteness, unswayed by a clean, flowing wind?
Then the 'plane donned a thick cloud. All it left was a cargo

of loaded silence. I supposed that I must be lost.
It grew evening. Trees fluttered in the dusk sough

like winged, palaeolithic moths eddying towards
the closing eye of the sun. I asked someone, 'Do you know

where the Bandra Medical Store is?' The directions
he gave me were motionless gestures scrawled on

a darkening fresco. I stepped forward, intentionally
trampled a crisp leaf, which then made the only

intelligible comment of the evening. But I took care
not to squash a warrior ant that scuttled before me.

He was so dignified, so black. Had I been smaller, I'd have
ridden him back home, or off into the sunset.

I sent this and four other poems to Alan Ross, and he wrote back
to me in two weeks, a note with a few scribbled comments on the
poems, saying he would keep it and another one for publication. The
poems would appear in the *London Magazine* during my first term
in Oxford, in October 1987. But the lane itself was changing; the
cottages were being torn down; six- or seven-storey buildings, like the
one we lived in, were coming up in their place.

At around this time, when I was writing these poems, I also began
to write a novel. I went to one of the small Gujarati-run shops on
Turner Road and bought a lined notebook, such as shopkeepers
and accountants use; its hardboard cover bore the legend 'Jagruti
Register'. I wrote a few lines every day; and, on certain days, I wrote
nothing at all. I wrote without anxiety, and tried to allow the petit-
bourgeois life of my uncle's family in Calcutta into the excitement of
the written word. I tried to solve, as I wrote, the paradox of why this
life, so different from the world I'd grown up in on Malabar Hill and
in Cuffe Parade, had been a joy to me; the same paradox that made
the location of my father's post-retirement life a joy.

Film stars came to see the flat (who but film stars, businessmen
and companies can afford Bombay real-estate prices?). I was told that
Naseeruddin Shah was looking to move from his two-bedroom flat
to a three-bedroom one; and, one morning, I saw him in our sitting

room with his mother-in-law, Dina Pathak, who, right away, seemed to know her own mind, and his. I struggled not to look too hard at him, because he had recently won a prize at an international festival. He was shy, if stocky and muscular after his workouts for *Jalwa*, and sent a momentary smile in my direction. Then he went about peeping into our rooms.

A property takes time to sell in Bombay, for the same reason it takes time to buy one. And so the final transaction – and my parents' departure to Calcutta, and the flat itself – remained in abeyance. 'White' money was scarce; my father wanted payment in 'white'. Helen came to see the flat, Helen, who had danced for us so many times, settled into matrimony and middle age, wearing a salwar kameez. She was an utterly charming woman; she had deliberately exchanged her sensual aura for an air of ordinariness; and yet she had a style of interaction that was seductive in its openness and warmth. She loved the flat and the lane; she had the thrilled air of a convert that I'd had when I first moved here. 'I *must* have the flat, Mr Chaudhuri,' she said to my father irresistibly, and I could almost visualise her living in it.

By the time I returned home from Oxford in the summer of 1988, I had a first draft. An extract – chapter seven in the finished book – had appeared in the *London Review of Books*; publishers had written to me, enquiring after the novel. As potential buyers wandered through the flat, I found, going through the pages of the notebook, that, to my alarm, I would have to excise the first two or three chapters, for which, now, there seemed no need, and rewrite the beginning and several other chapters. As I began to cut out and jettison what I had once thought were necessary links and coordinates, I noticed a form taking shape, a form that absorbed and pleased me. And then I fell ill, probably with the strain: my condition was diagnosed as hepatitis. I couldn't fathom how I'd got it; I never drank anything but boiled water.

Nine days in the Special Wing of Nanavati Hospital, on the drip; then back to the flat in St Cyril Road. I missed Michaelmas term in the new academic year in Oxford. 'Oh, hepatitis!' said the hushed voice of the accommodation officer at Holywell Manor, wondering if she might catch it from a long-distance call. 'Yes, *do* take your time.'

That Christmas, as in my poem, the young men came to the lane, guitar in hand, singing carols. I had finished revising the novel, after a horrible, protracted period, and then typed it on my father's Olympia typewriter. The typescript, after my excisions, came to eighty-seven pages. I sent this to the agent who'd been in touch with me after the publication of the extract. At first, she was worried by the size of the manuscript; later, she said she'd send it to William Heinemann. Recovered from hepatitis, back to health and normalcy and the routine disappointments they bring, I returned to England in January 1989, after it had lately snowed around London. I got a phone call which informed me that William Heinemann were 'excited' about the manuscript. I was still to become familiar with the language publishers use.

The flat was sold – not to Helen, but to a Punjabi businessman called Chandok. He could pay the entire amount in 'white'. Two months ago, when I went to Bombay, I walked into the building on St Cyril Road and saw that Chandok's name is still there on the nameplate. I have no idea what this small investigation was meant to confirm.

My agent, after a considerable silence, called me one evening to say, 'Amit, I have two pieces of bad news for you. The first is that Heinemann have turned down your book.' 'What's the other one?' I asked. 'I've stopped being an agent.' She was getting married.

I then went to another agent, Imogen Parker, who too had expressed enthusiasm for my work. She was one of the most determined and plainspeaking and intelligent people I met in the business; like Helen, she was a survivor, and had an odd, sparkling beauty. 'Don't worry,' she told me (she would herself marry and leave the agency in a couple of years), 'your book will be published.'

Listening

I did my best to escape music as a child, running very fast whenever my mother tried to teach me the Tagore songs she sang so beautifully, but my genes ensured that music would eventually return to me, or I to it. On the other hand, the desire to be a writer, or someone who dealt with words, came early; from wanting be the commander of an army, I graduated quite seamlessly towards the ambition of being a famous poet and sage by the time I was eight or nine. Still, growing up in the microcosm of a nuclear family located in a twelfth-storey apartment in Bombay, I was surrounded by music. There was my mother, of course, possessed of an extraordinary voice that never wavered from perfect pitch. There were other kinds of music as well: the songs of the Raj Kapoor film *Sangam*, which I had by heart when I was three, then duly forgot – as you might forget a language you're fluent in in early childhood. Both my parents were admirers of Julie Andrews, and brought the recording of the West End production of *My Fair Lady* back to India when they returned from London in 1961.

My father bought a hi-fi in 1970, and received two complimentary records in the process. I made a sudden leap from Julie Andrews towards the Bee Gees' delectable early pop sound, and The Who's mixture of lovely melodies and discomfiting lyrics. That year, on a Polydor compilation, I heard the transfixing opening riff of 'Hey Joe', as well as James Last's brassy version of 'Never on a Sunday'. This first wave of listening was eclectic, if not downright erratic.

For an Indian apartment, my home was, by Indian standards, relatively silent – given the fact that we were on the twelfth floor. This must have been an early, and subterranean, cause of unhappiness. My memory of growing up in Bombay is vaguely, but firmly, unhappy: I always presumed this had to do with the loneliness of being an only child, and the stratospheric nature of my father's corporate life. But I now see I've felt unhappy whenever I've been surrounded by silence – as I was as an undergraduate in London – and been content when sound is at hand: such as in my uncle's two-storey house in Calcutta, and in the second-storey flat in Bandra in suburban Bombay to which my parents moved after my father retired. Living closer to ground level makes it easier, in a country with a warm climate, to listen and be continually distracted.

My intolerance of silence is something I became more aware of after moving to England as an undergraduate in 1983. Sitting in a studio flat in Warren Street with windows shut, I began to recall how sound would ramify around my uncle's house in south Calcutta, always suggesting an elsewhere; around this time, I became aware that the soundtracks in Satyajit Ray's and Jean Renoir's films were as intent on capturing this elsewhere as they were in attending to the main story. This dimension of the world – its constantly shuffling, coughing, whistling, semi-visible presence – would go into my first novel, *A Strange and Sublime Address*, set in the Calcutta I visited as a boy. When I'm asked what continuities exist between my practice as a writer and as a musician, I'm at a loss; except, now, I can begin to acknowledge that the act of listening is a thread running through both.

Meanwhile, by the time I reached London, my musical propensities had taken an unexpected turn: I'd discovered the beauty and difficulty of Indian classical vocal music, and begun an arduous regime of training. At the same time, I stringently shut out 1980s popular Western music; this state of affairs continued till I returned to India in 1999. Scott Fitzgerald, wryly analysing the effects of his decades-long alcoholism on his career, said it was as if he'd been asleep (Van Winkle like) for twenty years. I, in the sixteen years I lived in England, eventually became a published writer and a concert performer in Indian classical music, while behaving as if Western popular music no longer existed. This idiosyncratic mental geography I'd created made it possible, in the early years of the twenty-first century, for my project in experimental music to come into being. It was a project that required disorientation, discontinuity and surprise, and for listening and remembering to suddenly come together. In 1999, on moving to Calcutta, I'd begun to play my old records again. And, listening to a posthumous release of Hendrix playing the blues, I started, for a while, to hear doubly – to hear the Indian raga in the blues scale, and vice versa. This was because both the blues and certain Indian ragas are pentatonic: they have five notes. One morning, as I was practising raga Todi, I had my first experience of what I now call a 'mishearing': I thought I heard the riff to 'Layla' in a handful of notes I'd been singing. A few days later, a recording of the santoor (a Kashmiri stringed classical instrument) being played innocuously in a hotel lobby seemed to embark inexplicably on 'Auld Lang Syne' before returning to raga Bhupali. These peculiar transitions were made possible by the recurrence of the pentatonic in different traditions; they were also enabled by twenty years of, in a sense, aural slumber, and of now beginning to recover, in a new but accidental way, what I'd long ago heard and cast aside.

When I think of how I make my daily journey from writing to music, and back again (which, in a sense, I'm enacting at the moment), I grope for analogies. It's not a question of being able to 'do' various things. I can cite two roughly analogous activities: global travel (which has defined my life for about thirty years); and writing bilingually.

To begin with the first: when I leave India, it is, each time, a great wrench, because I'm essentially casting myself aside – it's a little death. I struggle against it, but, in the country of arrival, I begin to let go, to form new alliances, to learn and see. Echoes and chance concordances direct me: in a street in Geneva or Brussels, I'll see a floor or wall or balcony that I've seen in Calcutta. These resonances complicate my certainties about history; those inert categories, 'East' and 'West', start to disintegrate. Something similar happens in my music. How, in my new album, do Rodrigo's 'Concierto de

Aranjuez', raga Kafi, Leonard Cohen's 'Famous Blue Raincoat' and two Hindi film songs come together in one long piece? It's like the resonances you discover, after years of travel, in a foreign city; when, unexpectedly, the correct comparison comes to you, bringing back to the world a memory you thought was dead.

As for writing in two languages, I think of the Indian poet Arun Kolatkar, who composed two great oeuvres in Marathi and English respectively. 'I keep a pencil sharpened at both ends,' he wrote in his notebook; and the same shrewd insight holds for the artist moving between art forms and genres. Music and writing are different languages, and each offers certain opportunities while foreclosing others; just as you become a slightly changed human being when you switch to French after speaking in English. When something stimulates me these days, when, say, I'm arrested by a sound, I ask myself what its best home might be: a story, an essay, a paragraph, a song? And then, after weighing the question, I take the plunge.

Writing Calcutta

I was in Berlin at the end of 2005 when my agent called and asked me if I'd write a book on Calcutta. It was a work of non-fiction he wanted: Indian non-fiction was going to be the new Indian fiction. I declined, saying, 'I'd rather write about Berlin'; but I saw where he was coming from. Suketu Mehta's compendious narrative of Bombay low life, *Maximum City*, had been a critical and commercial success. It wouldn't have taken much to guess that it, and a country transformed by fifteen years of economic deregulation, would unleash a stream of books on what, in journalistic shorthand, is called the 'new India'. I'd written three novels which had Calcutta as their setting, and my agent probably saw me as the ideal candidate for producing a non-fiction work on the city. The mid-2000s was a time of complete immersion in the present – a characteristic of free-market capitalism – so that things that had happened fifteen, ten, or even five years ago felt remote, and the frequent 'all-time best' lists in newspapers covered a span of, at most, twenty years. From the perspective of this compressed view of eternity, my novels about Calcutta might almost have inhabited another era. Perhaps it was time to write a new book about the city.

I instinctively knew that I couldn't, and didn't want to, do a *Maximum City* with Calcutta. Mehta's book, which I had reviewed and admired, wasn't just about Bombay; it was a creation myth for a new nation and its unprecedented, amoral provenance. History may not have ended, but the Nehruvian era had, with its 'mixed' economy of socialist development, Five Year Plans, idealistic hypocrisies and circumscribed private enterprise. Dams, the avowed temples of the older, industrialising nation, had given way to new temples where the rich and the aspirational classes could congregate in a kind of celebration, such as international airports (Katherine Boo's recent book, *Behind the Beautiful Forevers*, records the doomed theatre of a slum that festers, hidden, behind Bombay's Chhatrapati Shivaji International Airport).

I, who'd grown up in Bombay, leaving it for Britain in the early 1980s, had barely encountered the city Mehta described during my twenty-one years there – although the rise within it of new buildings, a new rich and underclass, the right-wing Shiv Sena and BJP had become disconcertingly visible by the time of my departure. The Bombay I grew up in – though it had long been India's financial centre – was genteel and tame in comparison. When P.V. Narasimha Rao, the prime minister at the time, officially deregulated the economy in 1991, the city that was most responsive to the event was Bombay. Post-Independence India had stricter, prissier demarcations – between the polite and the profane, the admissible and the inadmissible – than the India energised by the free market. One trivial instance will do: I recall how film stars were tacitly impeded from buying property in haut-bourgeois areas like Bombay's Malabar Hill until the late 1970s, and were forced, instead, to live in plush mansions on the outskirts of the city, in Juhu and Bandra. Deregulation allowed Indian cities to expand outward and gentrify internally, appropriating areas that had earlier been peripheral. Mirroring, and arising from, this sudden jostling of old and new spaces was a new, somewhat bizarre set of juxtapositions, a new kind of neighbourliness, that at once galvanised and troubled the country, bringing together criminals and politicians; the Indian novel in English, the paintings of M.F. Husain, and religious fundamentalism; Bollywood actors, sportspeople and celebrity activists; a smart, Anglophone middle class, fairness creams and female foeticide.

A new universe was at hand, comprising an impatient aspirational class. To write of it, one would probably need to adopt the epic mode, or the expansiveness of the nineteenth-century novel, one of whose themes was the invention of fortunes – albeit of families, rather than of nations and cities. One could partake of this creation myth by writing of Bombay, because it embodied its ambitions so vibrantly, and of New Delhi, which had benefited even more tangibly than Bombay in terms of political power from the new dispensation. Bangalore, too, and even Chennai and smaller cities could be part of the new epic. But not Calcutta, which was out of joint.

I knew this, and it was one of the reasons I said no to my agent. At the time of our conversation, West Bengal, the state of which Calcutta is the capital, had had twenty-eight years of Left Front rule: already a world record for a democratically elected communist government. The Left Front, throughout the 1990s, had made noises about the necessity of attracting investment, even foreign investment, to the state to boost its largely agrarian, badly ailing economy. But Calcutta, and Howrah, its manufacturing suburb, had become well known for lock-outs, strikes and 'sick' companies; and West Bengal for its *bandh* days, or closures, observed as stringently and frequently as religious and national holidays.

In fact, Calcutta had become synonymous with politics, nationalism and trouble in general from the late nineteenth century. For this, it was penalised by the British government; the capital of British India since 1772, it ceased being so in 1911, when the seat of power was transferred to Delhi. The home of Subhas Chandra Bose (a leading light of the Congress Party who had differences with Gandhi and went on to found the ragbag but influential Indian National Army), it was seen to have often embraced a mode of political agitation counter to Gandhian *ahimsa*. After Independence, the city moved increasingly leftward, especially with the emergence in 1967 of a militant, Mao-inspired faction in the Left's ranks called the Naxals (after Naxalbari, the place where the movement originated), who wanted not so much to change the system through electoral means but, in the Bolshevik manner, to overthrow it, and among whose progeny are today's Maoists, creating serious disturbances in far-flung areas and bringing a sense of crisis to upbeat, liberalised India.

Some of the old Naxals survive today, either in anonymity or rehabilitated as respectable academics; but most – including, so we were often told, a number of that generation's most 'brilliant students' – disappeared when that movement was brutally crushed at the end of the 1960s. In 1977, ten years after the Naxals first appeared, the more dominant, less radical group in the left, the Communist Party of India (Marxist), was voted into power in the state with its allies, and so began thirty-four years of Left Front rule, with the party winning seven successive assembly elections, not only because of its splendid achievements, but also because of total political disarray among its opponents.

Left rule in Bengal was, in one sense at least, akin to a colonial presence, in that it thrived, as British rule had, on the splintering of the opposition, and on the political void outside itself. But it had two great achievements. The first took place early, and was almost undone later: Operation Barga, by which land was 'redistributed' from landlords to sharecroppers and peasants in rural Bengal. The second is less advertised than the first, but is undeniable: a largely secular governance, which – though the Left by no means eschewed vote-bank politics – did not foster religious polarisation. This couldn't stop the egress of industry. Three decades under a single party brought a certain kind of stability to Bengal, the kind that became hard to distinguish from a fatal stasis. India changed rapidly, often disturbingly, after 1991; Calcutta remained resistant to globalisation and the new world order, cultivating their irrelevance to itself, and its own to theirs. For this reason, an exemplary epic about Calcutta – in the manner of the new non-fiction work about India – was difficult to write.

As a child, I escaped Bombay and school, during my summer and winter holidays, into Calcutta. It was like a journey towards the pastoral. But it was a strange pastoral, given that it comprised low houses with terraces, Maoist graffiti, acrid smoke from charcoal ovens in December, neon signs on Chowringhee and Park Street, and Naxalite violence in the area where my uncle lived. It wasn't exactly tranquillity and nature, but I was electrified by it, as Wordsworth claimed his younger, unthinking self had been by rocks and trees.

'Deprivation is for me what daffodils were to Wordsworth,' said Philip Larkin once, speaking as a resident of Hull. I could repeat that statement, replacing 'deprivation' with 'Calcutta'. Calcutta was an antithesis of both the suburban and the natural; it constituted, for me, during those visits to my uncle's house, my first, and at the time only, encounter with urban modernity. I was bored by nature and trips with my parents to hill stations; like Martin Amis's John Self in *Money*, who was 'addicted to the twentieth century', I became addicted, in Calcutta, to modernity and its smells, the combination of petrol, *dhuno* (for worship, and to ward off mosquitoes) and urine.

One thing that gave Calcutta the characteristic of a special region, and therefore of the pastoral, was the ubiquity of Bengali, the language spoken there. It was a language without classical antecedents and pedigree (though it had a rich devotional phase in the fifteenth century). It was in the early nineteenth century that it gained the modern provenance by which it is now identified; by the 1860s, it had been made respectable as the principal language of the Bengali *bhadralok*, or 'gentle folk'. This language helped create a particular world in Calcutta. People outside that world in India knew of it by reputation; outside of India, it was hardly known, except, occasionally, through the luminous cinema of Satyajit Ray and through translations of Tagore that teetered between the parodic and the perplexing.

This meant that, when I visited my uncle's house, I encountered a self-sufficient world of secrecy that spoke to me as a child. This was notwithstanding the public figures that this culture had produced in the nineteenth and twentieth centuries, such as Ray and Tagore; Raja Rammohan Roy ('the father of modern India', according to school textbooks, and Asia's 'first secular intellectual', in the words of the historian Chris Bayly); the religious revivalist Swami Vivekananda; the nationalist Bose; and, even later, Ravi Shankar and the economist Amartya Sen. To the sciences it had given two shadowy figures who altered the course of modern science: Jagadish Chandra Bose, who, using the woeful infrastructure of Calcutta University, discovered the radio waves on which not only the early 'wireless' was dependent, but also much of life as we live it now, including our use of mobile phones; and Satyendra Nath Bose, whose 'Bose-Einstein statistics' made the transition to quantum mechanics in physics possible, and through whose work the particle that the physicist Paul Dirac named the boson was discovered. Despite all this, that culture is little known; which is why I have to recite that litany of names, and why it means so little.

This boundedness, this simultaneous obscurity and centrality, gave to what I found in my uncle's house its air of the bucolic, of being at once fantastic and real. Ordinary things – the Bengali letters on the spine of a book; a toy; the cover of a children's annual; a photo album – became extraordinary, because I could sense they were deceptive markers of a great historical change of which I didn't know enough. When I came to write my first novel, *A Strange and Sublime Address*, about a ten-year-old boy from Bombay visiting his uncle's house in Calcutta, it was the quotidian, as a result, that became my subject. At the time – the late 1980s – Calcutta, if it was at all thought about in the larger world, was hardly associated with the quotidian. It was famous primarily for Mother Teresa, and through Dominique Lapierre's book *City of Joy* (about a real-life-inspired Polish priest working in a slum), and the film, starring Patrick Swayze, of the same name. For me, Calcutta's ordinariness was its most compelling feature – the word 'strange' kept recurring in my tale of everyday objects and occurrences – and, to convey this, I had to go against the grain not only of a certain kind of narrative about that city, but also the sort of novel in which character and psychology on the one hand and historical sweep on the other was predominant. *A Strange and Sublime Address* was not going to be a novel of the nation. In fact, to write about Calcutta meant risking not writing a proper novel (in terms of plot and character) at all.

Just as I'd escaped to Calcutta as a boy, to write about it was to escape the unspoken, but increasingly palpable, duty – for the Indian writer in English – to write about India. It was also to remove the experience of the city from the Lapierrean 'joy' with which it had been made one in the media, out of angelic, Christian, Western, even corporate acts of charity. This is not to say that the way I thought of Calcutta was joyless; in fact, my sense of the commonplace aspects of its petit-bourgeois life was fundamentally joyful. In the novel's seventh chapter, Sandeep's uncle, Chhotomama, shaves in the balcony on a Sunday; then goes into the toilet armed with cigarette and newspaper; then has a bath during which he sings two songs – an old popular Bengali song, and another one by Tagore: *'bahe nirantar ananta anandadhara'*, or 'endless and unbroken flows the stream of joy'. Chhotomama's 'joy' (*ananda*), unlike Lapierre's, goes back to Tagore's belief that *ananda* was essential to creation, both aesthetic and divine; a belief not so far from the young James Joyce's that 'the spirit which proceeds out of truth and beauty is the holy spirit of joy'.

Joyce's self-appointed task was to relocate this spirit in the everyday in Dublin; when asked by an interviewer if Molly Bloom's climactic monologue in *Ulysses* was an example of 'stream of consciousness', he reportedly said, 'When I hear the word "stream" . . . what I think of is urine and not the contemporary novel . . . Molly Bloom . . . would never have indulged in anything so refined as a stream of consciousness.' In retrospect, I see it's logical, given that the 'holy' could now only be discovered in the commonplace, that Chhotomama should have been singing of 'the stream of joy' in the bathroom, in neighbourliness to the toilet he'd just departed. These analogies may not be altogether fanciful. There were convergences in the nineteenth century that made both Calcutta and Dublin major cities of modernity, and which metamorphosed humdrum, low aspects of their lives – in rebellion against grand, national histories – with a new kind of comedy and affirmation.

By the time my agent asked me to write about Calcutta, this idiosyncratic, middle-class incarnation of the city had been put to rest for decades, and I too felt I had nothing more to say about it. Calcutta had not only become more inconsequential, it had also been renamed: Kolkata, a city not subterranean, unlike its predecessor, but provincial and with little except a utopian sense of its history, this utopianism reflected in the city's new name. In 1999, I moved back to India from Britain. Having lived all my life in Bombay and Britain, I set about fulfilling my childhood fantasy, of living in Calcutta; but it wasn't the city I'd daydreamed about. It wasn't just that the relentless departure of capital, of its intelligentsia and middle class, had left it hollowed from inside; it was also the way local politics had territorialised it. Policies, neighbourhoods, streets, universities and projects were carved out among the Left Front and its allies; the main political party in the opposition, the Trinamool Congress, led by a charismatic but volatile woman, Mamata Banerjee, appeared to have no long-term purpose but getting the Left Front out. When I'd said to my agent that I wanted to write about Berlin, I wasn't being flippant. Berlin proved that the modern city as I'd come to know it wasn't entirely dead; the way it bore the marks of its history – of the Second World War, of reunification – gave to it, as I'd journeyed daily within it from west to east, something like the atmosphere of concealment and strangeness that Calcutta had had.

In 2007, a friend of mine, the poet Utpal Kumar Basu, gave me a perspective on present-day Calcutta: the city I now lived in but was studiously ignoring. He told me that he sometimes went to the major railway station in the north, Sealdah, where large numbers of commuters (many of them daily wage earners) arrived and departed. He'd get there about 10 p.m., and hover discreetly; his main purpose was to eavesdrop on the homeless who lived around the station. He was particularly drawn to an elderly woman with a vivacious turn of phrase, whom he named *khurima*, or 'aunt'. Once, he heard her reprimand a policeman who was harassing her and her comrades with the words *'Ami bhikeri hote pari, pagal noi'* – 'We may be destitute, but we aren't mad.' It then dawned on Utpal Basu that sanity was a prized, probably a proud, possession for the homeless; to have neither home nor sanity in a city meant you had nothing.

Another time, he overheard the woman say to a man who'd come looking for someone with an 'address' scribbled on a piece of paper, *'Theekana diye ki hobe, soye kothhai seta bolo'* – 'What use is an address, tell me where he goes to sleep.' Again, it occurred to Basu that an important distinction was being made: the homeless have no address except the spot where they sleep at night. Referring to *khurima*, Basu said gravely but simply to me, 'These are our citizens.' Although the city was blithely obliterating its history, the anecdotes made me wonder if there was more going on in it than I admitted. The fact that stories could circulate about, and emanate from, people who lived here now, including those I didn't notice, perhaps pointed to a sort of subtle but vigorous regeneration. And was my move here – to a city I no longer admired – as a sort of reluctant 'citizen' one of these stories too?

As I began to feel, for the first time, that a new book about Calcutta was possible, precipitous political changes were taking place. I wrote an opening paragraph in 2008; by the time I resumed writing in 2009, it was clear that the Left Front government might not be re-elected in the state assembly elections that would take place nationwide in 2011. The signs for the Left Front were worrying; it had emphatically lost seats in the general elections in 2009 to Banerjee's Trinamool Congress. Everyone knew this had to do with its panicky mishandling of industrialisation. Bankrupt, it had tried to hasten investment by creating special economic zones (as the rest of India was doing), peremptorily wresting agricultural land from farmers – land it had once 'redistributed'. The way it invited, in particular, Tata Motors to Bengal to produce the Nano, 'the world's cheapest small car', reserving almost a thousand acres of farmland in the village of Singur for the factory, met with militant opposition from villagers and censure from celebrities. Banerjee and the Trinamool Congress stepped in to mobilise dissent, and Tata's Nano never crystallised in Bengal; Tata moved to the industry-friendly, right-wing Narendra Modi's Gujarat to bring the project to fruition. In Bengal, there was rejoicing that an unjust form of development had been rebutted; but there was also melancholy about the fact that Tata's departure confirmed that investment in the state seemed impossible. Could things get any worse?

It was on the back of this triumphal despair that Banerjee looked poised to sweep into power, promulgating *paribartan*, or 'change'. The story of Calcutta was now the story of being between a rock and a hard place. Did Bengal want to become part of the 'new India', and of a mode of development often based on state violence and inequity? Banerjee's punitive approach to industry made that look uncertain, anyway. Or did it want to continue opting out of globalisation, preferring instead to be in the grip of local politics and power struggles? Living in such a Calcutta for decades had made that alternative untenable. Would Bengal, in 2011, choose more of the Left Front; or would it go for a party without clear policies and no discernible core but its restive, combative leader?

I wrote my book in real time, experiencing the changes as they happened, witnessing the Left's debacle and the Trinamool's victory; but also absorbing the passage of seasons, the way the city responded with festivals, and trees with repeated flowerings; taking in, too, the destruction of old houses as the topography altered; and returning to the question of my presence amid these events and localities. Just as the experience of reading changes your perception of your immediate environment – when you look up from the page there's a small adjustment to be made – so does a period of writing. The book I have written is as much *of* the city as about it, bringing to me a new sort of immersion in where I live.

Art-Delusion

What is it that makes an artist? For a long time, like everyone else, I thought it was a particular gift or ability – and I still believe that ability is a prerequisite. I speak of ability because there are certain activities that seem to require none. Writing is a case in point: there are lots of people who think that knowing a language is enough reason to begin a career as a writer. Acting is another; many of us secretly feel that if we were a bit better looking and less shy, we might well have been actors. Politics, especially; almost anyone, if they're venal enough, and have the right connections, can be a politician. Art, music, sports, mathematics – these, however, are different. You are singled out, either by the kind of physique or brain you have, or by a peculiar, inexplicable aptitude.

Of course, much of twentieth-century avant-garde artistic practice is meant to put that very practice into question; to – whether it always intends to or not – provoke the irate viewer into commenting, 'Even I could do that!' Crucially, this category of viewer didn't then go on to 'do that', as 'that' would have been a waste of time; this viewer comprised the market for the prints of the Old Masters, and contemporary landscape painting. This viewer believed, as we all do in secret, that the vocation of art is hard-earned and hard-won.

A few years ago, I began to entertain fantasies of becoming an artist. These were noticeably different from the fantasies I'd had, since I was a boy, of being a writer. Naipaul speaks about how, for him, the mysterious urge to 'be a writer' preceded, powerfully, having anything to actually write about. He speaks about it almost as a necessary component of the writer's psychology – the attractions of the role, which are then set aside, temporarily, when the writer, at long last, discovers their subject matter. At least as difficult as the education in technique is for the artist and musician is (Naipaul appears to suggest) the discovery of subject matter for the writer – as difficult, but more unpredictable, unforeseeable and enforcing a radical break. To move from wanting to 'be a writer' to addressing your subject matter is to also experience, suddenly, a new awkwardness and fraudulence – Naipaul mentions how he lacked the confidence to put 'writer' under 'occupation' in his passport until he'd published his sixth novel. All these elements in the trajectory have resonances for me.

My lack of confidence in declaring myself an artist has a more straightforward reason: I am not one. And if I've been daydreaming about artistic practice, it's for very different reasons from those pertaining to the writer manqué. 'Being an artist' never held any particular glamour or promise for me, as, at various stages in my life, being an army commander, a chauffeur, a singer-songwriter, a filmmaker or a poet all did. Either the stamp of authority or that of sexual desirability (or both) confers to the dream role its magic; why the artist wasn't one of these multiple assignations I've no idea. It may have been that I suspected that, while I might make an astute commander or a respectable chauffeur, I had simply no talent for art.

In the last three or four years, though, I've begun, infrequently, to be visited by ideas for artistic projects and exhibitions. Are ideas, in themselves, any good; moreover, are they good ideas; and what does one do with them? We all know what happened when Degas, who occasionally wrote verse, but found the writing laborious, told his friend Mallarmé, 'I have so many ideas for poems, but find it hell writing one.' Mallarmé remarked witheringly, 'You don't write poems with ideas, Degas, but with words.' Could an artist turn to me with a similar reprimand: you don't make art with ideas, but with paint? It doesn't seem clear, any more, what an artist works with. While poets and novelists continue to use words, it's plausible that an artist might use words as well, or music, or other media. Ever since the impulse towards representation – even the representation of abstraction –

ceased to predominate in the art world, the artwork has become a sort of essay: a completely hybrid form. Naipaul's account of the writer's discovery of subject matter involved a flight from the apprentice's obsession with the 'literary' – great themes, ideas, forms – towards lived life, experience and, significantly, locality: whether that was a lane in Trinidad, a small town in Texas or a village called Nischindipur in Bengal. But I doubt if finding one's métier as an artist today entails a comparable flight, from the world of 'themes' to that of lived life.

Having said that, many of the art impulses I feel have to do with the city in which I now live for most of the year, Calcutta. Though I didn't grow up here, I've observed it since childhood – but observation and recollection, which have gone into my writings on the city, don't necessarily have much to do with the impulses I'm speaking of. They probably emerge from the shock of living here, up close, the digestion, over eleven years, of that shock, and from momentary reassertions of distance. I live here anonymously, like a migrant, and these impulses, these idle flashes, are directly related to my daily movements and activities.

I'll provide an example. After performing (as a singer in the north Indian classical tradition) at an expatriate Bengali's house in Salt Lake, I was given, in lieu of a fee, a gift. The gift was, in its way, a progeny of the time – a lamp (a faux Tiffany lamp, my wife instructed me) with a 'sensor switch', so that it would light up every time you touched it. What to do with it? Usually, we'd donate it to an unsuspecting but appropriate recipient, but this time I had a sort of mock epiphany, an artistic solution that came seemingly from nowhere: I'd exhibit it. The rubric would be 'Unusable Gifts' – we had many of those, but had simply not thought of collecting them. I could enumerate two other exhibits instantly: a violently purple shawl that was a wedding gift to my wife from a relative, and something she'd instantly known she'd never wear; and a rather beautiful black horn from Assam, given to me on a visit to Guwahati, which made a sound if you blew on it, but which I had no real reason to blow on, and no place to display except a cursory bookshelf. The next exhibit might arrive in the next few days, or in a year, or more. Marcel Duchamp said of his readymades and 'found objects' that you couldn't go looking for them; they couldn't be *anything* – you had to wait for them. The same was true of the project germinating in my head: patience, vigilance and cunning were all essential for it to take shape.

Having mentioned Duchamp, I should recount a rather frivolous idea – a direct spin-off from the Frenchman, maybe a homage. As we know, Duchamp's most famous readymade was a urinal, which he shifted to an exhibition space, turned upside down and named *Fountain*. Here in Calcutta, the public urinals are outnumbered by public urinators, at street corners, whether or not there's cover, standing by a low bush or a wall. At some point, the irritation I felt on my sightings melted into a theme: crucially, but unavoidably, invoking Duchamp, 'Indian Found Objects'. But how to transport a urinator to an art gallery? The simplest solution would be stealthy hand-held handycam (since CCTV on the streets is rare), perhaps inverting the image (though that may be stretching the parallel thin); yet it may well be intriguing to see the arc of piss shoot skyward, rather than down.

I'll share a last idea before returning to my other lives. It has to do with Calcutta's renowned sweet shops, most of them little more than cubbyholes that somehow withstood, fortified by an indelible soot, globalisation and change. I've often been struck by the large, framed picture that invariably hangs on the wall, a portrait in sepia of the founder-owner, whose vision of the future unfolds in his absence, as sweets are selected and rupee notes exchange hands. These figures have the air of the great men of the Bengal Renaissance (which they probably are, without so being acknowledged), the air of the extraordinary possibility of the time, of coming more or less out of nowhere and yet leaving an impress on history. In tone and texture and demeanour, they're often like the pictures you see on the flyleaf of Bengali modern classics, of novelists, playwrights. I've long been planning to take pictures of these pictures – from the walls (for example) of Bhim Nag, Ganguram, K.C. Das and Balaram Mullick

– till I have a whole album of these personages: then put them up in a gallery. Alas, I don't have a good camera, let alone any training in photography. However, I notice that many artists weren't born artists, or even trained to be one. Jeremy Deller, whose work I much admire, confesses he was never any good at art. Increasingly, it all begins to look like a scam.

Four:
The Unheroic

Conquests at Home and Abroad:
The Obelisk and Other Stories
by E.M. Forster

These are extraordinarily funny and revealing and persuasive stories, concerning English manners, propriety and appearances in the colonial world, and their being compromised by sex and low impulses and desires. That, in itself, is not a new theme: Kipling offered a brilliant diagnosis of such a situation as early as 1888, in his brief tale 'A Wayside Comedy', where a few English people who find themselves in an obscure hillside town in India manage to make history and the universe around them seem negligible in comparison to the narrative of their own deceptions and liaisons. Colonisation had a strange effect; it transported people to far-off places; it made the colonial, in his new habitat, seem at once emblematic and larger than life, and it also cocooned him and his family in a false Edenic calm – the calm of the expatriate ruling bourgeoisie – that is one of the most powerful fictions of colonialism. In that Eden (from whose vantage point the rest of the world principally constituted a problem of governance), the colonial and his wife were doomed to fall – from god-like control, Adamic innocence or Eve-like susceptibility – again and again; through some minor but unseemly misdemeanour; through, often, embarrassingly, sex. Kipling describes the nature of that Eden, the microcosm contained within it, and the constant expectancy of danger in a handful of sentences in 'A Wayside Comedy':

There are no amusements, except snipe and tiger shooting
. . . Boulte, the Engineer, Mrs Boulte, and Captain Kurrell . . .
are the English population of Kashima, if we except Major
Vansuythen, who is of no importance whatsoever, and Mrs
Vansuythen, who is the most important of us all . . . There was
deep peace in Kashima till Mrs Vansuythen arrived.

The idyll, the 'deep peace', of the non-Western world, then, was
agitated once and for all not only by the arrival on its shores of those
two great missions, Christianity and Western civilisation, but of sex.
Sex compromised those two missions, with their attendant moralities
and pieties, from within. But it also did other things. It gave to the
colonised world, partly, its misplaced sense of urgency and adventure;
it inverted elements of the landscape, making small seem large,
big appear inconsequential, secret trysts seem more pressing and
absolute than historical pacts. Donne, writing in the heat of English
expansionism, had sensed the comedy of inversions that sex wrought
upon territorialism, where 'one little room' became an 'everywhere',
and sex itself an epoch-marking voyage: 'O . . . my Newfoundland . . .'

These stories by Forster, in many ways, continue and consolidate
that ironical, comic tradition of making sex function, resiliently, as
a narrative device at once expressing, dramatising and undermining
colonisation and conquest; and, through sex, bringing to the colonial
protagonist what neither the administration, a higher authority,
conscience, the colonised, nor travel could: an intimation of crisis and
shame. The stories are full, too, of metaphors of the forms and genres
of interaction that shaped the late nineteenth and early twentieth
centuries, and through which strangers and classes (and, crucially,
cultures) came into sudden contact with one another in a way that
strained decorum and even credulity: excursions, tourist expeditions,
an afternoon spent in a country house, a cruise. All these innocent,
even genteel, activities, are, in this tradition, weighted and fraught
with the possibility of disrepute and scandal; with the possibility,
really, of confronting utter strangeness – the end of civility. In a novel,

they'd take up a chapter or episode (often of great significance), as they did in Forster's; in these stories, we are allowed to dwell a little longer as readers on how much of the episode in question was meant to draw attention to itself as construct and how much pass off as reportage.

In one all-important sense, of course, these stories represent a departure from the classic type that 'A Wayside Comedy' consists of: their subject is not only the subterranean incursion of sex in the colonial enterprise (the stories becoming accounts, as a result, of subversion), but – and this is achieved with a striking candidness and an almost shocking equanimity – of sexuality; they are really studies of, thus, dislocation. The problem of sexuality gives to these stories – perhaps to all of Forster's mature fiction – its modernist disquiet, its obsession with duplication, alterity, otherness, and with echoes. The echo would lead to a profound crisis of revaluation in *A Passage to India*; and the echo is very much present in these stories too, asking the question, interrogating memory, as Adela Quested was cross-examined in the courtroom till she realised she'd got it wrong. So, in 'Dr Woolacott', a young man who is ill imagines he's had a romantic and sexual interlude with the man working outside, until he begins to wonder if the entire episode was a fantasy:

'. . . And when the others came in and opened the cupboard: your muscular and intelligent farm hand, your saviour from Wolverhampton in his Sunday suit – was he there?'

'No, he was not,' the boy sobbed.

'No, he was not,' came an echo, 'but perhaps I am here.'

Again, in 'Arthur Snatchfold', as the first moment of attraction is registered and noted (here, the recipient of attention has temporarily disappeared after a flirtation), so is the intimation of disjunction, the unsettling presence of the echo: 'Where had he gone off to now, he and his voice? . . . What was his name? Was he a local? Sir Richard put these questions to himself as he dressed.' Later, Sir Richard will hear from one of his peers how that young man who worked at the house he was visiting, and with whom he had an encounter mutually relished, was spotted by a policeman and prosecuted, but could not reveal who his anonymous, well-to-do lover was. The terrified Sir Richard nevertheless remembers what his partner in crime was called: 'Arthur Snatchfold. He had only heard the name once, and he would never hear it again.'

In *A Passage to India*, the echo ('ou boum') was India and its infinite intractability; it undermined the name, and, with it, English identity (the sympathetic Mrs Moore's name is translated, by the 'native' crowd chanting outside the courtroom, into another echo: Esmiss Esmoor). Here, in these stories, we see what's arraigning Englishness is the otherness contained within desire; it takes the recognised symbols of that Englishness – names; even monuments, such as an obelisk in a seaside town – and either turns them into syllables, or puts them on hold, in abeyance, and subjects them to deferral: the obelisk is never actually seen; Dr Woolacott, after whom the story is named, is not an actual character in that story. This is akin to a Beckettian sense of the absurd, linked to Forster's delineation of the absurd in a British civilisational mission seen through the prism of a constantly present, but constantly suppressed, sexuality. In the longest story in this collection, 'The Other Boat', the result of the disgrace of homosexuality is the protagonist Lionel March's complete obliteration – not only the physical obliteration of his suicide, but a disintegration of the Englishness that was embodied in his identity: his mother 'never mentioned his name again'.

Unlike Kafka

The shame of being on the wrong side of history: this is what Kazuo Ishiguro's first three novels have been about. It is not a condition that has been written about a great deal in English, because the English language, ever since 'literature' was created and taught, has been on the winning side; and the once-colonised, who have been writing in English for about the past forty years, have always had the moral rightness of their exploitedness, and the riches of their indigenous cultures, to fall back on. But for the story of the personal implications of national shame or guilt in English, one has to turn to a Japanese writer, Ishiguro, and to his mentors, the Japanese film-makers; not the flamboyant Kurosawa, but the equally gifted Ozu.

Ishiguro's first two novels were profoundly cinematic in their technique: the subtle shifts of light – the medium out of which, and into which, cinema is created – were interwoven deeply, in these novels, with their subject matter. Even the title of the first novel, *A Pale View of Hills*, with its juxtaposition of 'pale' and 'view', used light to suggest both a visual and an emotional register. 'It was with interest,' Ishiguro writes towards the beginning of the novel,

> that I listened to those women talking of Sachiko. I can recall quite vividly that afternoon at the tram stop. It was one of the first days of bright sunlight after the rainy season in June, and the soaked surfaces of brick and concrete were drying all around us. We were standing on a railway bridge and on one side of the tracks at the foot of the hill could be seen a cluster of roofs, as if the houses had come tumbling down the slope.

Beyond the houses, a little way off, were our apartment blocks standing like four concrete pillars. I felt a kind of sympathy for Sachiko then, and felt I understood something of that aloofness I had noticed about her when I watched her from afar.

In its working and effect, this is fairly typical of the first two novels: light used to suggest movement where there is none ('as if the houses had come tumbling down the slope'), indicating both the precariousness and preciousness of human habitation in bombed-out Nagasaki. The play of light and shade as the rainy season ends narrates, with great economy, the insecurity and uncertainties of a drifting Japanese urban population in the post-war years. And, in the last sentence, a purely visual sense of distance from a character, brought about as if by the lens of a camera, coincides with an odd but touching intrusion of closeness, kinship and 'sympathy'.

In *An Artist of the Floating World*, Ishiguro's most accomplished and moving book, and one of the best novels published in the 1980s, the cinematic effect is used with even greater sensitivity, leading to the creation of a world of subtle perceptual richness unsurpassed by either Ishiguro's other work or the works of most of his contemporaries. Very near the start of the novel, the narrator Ono describes the house he lives in; it was designed by, and once belonged to, the eminent architect Akira Sugimura. In the following passage, one of his ageing daughters who had sold it to Ono revisits the house after the war; once more, the effect of light lies at the heart of the writing, and is used to convey loss and the passing of time:

The house had received its share of the war damage. Akira Sugimura had built an eastern wing to the house, comprising three large rooms, connected to the main body of the house by a long corridor running down one side of the garden. This corridor was so extravagant in its length that some people have suggested that Sugimura built it – together with the east wing – for his parents, whom he wished to keep at a distance. The corridor was, in any case, one of the most appealing features of the house; in the afternoon, its entire length would be crossed by the lights and shades of the foliage outside, so that one felt one was walking through a garden tunnel. The bulk of the bomb damage had been to this section of the house, and as we surveyed it from the garden I could see Miss Sugimura was close to tears. By this point, I had lost all my earlier sense of irritation with the old woman and I reassured her as best as I could that the damage would be repaired at the first opportunity, and the house would be once more as her father had built it.

In this novel Ishiguro developed to the fullest extent, yet at the same time obliquely and with great economy, what have turned out to be some of the central concerns of his other books: old age and the human capacity to survive disappointment and humiliation. Ono, in *An Artist of the Floating World*, represents the marginalisation of a set of political and cultural values which are no longer believed in by the new generation, and which are, indeed, considered disgraceful after the war. Ono's consciousness thus becomes a series of hauntings of images and ideals from the past; simultaneously, he adopts a compensatory series of rhetorical ploys to erase or escape self-awareness, and salvage whatever dignity might be left to him. Age, then, is associated with self-deception and a circumlocutory evasiveness that is both escapist and curiously life-affirming, in that it helps the old to survive disappointments, to continue at once to fool and rejuvenate themselves in a way that the young possibly could not. Banal politeness, for Ishiguro's characters, becomes a complex form of sympathy, a crutch for existence; at worst, as in *The Unconsoled*, it becomes a substitute for sympathy, an end in itself.

A notable feature of Ishiguro's last two novels is the absence in them of compelling women characters; one of the things that most distinguishes the first two books is their depiction of female responsibility (and male irresponsibility). The woman as mother, wife, daughter, daughter-in-law and breadwinner, the working woman who is still part of the decorousness and formality of the traditional family: all this reminded me of the working woman – the working mother and wife and daughter-in-law – in middle-class India.

In all the elements I have mentioned so far – the use of light, the exploration of old age, national guilt, women in relation to family and to work – Ozu, the maker of the superlative *Tokyo Story* and of its sequel *Autumn Afternoon*, among other films, seems to stand as a precursor behind Ishiguro's first two books. In his films, Ozu, by and large, eschewed the close-up, keeping his figures in the middle distance, in relation to their surroundings – a room, a façade, a balcony. In *Tokyo Story*, an old couple who arrive in the city to visit their sons and daughters and their spouses are made, increasingly, to feel a burden on their children; the only kindness they get is from a daughter-in-law, widowed by the war and working in an office, who, towards the end of the film, seeing her parents-in-law in their particular plight, says something that might be a sort of motto for Ishiguro's work so far: 'Life is disappointing, isn't it?' The film ends with the parents returning to their town, the old woman dying, and the children gathering in the old house for her funeral. Both this film and *Autumn Afternoon*, in which the old man is a widower living with his daughter, are imbued with the sense of a war that has been lost, and of a family and a country in mourning and transition.

With *The Remains of the Day*, the third novel, the predominance of the image and the delicacy of the style that captures its complexity largely disappear; many of the former preoccupations and character-istics remain – old age, guilt, evasiveness of speech – but although, like *The Unconsoled*, this is a love story, the portraits of the female characters do not take us into fresh territory as they subtly did in the first two novels. Moreover, in *The Remains of the Day*, the houses and places which are so marvellous in the second novel – for instance, Ono's house and the Migi hidari bar, with lanterns and deep-fry smells in its interior – have been replaced by Darlington Hall, a Kafkaesque building which is more a metaphor than a real place. The following passage from that novel bears remarkable similarities to the passage from *An Artist of the Floating World*, but one can see in it the germ of the dreamscape that entirely takes over the new novel:

> As for Miss Kenton. I seem to remember the mounting tension of those days having a noticeable effect upon her. I recall, for instance, the occasion around that time I happened to encounter her in the back corridor. The back corridor, which serves as a sort of backbone to the staff's quarters of Darlington Hall, was always a rather cheerless affair due to the lack of daylight penetrating its considerable length. Even on a fine day, the corridor could be so dark that the effect was like walking through a tunnel. On that particular occasion, had I not recognised Miss Kenton's footsteps on the boards as she came towards me, I would have been able to identify her only from her outline.

This is less a description of an old British building, with its resonances of personal memory and history, than a Kafkaesque castle, a place to get lost in; the disturbing but unconscious repetition of 'the back corridor' is typical of the style of the new novel, and exemplifies the problems that both form the subject matter and dog the writing of that book.

Although *The Remains of the Day* is not a particularly cinematic book, since in it the visual and perceptual are replaced by concepts – dignity, self-esteem, embarrassment, shame – it was made, perhaps unsurprisingly, into a very successful film. Today, filmmakers and audiences are less interested in film as an independent visual medium or language, and more in (I use a current television word) 'drama'; what we have witnessed, in the 1980s and 1990s, is the annexation of cinema, in terms of technique and approach, by television, rather than the other way round. In an earlier age of filmmaking, *An Artist of the Floating World* might have seemed promising material to a director: in today's climate, *The Remains of the Day*, with its muffled human drama, is probably the logical choice.

One of the main problems I had with *The Remains of the Day* was its treatment of the protagonist, the butler Stevens, and, by implication, the English class system. The idea on which the novel is based is a highly interesting one: it is the story of someone who served a distinguished man whose political life and sympathies now appear discredited. But the peculiar pathos of the story does not quite fit, for it depends on Stevens's identifying with his occupation – he is a butler – and with his employer in, dare one say, an almost Oriental way, a way more suggestive, in the novel, of the fixed, immemorial and metaphysical structure of caste, rather than the mildly profane, earthy, tragicomic interactions of the class structure, embodied in the relations between servants and employers in, for instance, *La Règle du Jeu*, Henry Green's *Loving*, in Wodehouse's writing or *Upstairs, Downstairs*.

In *The Unconsoled*, the themes of guilt and fear of humiliation persist, as do the means of negotiating them: excessive, insincere flattery, elisions, voluntary or involuntary amnesia. But it is a strangely ahistorical book, and in spite of the social decorum that both the prose and the characters obsessively attempt to maintain, it is a novel without any discernible cultural, social or historical determinants (surely fatal to any novel). Stevens, the butler, has multiplied here into several proto-selves: the almost imperturbable narrator, Ryder, and an array of socially subordinate characters such as the hotel manager, Hoffman, and the porter, Gustav, and his many friends. Butler, hotel manager, porter: all these, in turn, seem to go back to Kafka's doorman, the official subordinate who, though seemingly insignificant, has the hidden power to postpone your access to your destiny, to keep you from entering the room you have been waiting to enter. But Kafka's doorman also represents the face of European bureaucracy, part stunningly ordinary, part terrifying, part human; we're not sure what the strange behaviour of Ishiguro's porter represents.

The story is this: Ryder, a renowned pianist, arrives in an unnamed European town seemingly to give a performance. He puts up at a hotel, but is kept from sleeping for much of the night because of the constant requests, none of which he can refuse, from Hoffman and others. The entire town is suffering, it turns out, from collective shame and low self-esteem, a state of affairs mysteriously connected to the decline in the reputations and abilities of the local musicians. Everyone expects Ryder's arrival and his recital to be a new beginning for the town, a moment of positive reappraisal. For Hoffman, organising the event, it is to be a peak in his life and career; for Hoffman's son, Stephan, the event is to be an occasion to prove to himself, to others, and mainly to his parents, his own talents as a pianist; for Brodsky, once-famous local musician, now famous local drunk, it will be an occasion to forsake drink and conduct the town orchestra, restoring his and the town's reputation, and making himself worthy in the eyes of his beloved, Miss Collins. All these optimistic expectations are, in one way or another, belied.

The main action consists of a complicated but predictable back and forth dance involving Ryder and the other characters, each of whom has at least one absurd but urgent request to make of him. He cannot say no, however, and is thus delayed from honouring his many commitments in the town, most of them urgent but absurd. Ryder, we find out early on, has been to this town before, was once involved with the porter Gustav's daughter, Sophie, and is possibly the father of Sophie's son, Boris. All this he begins to recall or, rather, deduce as the story unravels; indeed, he seems to know little more of his past than we do – his knowledge is our knowledge. Often, he encounters friends from his childhood on his strolls; objects from his past – a family car, a rug – reappear at different points in the town. And however far away he goes on his tours through the town, he finds himself in a building which is just another wing of the hotel.

The echoes of Kafka are many, but eventually superficial. For one thing, the poetic fastidiousness of Kafka's prose confounds binary oppositions of fantasy and reality; so that, even when describing so fantastic a thing as a human being turned into a giant insect, Kafka speaks of the 'dome-like brown belly divided into stiff arched segments on top of which the bed quilt could hardly keep in position', an image that is defamiliarising both in its biological naturalism and in its domestic detail. Kafka points out that Gregor Samsa's legs were now 'pitifully thin compared to the rest of his bulk'. Ishiguro, although surely capable of this minuteness of observation, denies himself the joy of fidelity to detail; the world hardly impinges on his dreamscape, except as generalised settings and landmarks – a lake, a motorway, a theatre. Even music, which is supposed to be a central concern to most characters in the novel, seems marginal to the story.

Another feature of Kafka's writing is its extraordinary social and cultural pitch; its exploration, not just of existential man alone in the universe, but of the life of the middle-class individual, and, especially in *The Trial*, of the European bourgeoisie in the early twentieth century, with its crushing, illogically simultaneous emphasis on material success and old-world dignity and culture. In 'The Metamorphosis', Kafka uses music to define class and social position: Gregor's sister's violin playing betokens the family's desperate pretensions, with the violin a means of distinguishing oneself both from the desolation of the working class and the vulgarity of the nouveau riche. The lodgers' growing boredom as they listen, and the image of Gregor, turned into an insect, hidden behind the door, the only one truly engrossed in the music, evoke, among other things, a profound nostalgia for one's absolutely ordinary, but, to oneself, irreplaceable position in society. Food, too, is part of Kafka's social exploration, and, in his list of what is appealing to Gregor's appetite, Kafka gives us a parody of food as a social code. The list is both playful and painfully attentive, reminding us once more that the real 'metamorphosis' in the story is the transformation of the stable and precious symbols of a middle-class world into something else: 'There were old, half-decayed vegetables; bones from last night's supper covered with a white sauce that had thickened; some raisins and almonds; a piece of cheese that Gregor would have called uneatable two days ago; a dry roll of bread, a buttered roll, and a roll buttered and salted.' It is not that Kafka's allegories *represent* the social: they are in complex ways informed and transformed by the social.

What is un-Kafkaesque about Ishiguro's Kafkaesque novel is its refusal to allow its allegory to be engaged, in any lively way, with the social shape of our age. The themes of guilt and embarrassment have been exhausted in terms of Ishiguro's own oeuvre. The language, as usual, is lucid, but completely lacks the delicacy that Ishiguro is capable of; the words 'in fact' occur on almost every page, sometimes more than once, but are used without variation in emotional register, in contrast to the way that Kelman, for instance, can use different conjugations of the f-word; one of the startling defects of the language of this novel is that, despite its repetitiveness, it fails to use repetition as an inventive artistic strategy. The only positive way of looking at this Kafkaesque work is as a sort of revenge on the increasingly intractable and Kafkaesque world of publishers and the publishing market (previously known as 'readers'): the parallels between Ryder's life as a musician on the international circuit and Ishiguro's as a successful author are obvious. The novel is a failure, and that itself is a brave and old-world thing to be in a time when the idea of artistic success and failure no longer really applies; when literary success, too often, is the product of carefully manipulated kitsch which is then cleverly marketed. Ishiguro's novel is not kitsch, and it defies marketing; it is a failure, and failure usually implies the presence of artistic vision and talent.

There Was Always Another:

Introduction to Shiva Naipaul's Fireflies and The Chip-Chip Gatherers

W riting is not, generally speaking, a family profession. Law, engineering, even dentistry, are known to be taken up by siblings. But writing and the artistic temperament constitute a turn in the family's fortunes, as Mann so vividly showed us in *Buddenbrooks* and *Tonio Kröger*; and this has been true of modernity everywhere, whatever adjective we append to it, European or colonial. Nevertheless, there are anomalous instances of siblings producing serious additions to the realm of letters. Those families must have been quite odd in their intensities, you think; the Brontës come to mind. In Bengal, in the second half of the nineteenth century, there was the Dutt family, who wrote in English, and whose most extraordinary member, Toru Dutt, died when she was twenty-one. In that same age of great change lived, in Calcutta, the Tagore family (itself a precarious breakaway faction from the larger, more orthodox Tagore clan), whose youngest son, Rabindranath, overshadowed the other brilliances among his brothers. In the new world, but frequently travelling out of it, were William and Henry James. To these pairings and constellations must be added V.S. Naipaul and his short-lived but immensely gifted brother Shiva, born in a country remote enough for the Brontës to have daydreamed of.

The name 'Naipaul' today provokes a range of emotion: from adoration and supplication of a very pure, literary kind to liberal and postcolonial distaste. It's one man this emotion is directed towards, and this man, despite writing repeatedly, unforgettably, about his family (especially his father) in his fiction and non-fiction, is viewed *sui generis*, as if he came to the twentieth century and the English language like the infant Moses, solitary and untrammelled. Naipaul (V.S., that is) is partly responsible for the way he's constructed his biography. Given his difficult relationship with his country of origin, Trinidad, and his ambivalence towards his country of cultural ancestry, India, Naipaul has been pursued by, and subtly pursued, erasure, even while giving to us accounts of those places that are life-like and often revelatory. Secondly, Naipaul's contribution to the aura of the 'writer', both in terms of single-mindedness ('He has followed no other profession,' his biographical note famously declared) and as a conceit governing his work, has been unparalleled, and further given him that air of aloneness. But, in reality, there was always another one, who was closer to home.

The younger Naipaul's novels and essays were received enthusiastically, with praise and awards, before his abrupt death – albeit there were only so many Naipauls the world could cope with. Notwithstanding the admiration of readers like Martin Amis, one suspects that Shiva Naipaul was not only misunderstood and underestimated ('misunderestimated', to use a Bushism), but read lazily. Paul Theroux spoke of Shiva unflatteringly, as a sort of paradigmatic black sheep. The journalist Stephen Schiff, already, in 1994, writing in the past tense, said, 'The trouble was that Shiva's view of the world was rather like his brother's and so were his travels (Africa; South America); he never fully emerged from Vidia's shadow.' Speaking for myself, I grew up with at least a couple of misconceptions about the Naipauls: that V.S. Naipaul was famous principally for one book, *An Area of Darkness*, and that his chief preoccupation was finding fault with India; and that there was a younger brother somewhere, whose chief preoccupation was trying to become Naipaul, and failing at the task. For a family to be plagued not only by talent but by mythology must be hard.

This is not to say that Shiva was not in awe, and, in some senses, even oppressed by his older brother. Schiff reports V.S. Naipaul's editor Diana Athill's account of a lunch during which '. . . in Vidia's eyes Shiva couldn't do anything right. He had this picture in his mind that Shiva was going to utterly disgrace himself and the family . . . Vidia loved him but he thought Shiva was going to come to some terrible end.' Naipaul told Schiff that, when Shiva died at the age of forty in 1985, his mourning translated into a kind of physical ailment: '"My body began to burn," he told me. "I was doing a television program and my hands began to erupt. My body was covered with an eczema – the eczema of grief."'

The 'intimidating burden of expectation', as Shiva Naipaul calls it in his great essay, 'Beyond the Dragon's Mouth', was created early. To succeed in Trinidad, you had to – besides being intelligent and competitive – get out of Trinidad. To succeed at being successful, you had to win one of four 'Island Scholarships', the probable outcome of a punishing regime of studies, the 'distant goal of all this torment'. There was 'no higher reward, no greater accolade than these': England awaited at the other end; possibly Oxbridge. There were more immediate incentives: 'Island Scholarship winners were . . . the elected, the anointed. Their photographs appeared on the front page of the local newspaper; they were feted; girls of dubious but ambitious intent offered assignations amid the sombre glades of the Botanical Gardens.' Shiva Naipaul's family's reputation for intellectual achievement had, for him, a watchful, Big Brother-like quality: 'At Queen's Royal College – the secondary school I attended – the names of the winners were inscribed in black letters along the walls of the Assembly Hall . . . The name of an uncle of mine was there; so, even more intimately, was the name of my elder brother.' In the event, the younger Naipaul won the scholarship, though, characteristically, he managed to pull this feat off with the air of one who's missed his target, his name remaining outside that Assembly Hall pantheon: '. . . for, though I did win an Island Scholarship, I did it at another school which, regrettably, did not celebrate its heroes in the same way'. No wonder, given the striving for excellence to no clear end except independence, given the ghosts of former selves swiftly put to rest in such a childhood and youth, Shiva Naipaul had a nervous breakdown in Oxford, just as his older brother once had had. On 'a fine summer afternoon, soft and blue and unportentous', in 1966, 'when skirts were extravagantly short', Shiva Naipaul 'suddenly became aware that something peculiar was happening' to him; 'barely able to breathe, I huddled against the wall of Balliol'. English undergraduate life brings to some people their first heartbreak or their first premonition of the future; in Naipaul's case, the trigger was the death of a contemporary from Trinidad, Steve, a 'tolerant, indulgent' Presbyterian who'd come to Oxford on a different scholarship to read Politics, Philosophy and Economics, that celebrated Oxford cocktail of disciplines, and been found dead in his room. 'Even now, nearly twenty years later, I still do not altogether accept it,' he wrote, in this essay collected in a book that came out a year before his fatal heart attack. 'The fact of his death remains unassimilable . . . inadmissible. I know no other fact quite like it . . . His death was like a sermon.'

The end of this long piece signals, as such reflections do, a fresh start: 'On a sunny summer afternoon I turned my back on Oxford . . . My dreams of philosophical wisdom had ended a couple of years before.' He married, and the couple 'found an affordable bed-sitter in Ladbroke Grove' in London; there, he 'bought a ravaged leather topped desk with brass-handled drawers . . . That is the beginning of another kind of story.' This 'beginning' and its aftermath didn't last very long – barely two decades. In this span of time, Shiva Naipaul had to make a case for himself as a novelist, as someone who had, problematically, inherited what his older brother had triumphantly and movingly called his 'early material'. This 'material', though it risked coming to him second-hand, was also Shiva's own; and, when approaching it as he did in his first novel, *Fireflies*, he had to, among other things, pretend his brother's acclaimed 1961 novel, *A House for Mr Biswas*, didn't exist, and produce, out of the same, richly visited terrain, his own masterpiece. V.S. Naipaul often speaks about the act of writing, and of discovering one's own 'material', as not being 'easy'; despite its immaculate formal progression and its beady-eyed assurance, writing *Fireflies* couldn't at all have been easy for Shiva Naipaul. The story covers the same ground that *Biswas* did: a young woman, Baby, from an all-powerful Hindu family, the Khojas, is married off to an outsider, Ram Lutchman, a bus driver of no particular social status. Ram Lutchman, a little man, is a sort of prototype of and antithesis to Biswas, to modernism's 'little man'. For a time, it seems that he'll be the story's protagonist, a character without distinction, generosity or even real ambition, marked more by resentment and fitful preoccupations, without recourse to, then, the air of eccentric imaginative liberation that Biswas and modernism's 'little men' have. Lutchman is simply a little man, without a great deal of either personal or literary history. He has some of Biswas's enthusiasms, which, anyway, both characters share with the figure on whom they were partly modelled, the authors' father, Seepersad Naipaul; gardening, for instance, and, especially, the cultivation of a particular tree on which a great deal of energy and hope is focused. In *Biswas*, in the new house at the end of the story, they 'bought rose trees and planted a garden . . . At the side of the house, in the shade of the breadfruit tree, they had a bed of anthurium lilies', a species of the flower that will grow again in Mr Lutchman's garden. Besides these, in 'the extra space Mr Biswas planted a laburnum tree . . . Its flowers were sweet, and in the still hot evenings their smell filled the house.'

Before he dies, Biswas writes a letter ('It was a letter full of delights') to his son Anand, reporting to him, among other things, the progress of the garden. Mr Lutchman's garden is one of – and the most enduring of – his several excursions and essays into doing something, excursions that always end in a fiasco. It's on a trip to a well-known public garden with his two sons and one-time mistress, the American-educated would-be anthropologist Doreen James, that Mr Lutchman is caught stealing an avocado by the old but sly caretaker, and his transgression overlooked for a price. Both indiscretions – the half-hearted affair with Doreen; the stealing of the exotic fruit – would be unusual in the world of the early V.S. Naipaul, but are symptomatic of Shiva's characters – their semi-socialised, spasmodic restiveness. Although Rousseau's *Confessions* and Stevenson's *Treasure Island* circulate in *Fireflies*, and at least two of the children, Sita and Julian, in *The Chip-Chip Gatherers* appear to subsist on books, Shiva Naipaul's characters have relatively little access to the out of the way, concealed but tumultuous world of cosmopolitan excitement that surreptitiously but palpably nudges Mr Biswas, a world in which both great and obscure literary figures and serious and absurd literary projects grip and inform, comically but transmogrifyingly, people's daydreams – a world of (as Naipaul described R.K. Narayan's busybodies) 'small men, small schemes, big talk, limited means'. In Shiva Naipaul's universe, not only dreams, but daydreams – especially daydreams – are kept firmly in check. This partly happens because of the predictable, almost necessary, cycle of burgeoning and disappointment, hubris and humiliation, that all humans are subject to in Shiva Naipaul's scheme of things. Mr Lutchman returns home and plants the avocado stone; but the tree refuses to grow in a healthy, encouraging way. Then, almost whimsically, it decides to live. There's an anarchy of will in Shiva Naipaul's world which thwarts its characters' imaginations. His protagonists aren't 'small men' who indulge in 'big talk' about 'small schemes'; they're fish who live in brackish water, with little expectation of escape, but vulnerable to a multitude of agitations. A bit more than midway through *Fireflies*, just as the garden appears to be going fairly well, despite a rampant weed accidentally planted in it, Mr Lutchman dies. His life has been a series of abortive episodes that are not quite adventures – his marriage into the Khoja family; his brief, uncomprehending passion for photography; his liaisons with Doreen; the drive into the country during one such liaison, into obscure villages named after places in India (Bengal, Calcutta); the throwing of a disastrous Christmas party; the garden and the avocado tree. All these are undertaken without Biswas's quixotic gusto, but with a smouldering nursing of disaffection (besides stealing the avocado, Mr Lutchman also filches grass and flowers from a park, and a book on photography from the public library), as possible avenues and dance-like movements open to a man with little hope of social mobility. And, when he dies, we realise the true protagonist of the novel isn't Mr Lutchman at all, but his wife.

This decision on Shiva Naipaul's part means many things for *Fireflies*. Baby Lutchman is ingenuous, trusting, even gullible; she's also remarkable at appearing to doggedly move on from her many setbacks, rather than rehearsing, in a discomfited way, consecutive fantasies, as her husband did. By focusing on her, Naipaul delineates a relationship to power different from the one his older brother conceived in *Biswas*, where the eponymous protagonist, despite being equally beholden and resistant to his wife's family, embodies an idiosyncratic, comic sense of liberation. The portrait of Baby Lutchman (who has lived under the shadow of the Khojas and of her husband, been fettered to and then let down by her sons, and even been in thrall to a Scottish fortune-teller) instructs us that there is no real freedom – even from our own delusions. The only person who seems unencumbered by illusions in Shiva Naipaul's first two novels is the narrator; who, absorbed, almost helpless in this dubious lack of encumbrance, attends to the characters in the landscape as if from an infinite but clarifying distance, recording their arc from ritual contentments and unhappinesses to dissolution. V.S. Naipaul has often spoken of how he's been directed by a need for clear-eyed truthfulness, a need that occasionally makes his statements unpalatable; however, we're never quite certain if that compulsion to truth governs his life or his art. With Shiva Naipaul, there is no life; he is not, unlike his brother, a profoundly autobiographical writer, though he borrows constantly from personal memory. What we encounter, in the novels, is not so much memory, or personality, but a free-standing universe. It shares commonalities with both his past and his older brother's fiction; but it is, in the end, undeludedly and unconsolingly itself. Unlike V.S. Naipaul, who is at once haunted and tormented by a sense of completeness deriving from his lost Hindu, historical past, Shiva Naipaul has no real conviction in authenticity or wholeness; it's almost out of this state of negation that he creates his variously populated novelistic world. The world is what it is, says one of V.S. Naipaul's narrators; this is far more true of Shiva Naipaul's fiction than it is of his brother's. V.S. Naipaul *will* succumb to enchantment; but not so Shiva. This reining in, this holding in check, might be the outcome of temperament; but it is also a response to a sense of belatedness. Shiva's determination to be unillusioned and truthful is inextricable from his determination not to be V.S. Naipaul.

This doesn't mean these two novels aren't enthralling; they are. Shiva Naipaul's work is animated by a mad, destructive comedy, which is near-perfectly orchestrated by formal mastery. Here, for example, is the opening of an episode in *Fireflies*, where the sisters and relations of the clan have gathered at the Khojas' house for a *cattha*, or an annual religious celebration:

> No Khoja function was ever considered complete without a beating. Any infringement of the rules (they could be invented on the spur of the moment) could be made the occasion for one of these entertainments, and children who were rarely beaten at home would suddenly find themselves liable. The choice of the victim was, in the normal run of things, capricious. At such times the sisters became unpredictable forces and, a beating once administered, its influence percolated through the clan. Several more victims were hastily assembled, although none could surpass the grandeur of that first beating.

This mixture of random justice and predestination gives to Naipaul's fiction – in lieu of straightforward linearity – a tantalising, slightly alarming, circular musicality, a kind of pass-the-parcel sequence of shifting the weight from one person, one centre, to another, while, all the time, you're listening intently to the music and wondering where it will stop. No one is free of this musical pattern of reward and punishment, self-satisfaction and grief, not even Govind Khoja, or, in *The Chip-Chip Gatherers*, Egbert Ramsaran, the phlegmatic patriarch. Naipaul's themes are fate, dissolution, bad luck; but he is also concerned with, beyond the story, the music – that is, a span of time, constituting a narrative or a life, comprising pauses in which the sword falls repeatedly, and in which nothing much is achieved. As a result, the matter of fate and destiny is something he deals with in a way that's unique, and which bears no resemblance to the plotted narratives of others who've had similar concerns, like Hardy. Scene after scene, episode after episode in this terrible pass-the-parcel game, Shiva Naipaul reveals himself to be less an adherent of character and story than a devotee of an exquisite, if deeply odd, formal beauty.

Only some of the minor characters are exempt, it would seem, from this fatiguing pattern; and that might be because we don't know enough about them. Those who perform these cameos are drawn delicately, and they possess an almost spirit-like mysteriousness that the main characters never have. One such bit player in *Fireflies* is Sadhu, whom we discover momentarily in the decaying house that a spinster among the Khoja sisters, Indrani, has withdrawn to: 'At some point, she had taken under her wing an ageing Indian peasant, a decrepit old man of about seventy . . . He lived in a tiny cubby-hole (formerly a broom cupboard) on the ground floor. Here, he slept on a collection of rags which Indrani had made up for him as a mattress. On the floor next to his bed were the scattered instruments of his existence.' The only living thing of any kind in either novel that is entirely and transcendentally blameless is the dog that Mrs Lutchman acquires after her husband's death and names Rover. Almost inadvertently, Naipaul turns it into one of modern fiction's most unwittingly engaging creatures; despite the optimistic 'Beware of the Dog' sign that Mrs Lutchman puts up, the narrator informs us that 'Rover's meekness was almost legendary. It was a well-known fact that he only barked at strangers from behind the safety of the closed gate. The moment they entered . . . he either licked joyfully at them or, tucking his tail between his legs, retreated with an ineffectual snarl . . .' When Mrs Lutchman begins to visit the newly formed Hindu League, and return with the customary *prasad*, or sacred offerings, everyone finds it inedible except Rover, who 'fell upon it with a joy that never diminished . . . "You is a real little Hindu," she would say, watching his tail wag as he buried his head in the paper bag. "A real little Hindu." ' This is one of the relatively few allusions Shiva Naipaul permits himself to the land of his ancestors, particularly to the dog Dharma ('faith' or 'calling') in the epic, the *Mahabharata*, who mysteriously follows Yudhishthir as he journeys into the afterlife. By inserting this sly and subterranean reference, Naipaul reminds us that his story of unjust dispensations and abortive plans is, in its way, no less far-reaching in its scope than an epic might be.

Children aren't exempt either. The world of childish desire, dashed hopes, rivalry, manipulation, sex and play is evoked with marvellous precision and intelligence in *The Chip-Chip Gatherers*. But the book – while it can often be hilarious – isn't a comedy or by any means a celebration, as books about beginnings can be. Unlike Joyce's first novel, or Lawrence's *Sons and Lovers*, or *Biswas*, where memory is not only transformative but forgiving, and those books themselves delighted records of encountering the world and words for the first time, Shiva Naipaul's novel is an assessment of how shaky beginnings are, and how they don't contain (as character was supposed to) any inkling of how the future will turn out. The latter, again, seems dependent on fate, luck and inexplicable inner demons: not some fatal flaw, not the gods (since there don't seem to be any, despite shrines, portents and pictures on the wall), but something more intractable. Fate favours some, and doesn't others: but we can't be sure, in these novels, if the protagonist is the favoured one or the one who is being cast aside. It's the democratic but unnatural workings of destiny that complicate our sense, until late into the novels, as to who their central characters are: for a long time, everyone's future seems to hang in the balance. In *Fireflies*, fate gives to Mrs Lutchman the dubious benefit of outliving her husband and watching her sons fail or disappear; and so, almost reluctantly, she becomes the novel's principal figure, carrying, literally, the burden of its narrative. In *The Chip-Chip Gatherers*, it's young Julian Bholai whom fate favours, by gifting him a scholarship to study medicine in England; but, eventually, it's the patriarch and businessman Egbert Ramsaran's son, Wilbert, who's had a more advantageous birth but who's less bright, less handsome, less lucky, whom Shiva Naipaul decides will take the novel to its bleak, unresolved but pulsating conclusion. In this way, Naipaul makes his protagonists mythic, in the sense that they're characters who have been assigned a task which only we, from the outside, realise is at once unheroic and stupendous – the curious and distracting task of living.

In writing his first two novels, Shiva Naipaul stubbornly, and surely unexpectedly, produced two masterpieces. I use that near-meaningless term to mean works that impeccably adhere to the most difficult of literary conventions while also uniquely subverting and exceeding them. This makes reading his fiction an experience for which reading about it can't be any kind of substitute. His feeling for perfection and its passing is very much his own; he should be on our bookshelves for giving us a region of the world and the imagination that very few other writers have with such skill and eloquence, such comic mischief and pain.

A Strange Likeness:
Walter Benjamin

One must begin, as Susan Sontag did in her great essay 'Under the Sign of Saturn', by looking at photographs of the man. This is because, despite our curiosity and ardent interest, we know relatively little about him, and the little we know is too familiar. So we go back to the man himself, to the likeness – as we sometimes study the faces of those whose lives were interrupted early, to see what they can tell us. Sontag notes that Benjamin, in 1927, at the age of thirty-five, is, with his 'high forehead' and 'moustache above a full lower lip', 'youthful, almost handsome'. His head is lowered in this picture, and 'the downward look through his glasses – the soft, daydreamer's gaze of the myopic – seems to float,' believes Sontag, 'off to the lower left of the photograph'. In a picture taken after about ten years, though, Sontag finds 'no trace of youth or handsomeness . . . The look is opaque, or just more inward: he could be thinking . . . or listening . . . There are books behind his head.'

Two things strike a chord in Sontag's summation, although it takes a long time to grasp what they are. The first is the portrait of the intellectual – in this case, Walter Benjamin – as contemporary, and contemporaneousness being a quality (bestowed on him by death) at once tragic and optimistic. Despite losing his 'youth' and 'handsomeness', Benjamin will never grow old, and we are always subliminally aware of this: Benjamin, thus, never forfeits his curious unworldliness – he never settles into success or hardens into conservatism, never disintegrates into infirmity or dependence. This

301

contemporaneousness, achieved through both the texture of the work and the arc of the life, is the essence of the photographs, and gives Benjamin, despite – or because of – his strange life, his anomalous, friend-like status in our imaginations. It makes this, in many ways, difficult and complex writer seem oddly accessible.

This brings me to the second thing that Sontag notices almost inadvertently: the recognisability proffered by the photographs. Sontag doesn't approach the man in them as if he were a stranger; instead, she speaks of him with intimacy. This note of intimacy allows her to draw the portrait within the essay, which elaborates upon a single remark that Benjamin made about himself: 'I came into the world under the sign of Saturn – the star of the slowest revolution, the planet of detours and delays . . .' Benjamin's 'melancholic self-awareness', ironically fortified by his fatalism, draws Sontag out, in this connection, on 'his phantasmagorical, shrewd, subtle relation to cities', on his famous *flânerie*, as a theory and a practice, and even on his 'slowness', his 'blundering', his 'stubbornness':

> Slowness is one characteristic of the melancholic temperament. Blundering is another, from noticing too many possibilities, from not noticing one's lack of practical sense. And stubbornness, from the longing to be superior – on one's own terms.

In this way, Benjamin is turned, by Sontag, into a familial figure, an obscure relative whom one had largely studied from a distance, and, somewhat peremptorily, thought one knew. There might be a reason for this sense of curiosity and recognition; Benjamin might belong to a family that many of us have a relationship to.

When I look at Benjamin's photographs, I realise now that I too experience that sense of recognisability – which Sontag builds her argument around, and uses to her advantage, but does not explain: so subtle and integrated into the personal, into memory, is that register of affinity. When I look at Benjamin's face, for instance, I realise that I don't see, first and foremost, a 'Western' man; I see someone familiar, someone who could also have been a Bengali living at any time between the end of the nineteenth and the middle of the twentieth centuries. Certainly, the 'high forehead' and 'the moustache above the full lower lip', and especially the 'soft daydreamer's gaze of the myopic', the features characterised not by nationality or caste but by introspection, gentility and the privileges of childhood, mark him out as a *bhadralok* – the Bengali word for the indigenous, frequently bespectacled bourgeoisie that emerged (mainly in Calcutta; but also in the small towns of Bengal) in the nineteenth century. The *bhadralok* boy was born to well-being and maternal affection, but well-being is not the only connotation of the word: it could denote anything from well to do to hand to mouth. Almost the only assured possession of the *bhadralok* was, in lieu of property (since the *bhadralok* often also comprised East Bengali migrants settled in Calcutta), what Pierre Bourdieu misleadingly called 'cultural capital', made material, commonly, in a collection of books ('There are books behind his head'). I say 'misleading' of Bourdieu's term because it misses the often self-defeating romance, the fantasy, of *bhadralok* pedagogy, learning and auto-didacticism, circulating as these are in a milieu of subjugation, migration and colonial history; it misses, too, the self-fashioning elitism and extravagance of the imaginary world of the *bhadralok*, often amassing cultural capital in a context of *mofussil* or small-town marginality, while at the same time exceeding that context. No one has formulated better than Benjamin the peculiar poetic resonance of the relationship of 'cultural capital' to marginality and imaginative extravagance. Thus, in the syntax of the following sentence from 'Unpacking My Library', the verb, which denotes performance, action and imagination (in this case, the verb is 'collecting'), is given a greater weight than the noun, which is commonly at one with identity, self and the source (the noun is 'collection'): '. . . my heart is set on giving you a sense of the collector's relationship to his possessions, something of an understanding of collecting rather than of a collection'. Not so much an ideal or an aim, but a form of daydreaming is being anatomised here. Culture, daydreaming and the imagination become interchangeable for both the *bhadralok* and the Jew, for those who are placed just outside of the mainstream of twentieth-century Western history: 'Of all the ways of getting hold of books, the most laudable is deemed to be writing them yourself.'

What is it that makes Benjamin, for me, so familiar? What is it that converges in the face of a certain kind of Bengali and Jewish bourgeois, a face that's now, to all purposes, a relic? It's a current of history that shaped the late nineteenth and the twentieth centuries everywhere, and brought a particular kind of individual – putatively, the 'modern' – into existence. The face of the 'modern' belongs to someone who's secular, probably deracinated, and whose face, in place of the old patrician certainties of class, caste and standing, possesses a new expression of inwardness; the glasses add to the refractedness of the expression. It's a face that inhabits a world in which various cultures are suddenly in contact with one another, and it is a product of that contact; but its inwardness refutes any easy formula – internationalism, miscegenation, hybridity – for how that contact takes place. Both Benjamin's and the *bhadralok*'s face, with their look of introspection and contemporaneity, conceal something: in Benjamin's case, the shame of Jewishness; in the Bengali's, the disgrace of colonial subjugation. This is what makes the secular Bengali, the secular Jew, political: his or her angularity in relationship to the mainstream. But, unlike today's postcolonial or proponent of identity politics, the *bhadralok* is unsure of his own identity: confronting world history has displaced him from his lineage, and his politics extends to a critique of his forebears. Many of us know what it means to occupy such a position, or to emerge from a tradition of individualism, of modernity, inflected by minority; and of minority not being a political certitude, but an experience of ambivalence. This is what makes Benjamin's face, and its pensiveness, recognisable to us; for a large numbers of twentieth-century moderns belong to, or are a progeny of, that peculiar, nomadic family. Even Sontag – a Jew, a lesbian – is shaped by world culture in such a way as to permanently complicate, for her, simple affiliations of race and sexuality, and to force her to constantly reinterpret minority; in the end, for the modern, ambivalence *becomes* identity, and modernity a very specific kind of problem.

What kind of problem is Benjamin pondering in these photographs? I think it's the problem of constructing tradition – his very special approach to which makes him unique in the annals of modernism, as well as integrally a part of it, and also makes him continually resonate for us. That war, capitalism, industrialisation and technology destroyed the unity, the presence, of the European past is a well-worn myth; so too is the consequent myth supporting the modernist aesthetic, of revisiting the past, or only being able to revisit it, through the fragment and the moment; to privilege that inheritance less, in a sense, than the talismanic bits and pieces through which it would henceforth be useful – thus Eliot's simultaneously resigned but assertive admission in *The Waste Land* about shoring fragments against ruins. Benjamin himself explored this nostalgia in 'The Work of Art in the Age of Mechanical Reproduction': 'We can say: what shrinks in an age where the work of art can be reproduced by technological means is its aura.'

This account misses how much of what's inadequately called 'European culture' was being reinterpreted, in this unprecedented way – a way that destroyed, in effect, traditional historical narrative – by those who, for reasons of race or religion or gender, had no 'natural' proprietorial claim to it: that the mode of disjunctiveness, and the problem of constructing a tradition, was not to do with the onset of industrialisation alone, but liminality and disenfranchisement: for, say, Jews, Bengalis and women, both political disenfranchisement and cultural inadmissibility. And so, for example, in Virginia Woolf's *A Room of One's Own*, the act of perusal, the right to access books (especially in Oxbridge), or, in the case of women, the dismemberment of that right, is directly connected, in an arc, to the act of writing, in a tale of humour and frustration that echoes Benjamin's 'Of all the ways of getting hold of books, the most laudable is deemed to be writing them yourself.' Not only writing them, but, as in the case of Woolf and Benjamin and others, abandoning the safety of a certain mode of telling for disjunctiveness as an entry into a tradition one has no natural right to, but in relationship to which one harbours both a deep kinship and a concealed sense of alienation. 'The world changed in 1910,' said Woolf; this is taken to be a reference to many things, including the loosening of sexual mores in Woolf's own family; but it could also include a subterranean awareness that the emergence of the disenfranchised 'other' – the Jew, the female, the non-Western – was going to be increasingly coterminous with the career of the 'modern'; and this is one of the principal reasons why, from the prism of modernity, tradition, in a way at once theatrical and exemplary, becomes so difficult to access or even recognise.

The Romantic stereotype of the artist and the radical – who, in his propensity for wandering and towards exclusion prefigures, in some ways, the *flâneur* – is, with his exacerbated individualism, visibly 'different': 'flashing eyes . . . floating hair'. With the modern, a new and deceptive quality emerges worldwide – normalcy – where difference and even radicalism are formative but implied. The gentleman (literally, the *'bhadralok'*: 'civilised person'), the most characteristic face of normalcy, is the product of a complex contemporary history – to do with secularism, but also to do with colonial history, on both sides of the divide – where all sorts of inadmissible intellectual transactions (between languages, between cultures) are taking place within the domain of normalcy and sameness. It's worth recalling that both capitalism and colonialism generated an administrative class that was crucial to governance but which was disallowed real political power; from this class emerge Kafka's hapless protagonists as well as the doorkeepers who so bewilder and confound them. 'Sameness' and 'normalcy' become the mode, then, through which the governed and subjugated – let's say, Jews and Indians – share in governance through this new class, but are also denied absolute power: the 'world of chancelleries and registries, of stuffy, shabby, gloomy interiors, is Kafka's world', says Benjamin.

This, too, is the world that Macaulay intended when, in 1835, he spoke of conjuring, in India, 'a class of persons, Indian in blood and colour, but English in taste, in opinions, in morals, and in intellect'; an administrative class, predominant within India at first in Bengal, working away in rooms and creating refracted lives of the mind, and reshaping and relocating its difference under the illusion of the normal and the recognisable. The artists and radicals who are the products of this class and history also conceal their marks of departure and oddity, just as those administrative servants do; a safe and conventional (and secular) respectability is the defining air of the Jewish or *bhadralok* intellectual – indeed, of the modern – a respectability interrogated from within through both the workings of the imagination and, significantly, of radical difference. Baudelaire's description of the dandy provides a clue as to how this marginal but recurrent type will proliferate everywhere from the late nineteenth century onwards: 'the burning desire to create a personal form of originality, *within* the external limits of social conventions' (my emphasis).

Both the discourse of politeness and the one to do with the artistic or imaginative individual who emerges from the polite classes contain within them a paradoxical narrative to do with development, impairment and slowness. Tagore rhetorically exhorts the motherland, Bengal, to reform her genteel progeny: 'You are content, Mother, for your seventy million children to remain Bengalis, and not turn into men.' 'Bengalis', here, are not being configured as primitives, but quite the opposite: as super-refined, spoiled, genteel children – in the privileged familial world of the colonial bourgeoisie – who haven't grown up into 'manhood'; in other words, into self-governance. In this way, the modern is insinuated subtly, and seductively, into a vocabulary of backwardness. And so Benjamin himself draws attention to the sign under which he was born, Saturn, the sign of impediments, expressing, through a mixture of metaphor and superstition, the melancholy not only of the intellectual life but of minority; so Sontag recognises in him the subaltern or peasant characteristics of 'slowness', 'blundering' and 'stubbornness'; so Benjamin himself admits to his ineptness with objects, his inability, even in adulthood, to make a proper cup of coffee, his lack of mastery of the inanimate world. When writing of Proust, he describes him, revealingly, as a 'hoary child'; the quote he chooses from Jacques Rivière to comment on Proust's odd backwardness, his marginality, is instructive, and serves partly as a self-commentary on the scandal, the increasing unacceptability, on many levels, of being a Jewish modern: 'Marcel Proust died of the same inexperience as enabled him to write his work. He died of unworldliness and because he lacked the understanding to alter living conditions that had begun to crush him. He died because he did not know how to light a fire or open a window.' It's a fairly accurate, if figurative, account of the exigencies, as well as the peculiar creative opportunities, of the colonised bourgeoisie.

From somewhere within the interstices of the various themes and languages of development (the avant-garde, for instance, or the colonising mission) and backwardness (tradition; the 'primitive') that comprise modernity comes Benjamin's indictment of linearity and progress, and his strategic embrace of the backward, the slow. Thus, his famous observation: 'The concept of the historical progress of mankind cannot be sundered from the concept of its progression through a homogeneous, empty time. A critique of the concept of such a progression must be the basis of any criticism of the concept of progress itself.' This critique is what gives Benjamin's work its unresolved, anti-narratorial quality; and it embodies what is characteristic of modernism, but what's insufficiently acknowledged in the canonical versions of that phase – the coming together, as in Benjamin, of the primitive, the barbaric, on the one hand, and the 'high' cultural, the 'European', on the other, in one mind, one place, one personality, in such a way that, fundamentally for the modern, redefines these terms and oppositions. It's a problematic confluence that brings to civility and gentility their distinctive aura and slowness.